The Illustrated Encyclopedia of
AVIATION

Volume
17

Wings Prelims

Editorial Board

Reference edition published 1979

Reference edition © 1979 Marshall Cavendish Limited
© Orbis Publishing Limited 1977

Printed in Great Britain

Bound in the United States

Library of Congress Cataloging in Publication Data
Main entry under title:

The Illustrated encyclopedia of aviation.

First published in 1977 under title: Wings.
Includes index.
1. Aeronautics—History. I. Robinson, Anthony,
1947—
TL515.144 1979   629.13'009   78—12408
ISBN 0—85685—318—6 (set)
ISBN 0—85685—590—1 (vol.17)

Picture Acknowledgements

Cover: USAF—1921: S. Howe—1922: Fairchild—1922-23: IWM—1923: Fairchild; S. Howe—1924-25: Popperfoto; E.G. Gee—1925: USAF—1926: USAF; IWM—1927: P. Endsleigh Castle—1928: IWM—1928-29: IWM; USAF—1930-31: Jahr Verlag—1932-33: S. Howe—1933: API; S. Howe; USAF—1934: S. Howe; J. Goulding—1935: Fairchild—1936: API; Fairchild—1936-37: API—1937: USAF—1938: S. Howe; M.J. Hooks; API—1938-39: M.J. Hooks—1939: S. Howe—1940: Fairchild—1941: Fairchild—1942: API—1942-43: API—1943: Glenn L. Martin Co/Popperfoto; API; M.J. Hooks—1944-45: A.J. Brown—1945: P. Endsleigh Castle; API—1946-47: M.J. Hooks; Fairchild—1947: M.J. Hooks —1948-49: Fairchild; P. Endsleigh Castle—1950: Fairchild 1950-51: USAF—1951: API; K. Brookes—1952: Robert Hunt Library—1952-53: J. Goulding; IWM—1955: Canadian War Museum; E.F. Cheeseman; IWM—1956: USAF Art Collection; USAF—1957-58: USAF—1959: St Bees, Cumbria; Ray Rimell; IWM—1960: IWM; D.H. Robinson —1961: Military Aircraft Photographs; Popperfoto—1962: Hawker Siddeley; Military Aircraft Photographs—1963: A. Imrie—1964-65: A. Imrie; J. Goulding—1966-67: B. Robertson; IWM—1968-69: IWM; RAE, Farnborough—1970-71: IWM; J. Goulding; Military Aircraft Photographs; P.R. March; RAE, Farnborough—1972-73: F.K. Mason; Bundesarchiv—1974-75: Bundesarchiv—1976: P. Kilduff; J. Van der Heuval—1978-79: M. Jerram—1980: M. Jerram; M. Hooks—1981: Saab—1982: M.J. Hooks; Saab—1983: Saab—1984: M.J. Hooks; Saab—1985: Saab; P. Endsleigh Castle—1986: A.J. Brown; Saab—1987: Saab—1989: USAF—1990-91: J. Goulding—1991: M.B. Passingham—1992: IWM—1993: MoD; IWM—1994-95: IWM—1996: IWM; IWM/Tweedy—1997: British Hovercraft Corporation—1998-99: British Hovercraft Corporation; A.J. Brown—2000: P.R. March; M.J. Hooks—2001: M.B. Passingham—2002: Musée de l'Air; Achille Ghizzardi via M.B. Passingham—2003: M.B. Passingham—2004: IWM; M.B. Passingham—2005: P. Endsleigh Castle—2006: P.R. March—2007: Bundesarchiv—2008: Roger Bell; Bundes-archiv—2009: Orbis; Radio Times Picture Library—2010: J. Goulding—2010-11: Flight—2011: Musée de l'Air—2013: Flight; Smithsonian Institution; Radio Times Hulton Picture Library—2014: Orbis—2015: Popperfoto; IWM—2016: USAF—2017: IWM—2018: Radio Times Hulton Picture Library—2019: Stuart Howe—2020: Fokker-VFW International—2021-23: Popperfoto—2024: IWM—2025: P.R. March; M. Hooks—2026-27: J. Goulding; P.R. March; M. Hooks—2028-29: IWM; IWM/Tweedy—2030: IWM/Tweedy; Robert Hunt Library—2031: RAF Museum, Hendon; Military Aircraft Photographs—2032: P. Endsleigh Castle—2033: Popperfoto; IWM—2036: Shorts; M. Jerram—2037: Shorts; M. Hooks—2038: Shorts; M. Young—2039: Shorts; K. Brookes; M. Hooks—2040: M. Hooks

The Illustrated Encyclopedia of
AVIATION

Marshall Cavendish New York & London

Contents

Famous Aeroplanes

Republic's Juggernaut *by Simon Clay*   1921
Backbone of NATO *by Bill Gunston*   1941
The Thunderchief *by Bill Gunston*   1946
Sharks of the Air *by Alex Imrie*   1963
The Factory at Farnborough *by Bruce Robertson*   1969
Shield of the Northern Skies *by Pamela D Matthews*   1981
Yachts of the Air *by Philip Moyes*   1997
Builders of the Air Armadas *by M B Passingham*   2001
Prestwick Pioneers *by M J Hooks*   2024
Ships of the Air *by Philip Moyes*   2031

Fighting Airmen

Knights under the Black Cross *by Peter Kilduff*   1952
Hat in the Ring *by Peter Kilduff*   1956
Home Defence Hero *by Peter Kilduff*   1959
Stuka Pilot *by Frank Osman*   1972
Germany's High Flyers *by Peter Kilduff*   1976
Sportsmen's Airplanes *by Mike Jerram*   1978
Winged Samuri *by Christopher Shores*   1989
Chiefs of the Air Staff *by Chaz Bowyer*   1992
Flying Buccaneer *by Chaz Bowyer*   1994
The Midnight Ghost *by Frank Osman*   2007

Trailblazers

First Englishman to Fly *by Mike Jerram*   1961
High Speed Seaplanes *by Mike Jerram*   2009
Mildenhall to Melbourne *by Mike Jerram*   2018
Leading Lady *by Michael Heatley*   2021

War in the Air

Black Thursday *by Simon Clay*   2015
Storm Over the Sealanes *by F K Mason*   2028

Above: the Seversky Aircraft Corporation, based at Farmingdale, New Jersey from 1933, became the Republic Aircraft Corporation in 1939. Below: P-47s of the 390th FS, 366th FG, Ninth Air Force USAAF operating from East Anglia in 1944. Opposite top: designed in 1931, the SEV-3 amphibian was Seversky's first product. Opposite centre: 120 examples of the pre-war P-35 were ordered by Sweden, half of which were requisitioned by the US Army Air Corps in 1939. Opposite below: a line-up of P-47s preserved by the Confederate Air Force

As the Supermarine Spitfire eclipsed the Hawker Hurricane as the best-known British fighter of World War II, so the North American P-51 Mustang came to overshadow the Republic P-47 Thunderbolt for equivalent status in the United States. Yet the Thunderbolt was built in larger numbers than any other American fighter and had an excellent record both in air combat and as a ground attack aircraft. In the latter role it proved more successful than any other aircraft type of the combatant nations, even though originally designed as an interceptor. The Thunderbolt was also the largest and heaviest single-seat fighter in mass production, dwarfing its principal adversaries such as the Messerschmitt Bf 109. Despite comparative deficiencies in performance with these enemy fighters, the P-47 gave an excellent account of itself and was flown by the two top-scoring US fighter aces in Europe.

Seversky's pursuit aeroplane
The origins of the Thunderbolt can be traced to the original design concept of the Seversky Aircraft Corporation and its two *émigré* Russian principals, Alexander Seversky and Alexander Kartveli. Both had been absent from Russia at the time of the revolution and both declined to return.

Major Alexander Seversky had been a successful fighter pilot on the Russian front in World War I and had several German aircraft to his credit in air combat. As a member of a special air mission sent to the United States in 1917 to establish an interchange of technical data on air matters, Seversky decided to remain in that country and in the early postwar years became well known for his many aeronautical patents. From these he was able to raise sufficient capital to form a company, although this was not particularly successful. By 1931 he had obtained sufficient backing to form the Seversky Aircraft Corporation with the object of promoting an all-metal radial-engined monoplane design, which could be adapted for a number of purposes and thus have a wide potential market. Construction of a prototype—given the designation SEV-3, but commonly known around the works at College Point, Long Island as the Demonstrator—began in 1931 but was not completed until two years later after the Company had moved to a new site at Farmingdale. It was during this period that Kartveli joined Seversky and became the principal design engineer. Kartveli had begun his career in aeronautical design in Paris and had later moved to the United States, where he had been employed by two other companies before joining Seversky.

The SEV-3 proved highly successful and this lone prototype was to appear both with land undercarriage and with floats as an amphibian. There was great competition for orders among the many aircraft companies in North America at this time. The flamboyant Major de Seversky's talents stretched to salesmanship and, despite the years of financial depression in the United States, he was eventually successful in obtaining an order from Colombia for three of his amphibians and also in gaining a contract from the US Army for 30 derivatives to serve as basic trainers in the Army Air Corps under the designation BT-8.

In those days the US Army Air Corps had a policy of issuing a design specification and inviting various manufacturers to compete by producing a prototype for testing. As Seversky's monoplanes had superior speed to most of

the pursuit fighters then in service with the Army Air Corps, he decided to build a new design based on SEV-3 for entry in the pursuit fighter competition scheduled for June 1935. This aircraft was designed as a two-seater, but after being damaged in an accident was rebuilt as a single-seater and given the designation SEV-1XP. With a top speed of nearly 467km/h (290mph) and a range of over 1,610km (1,000 miles), its performance impressed the adjudicating engineers. However, it was not until April 1936, after further modification and delays, that Seversky won an order for 77 examples of his fighter, which received the Army designation P-35. Delivery of these dumpy, radial-engined fighters took place between July 1937 and August the following year.

Seversky's team exploited the original basic design to the full and a spate of variants appeared in the late 1930s. Several were used in races or other speed events and special versions were flown by such notable pilots as Jimmy Doolittle and Jacqueline Cochran. A modified P-35 type was offered to the US Navy, but did not find favour with that service. Seversky also explored the export potential of his design in Europe, personally demonstrating both single-seat and two-seat versions of his basic radial-engined fighter to the air forces of several nations. A large order was obtained from Sweden for a version of the P-35, although this contract was too late to stave off a financial crisis which had befallen the Seversky Aircraft Corporation. Further backing was obtained, but the new investors took over control of the Company from Major de Seversky, who then severed his connections with it. This was in 1939 and led, in the autumn of that year, to the firm adopting the name of Republic Aviation Corporation, signalling a welcome change in its fortunes.

Kartveli remained as chief designer and continued to further the basic design by refinements and new engines. The XP-41 had a more powerful Pratt & Whitney Twin Wasp radial and a cleaner airframe, principally through a flush-fitting retractable undercarriage in place of the exposed units on the P-35. Although the XP-41 was cap-

able of reaching 515 km/h (320 mph), it never went beyond the prototype stage as the Air Corps was more interested in another proposal from Republic which involved the installation of a turbo-supercharger to give better performance at high altitudes. This was ordered under the designation YP-43, 13 service-test models being built. Although the design was much refined, it retained the same semi-elliptical wing shape and other features which could be traced back to the original SEV-3.

Choice of power plant

While Republic still favoured the radial engine, other American aircraft manufacturers had turned to the Allison liquid-cooled unit, which offered more power and better streamlining. This was in line with the trend in Europe, where the Messerschmitt Bf 109, Hawker Hurricane and other types had performances far superior to the fighters currently in service with the US Army Air Corps. Kartveli felt that he could not ignore the potential of the Allison engine and in the summer of 1939 he began to develop the firm's basic airframe to take the liquid-cooled power plant. Top speed was expected to be in excess of 644 km/h (400 mph) at around 4,600 m (15,000 ft), but, while the projected fighter offered superior performance to its predecessors, the proposed armament of one 0·5 in and one 0·3 in calibre machine gun mounted in the fuselage was totally inadequate by European standards. Nevertheless, the Air Corps was sufficiently interested in the project to award a contract for two prototypes in November 1939, to be designated XP-47 and XP-47A.

The outbreak of war in Europe and the possibility that the United States might also eventually become involved caused the Air Corps to expedite the building of a prototype, so that flight testing could begin at an early date. To this end, the XP-47A was intended to fly first, being an aircraft without armament, radio and military equipment. However, the contract was never signed because the Air Corps considered the inadequate armament and the high wing loading which would result from a fully-equipped aircraft to be undesirable. Further discussions with the manufacturers ensued and it was decided to increase the armament to four wing-mounted 0·3 in machine guns and two 0·5 in weapons in the fuselage. This and other changes to reduce the wing loading were accepted by the Air Corps and a contract for the two prototypes was signed in January 1940.

Design work and construction of a mock-up went on apace at Farmingdale, but the indications are that the Air Corps was not entirely happy with the Republic Allison-engined fighter project, due to possible limitations in development. In June 1940 a special Air Corps Board, which had been taking a critical look at the whole experimental fighter programme, issued a report in which concern was expressed at the number of new fighters in the pipeline which relied on the one type of liquid-cooled engine. Republic engineers and executives were sent for and at a meeting at Wright Field, Ohio, the Air Corps suggested that Republic consider an alternative project making use of the new 2,000 hp Pratt & Whitney R-2800 radial engine. It was obvious to Kartveli that this powerful unit could not be embodied in a further projection of the original basic airframe, currently being advanced yet again as the P-44. Accordingly he decided to design a completely new airframe, although externally it would appear very much as a scaled-up P-43 and P-44.

The successful application of the General Electric turbo-supercharger in the YP-43 led to a similar unit being designed into the new radial-engined fighter. In fact, this and the ducting connecting it to engine components became the first feature of the design, with the fuselage being formed around it. The turbo-supercharger would give the aircraft its maximum speed at around 7,620 m (25,000 ft) and it was as a high-altitude interceptor that the new design was proposed to the Air Corps. Despite the fact that the proposed fighter would gross the then-phenomenal weight of 5,260 kg (11,600 lb), the proposal was accepted. Although a completely new design, the Air Corps decided that the prototype would be built on the existing contract for the XP-47. The new aircraft would be designated XP-47B and all work on the original Allison XP-47 and XP-47A would be scrapped. As it was, some 60,000 dollars had been spent on the Allison-engined design, including a full-scale wind tunnel model of the XP-47, which was to be completed and passed to the National Advisory Council for Aeronautics (NACA) for experimentation on the cooling requirements of inline-engined, high-performance aircraft. The amended contract called for a single XP-47B and this prototype was constructed during the winter of 1940–41.

Heavyweight fighter

The aircraft was quite unlike any other single-seat fighter through its massive proportions. The span was 12·4 m (40 ft 9 in) and the length approximately 10·7 m (35 ft), but it was the depth of the fuselage which surprised many experienced fighter pilots. Whereas most aircraft tended to be glove-like around the pilot, in the XP-47B he sat in an extraordinarily-spacious cockpit, above the mass of ducting connecting the turbo-supercharger to the engine. If the fuselage was enormous by current standards, it was nonetheless remarkably clean. The large engine cowling embraced an air intake under the engine, which supplied the turbo-supercharger with ram air, as well as cooling the oil radiators and other components. Exhausted and by-passed air was released from two shutters in the sides of the rear fuselage. As with the P-43, the 'turbo' was buried in the rear fuselage, the exhaust gases which operated the turbine being ducted from the engine – a layout which proved highly satisfactory.

The two fuel tanks were situated forward and below the cockpit and had a design capacity of 1,190 litres (262 gallons). Unlike earlier designs no fuel was carried in the wing; instead, following British fashion, the mainplanes housed an armament of Browning machine guns. Six were specified as normal, with eight as an alternative, although in production the eight-gun armament became standard. Unlike British fighters, which used the rifle-calibre 0·303 in weapon, the XP-47B was to be equipped with the 0·5 in heavy machine gun, which had a higher muzzle velocity and far more destructive power, although the rate of fire was less. A 3·65 m (12 ft) diameter four-blade Curtiss propeller was installed to make full use of the horsepower available. This created problems for the design team, in that an extremely long main undercarriage would be necessary to give adequate ground clearance for the blades. In order to stow this undercarriage in the wing, it was necessary to devise a mechanism whereby the main legs shortened by some 23 cm (9 in) during retraction.

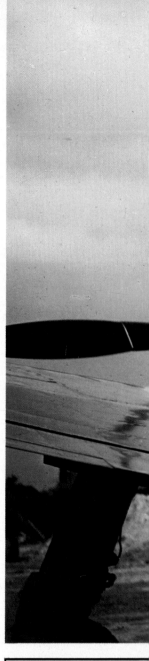

Above right: a US war correspondent photographs a P-47C of the 84th FS, 78th FG, flown by Major Eugene Roberts, the Eighth Air Force's second ace, in September 1943.
Right: a P-47D fighter-bomber of the 373th FG, US Ninth Air Force, seen over Mont St Michel, soon after D-day.
Far right: a P-47 of the US Eighth Air Force awaits a bomber escort sortie to Wilhelmshaven on 3 November 1943

In general the XP-47B perpetuated the familiar features which had come to be associated with Seversky and Republic aircraft: the semi-elliptical wing form and tailplane and dumpy fuselage. In flight the XP-47B appeared beautifully proportioned, the high fuselage decking behind the cockpit being a spine fairing which added to the lateral stability of the aircraft.

The first flight was made on 6 May 1941 with Lowry L. Brabham, Operations Manager at Republic, at the controls. At that date, the Farmingdale flying field was somewhat limited in area and, as it was anticipated that the prototype would need a long landing run, arrangements were made for the aircraft to make its initial touchdown at Mitchel Field a few miles away where a longer runway was available. Brabham found the aircraft behaved well on take-off, but he was soon concerned when the cockpit began to fill with smoke and fumes. Although fearing a fire, Brabham continued his flight to Mitchel Field, where a successful landing was made and the cause of the smoke identified as an accumulation of engine oil on the exhaust manifold. In subsequent flights the XP-47B showed an excellent performance at high altitude. The name Thunderbolt was adopted for the aircraft, being suggested by Republic executive C. Hart Miller. The prototype was retained by Republic as a test vehicle, but was lost in August 1942 when a fire developed in the rear fuselage and the pilot successfully baled out over Long Island Sound.

Development snags

Long before the prototype had flown, a contract for 773 P-47B aircraft had been signed and in October 1941 another 850 Thunderbolts were ordered. The first pre-production Thunderbolt was completed in December 1941 and four others followed in the following March. Mass production did not get under way until May 1942, albeit at a slow rate, and in June the first examples were issued to fighter squadrons. Production P-47Bs were very similar to the prototype, apart from having a sliding cockpit hood in place of the sideways-hinging type fitted on the XP-47B. High-altitude performance was good, with a top speed of 690 km/h (429 mph) being officially recorded at 8,470 m (27,800 ft), establishing the Thunderbolt as the fastest American fighter in service. Low-altitude performance was not quite as impressive and the aircraft's rate of climb was decidedly poor in comparison with European contemporaries. It took nearly 10 minutes to reach 6,090 m (20,000 ft), whereas the Spitfire could reach the same altitude in under five and a Focke Wulf Fw 190 in seven.

Nevertheless, the Thunderbolt's level-flight performance and acceleration in a dive was very impressive and it was at these speeds that the first serious problems with the design were encountered. In late March 1942 a Republic test pilot was killed when his aircraft broke up during high-speed manoeuvres. The cause was a mystery and speed limitations were put on the aircraft. Some weeks later another Republic pilot had to bale out when the aircraft went out of control due to failure of the tail and further investigations confirmed suspicions that the fabric covering on rudder and elevators was 'ballooning' and rupturing under the stress of high-speed flight. The solution was the installation of metal-covered rudder and elevators and these were introduced on the P-47C, which was otherwise very similar to the B model. Control problems at high speed were not, however, completely overcome until bob-weights were fitted in the control system; thereafter, no difficulties were evident.

There were many accidents involving the early Thunderbolts at airfields in the New England states where training on the type was concentrated. Some of these accidents were through pilot error in handling an aircraft so different from the other US Army Air Force (as the USAAC had become in June 1941) single-seat fighters of the day. Many crashes were due to engine or propeller troubles, both units being comparatively new and showing up various weaknesses when subjected to the strains of high-altitude operations.

Despite the Thunderbolt's conception as a high altitude interceptor, it was apparent by the summer of 1942 that the USAAF would be chiefly engaged in offensive operations and a decision was taken to send the type to the United Kingdom for use on short-range escort

missions and support of daylight bombing. The Pratt & Whitney R-2800 consumed fuel at an average 397 litres (87 gallons) per hour at moderate cruising speed, so that endurance of the fighter was about two hours under operational conditions. The radius of action for the Thunderbolt flying on high altitude operations from England would be about 320 km (200 miles), which did not do much towards satisfying the long-range escort requirements of the Eighth Air Force. In the absence of the more desirable Lockheed P-38 Lightning, which had double the endurance, ways would have to be found to use the P-47 to advantage.

Three fighter groups – each comprising three squadrons with a strength of 25 aircraft each – were established in

Top: P-47s en route to an airfield in England in February 1944 after having been shipped to Liverpool from the USA.
Above: Thunderbolts of an RAF South-east Asia Command squadron prepare to take-off. The RAF used the type almost entirely in Burma, initially as escorts but more successfully as fighter-bomber aircraft

Republic Thunderbolt MkI
of No 134 Squadron RAF

1927

eastern England during the early spring of 1943. The first operation undertaken by Thunderbolts was actually flown on 10 March that year, but this sweep over the enemy-held coastline proved notable for the amount of radio interference and no operations requiring radio to be used were conducted until this problem had been solved. The trouble was eventually traced to static electricity caused by corrosion in the magnetos. Although a temporary solution enabled reasonable radio communication to be re-established, the difficulties persisted until the advent of pressurised magnetos at a later date permitted full radio contact to be resumed.

Above: groundcrew load a 500 lb bomb onto the centreline rack of a P-47 at an English base. The P-47 could carry a variety of stores on centreline and wing racks for ground-attack duties.
Above right: USAAF ordnance men re-arm a P-47 on an advanced airfield in France shortly after D-day. The P-47 had a standard armament of eight 0.5 in Browning machine guns.
Right: a P-47D of the US Seventh Air Force leaves the flight deck of USS Manila Bay after being ferried from Oahu to Saipan, Mariana Islands in June 1944

Into action

The three Thunderbolt groups were placed on operational status early in April 1943, flying shallow-penetration fighter sweeps in company with RAF Spitfire squadrons to gain experience. The first known combat between Thunderbolts and German fighters occurred on 15 April, when the 4th Fighter Group engaged Fw 190s near Ostend and one of its leaders, Major Donald Blakeslee, made the first claim of an enemy aircraft destroyed by a pilot flying a Thunderbolt. However, the American unit apparently got the worst of the engagement, as three aircraft failed to return, although two of these were thought to be victims of mechanical failure. Considerable trouble was experienced during the early days of combat with engine seizure due to overstrain and pilots had to be cautioned on the use of extreme manifold pressures and the careful correlation of throttle, turbo-supercharger and propeller setting to avoid these failures.

While the Thunderbolt was no match in climb or turning performance for the enemy fighters encountered, it could outfly them at high altitude and easily overtake them in a dive. It was this latter advantage that was to be fully exploited by the leaders of the Thunderbolt groups, notably Colonel Hubert Zemke who commanded the 56th Fighter Group. Knowing that the USAAF Boeing B-17 Fortresses and Consolidated B-24 Liberators were the objectives of the enemy fighters, Zemke devised tactics whereby his Thunderbolt squadrons would be positioned above the American bombers in such a way as to dive and interecept the German fighters making their attack on the four-engined 'heavies'.

contracts for the P-47, Republic had established a second source of production at Evansville, Indiana. First pre-production examples appeared in September 1942, but the plant did not get into full production until a year later. Its Thunderbolts were identified by the letters RA following the production designation, whereas those from Farmingdale had an RE suffix. A third production Thunderbolt was a licence-built version by Curtiss at Buffalo, New York. The first examples appeared late in 1942, but various production problems led to a very limited output and Curtiss-made Thunderbolts, designated P-47G, were restricted to training use.

Continuous improvement

While a continuous programme of improvement · saw many changes incorporated into production P-47D models, it was not until late in 1943 that any of a really significant nature began to appear on aircraft reaching combat squadrons. The P-47D-10 and D-11 models introduced the R-2800-63 engine, which had equipment for injecting water into the cylinders, thus allowing higher power to be drawn for short intervals without damage to the engine. This gave a great boost to performance, particularly improving the rate of climb. The P-47D-22 and D-23 models introduced new propellers with so-called paddle-blades which were more efficient than the original types. The P-47D-22 used the Hamilton model, while the D-23 used a Curtiss version. Both water injection and paddle-blade propellers could be fitted to earlier D model Thunderbolts and many service aircraft were so modified before the first production models with these features arrived from the factory. The P-47D-15 model introduced modified internal fuel tanks with capacity increased from 1,154 litres (254 galllons) to 1,420 litres (312 gallons). This model was also the first to feature a jettisonable cockpit canopy, in response to complaints from combat areas where some pilots had experienced difficulty in baling out.

The first Thunderbolt pilot to achieve ace status (five or more enemy aircraft shot down in combat) was Captain P. London, a flight leader with the 78th Fighter Group operating from Duxford in Cambridgeshire. This was on 28 July 1943, the occasion of the first use of drop tanks to extend the P-47's radius of action. A month later London's squadron commander, Major Eugene Roberts, became the second Eighth Air Force Thunderbolt ace and thereafter so many pilots could claim this status that it was no longer novel.

The particularly-successful 56th Fighter Group was credited with its 100th enemy fighter shot down early in November 1943 and soon had several pilots with more than 10 victories to their credit. The high-scoring aces of this Group were: Gerald W. Johnson, who destroyed 18 enemy aircraft before being himself shot down by ground fire in March 1944; Walker H. Mahurin with 21 victories, who was lost to fire from the rear gunner of a Dornier bomber he attacked in March 1944; Hubert Zemke who commanded the Group and had 17 victories; Fred J. Christensen, credited with 22 victories before completing his combat tour in September 1944; David C. Schilling, the second combat commander of the 56th, who gained 23 air victories and also destroyed another 10 German aircraft by ground strafing; Robert S. Johnson, who brought down 28 enemy aircraft before finishing his tour in May 1944 and Francis S. Gabreski, also with 28 victories, who was shot down in July 1944. Another very successful unit on escort operations with the Eighth Air Force was the 353rd Fighter Group, which produced Walter C. Beckham with 18 air victories, who was lost

The Thunderbolt units sustained far more losses than victories during the first two months of operational flying, but by August 1943 the position was being reversed. Using hit-and-run diving tactics, Thunderbolt pilots began to shoot down large numbers of German fighters which tried to intercept the American bomber raids. The excellent stability of the P-47 and its heavy firepower was a major factor in this success. The American pilots found that a short, well-aimed burst from the eight 0·5in guns was often sufficient to cause an enemy fighter to disintegrate. This armament had originally been proposed for the Thunderbolt with a view to its use in destroying bombers in a single pass, so it can be understood that a concentrated burst on a small fighter aircraft was devastating. Many Allied fighter pilots who had experience flying cannon-armed fighters still considered the Thunderbolt's firepower to be the most effective armament in fighter-versus-fighter combat.

Range was of paramount importance in these operations by Eighth Air Force fighters and developments were quickly put in hand to use pressurised externally-mounted fuel tanks. Fuel could be drawn from these at high altitude on the penetration flight and, when empty, the tank could be dropped. These so-called 'drop tanks' enabled the Thunderbolt's range to be doubled, once suspension points had been installed under the wing.

The P-47C was followed by the D model, reaching the combat theatre soon after operations had started. The P-47D could only be distinguished from the C in minor detail and it was really the designation for a standardised combat model produced by two factories. With more

Republic P-47D Thunderbolt
of the USAAF

Dimensions
Span 12·43 m (40 ft 9⅜ in)
Length 11·02 m (36 ft 1¾ in)
Height 4·44 m (14 ft 7 in)

Engine
One 2,000 hp Pratt & Whitney
R-2800-21

Performance
Maximum speed 700 km/h
(435 mph)
Service ceiling 12,800 m (42,000 ft)
Maximum range 1,270 km
(790 miles)

Armament
Eight 0·5 in Browning machine guns
Up to 1,135 kg (2,500 lb) of bombs

1931

in February 1944 and Glenn E. Duncan (19 victories), commander of the Group, who was also shot down in the following July. All the ace pilots mentioned here as being shot down or lost survived the war–testimony to the substantial construction of the Thunderbolt.

Thunderbolt versus Focke Wulf

The Eighth Air Force had eight P-47 groups flying from England by the end of 1943 and most enjoyed considerable fortune with the fighter on daylight escort operations. The secret of success with the heavy fighter was to keep the speed above 400 km/h (250 mph) in a turning fight. In the spring of 1943 a captured Fw 190 flown by an RAF pilot had been tested with a P-47C. The results confirmed the Thunderbolt's superior speeds at high altitudes, but showed it at a disadvantage in most comparisons made below 4,570 m (15,000 ft).

Some 12 months after the 1943 trial, another test was run with the same Fw 190 and a P-47D fitted with water injection and paddle-blade propeller, which showed how the Thunderbolt's performance had been improved. The Focke Wulf had an initial advantage in acceleration, but it was soon overhauled by the Thunderbolt at all altitudes. The same was true of climb, with the German fighter going up quicker at first, only to be overtaken by the P-47 which then climbed 150 m (500 ft) per minute faster. In turning, providing the Thunderbolt kept the speed at 400 km/h (250 mph) or more, it could out-turn the Fw 190 at any height, the advantage increasing with altitude. The Republic fighter could easily dive away from the Focke Wulf, although here again the lighter enemy type initially accelerated faster and it would take between 300 m (1,000 ft) and 1,220 m (4,000 ft)–dependent on altitude–for the P-47 to pass it.

Despite the fact that in these tests the Thunderbolt grossed 6,350 kg (14,000 lb) and the Fw 190 4,310 kg (9,500 lb)–less than the empty weight of the former–the power advantage offered by the use of water injection had improved the P-47's performance very significantly, although this technique could only be used for brief periods if engine overheating was to be avoided. The tests also made it very clear that the Thunderbolt was highly vulnerable at low speeds and should avoid them at all costs while in hostile airspace.

Comparative tests conducted by the German authorities with a captured P-47 resulted in similar findings. Luftwaffe pilots engaging Thunderbolts were aware that to gain the advantage they had to slow the fight and to change flight attitude once their initial acceleration advantage had been lost. The Thunderbolt was also tested against the other major German fighter type, the Messerschmitt Bf 109G, where the contrasting weight and size differences were even more marked. Performance differences were comparable to those highlighted in tests with the Fw 190.

Above right: a P-47D restored by the Confederate Air Force in the markings of an aircraft of the 86th Fighter Group, US Twelfth Air Force. Above: a Thunderbolt representing a machine of the 355th Fighter Squadron, 354th Fighter Group, US Ninth Air Force, which operated from the Continent after D-day in the close-support role

Over the Pacific

In the summer of 1943 Thunderbolts were introduced to combat in the South-west Pacific Theatre, flying long-range escorts and sweeps over New Guinea. There, the Fifth Air Force was not very enthusiastic about the large, fuel-thirsty Republic fighter, preferring the P-38 Lightning, which was highly favoured. Special drop tanks had to be fashioned locally for use by the P-47s to obtain the required range for the long distances involved in reaching important Japanese targets. Even so, there were problems in employment, as the Thunderbolt gave its best performance and economy at altitudes far above those at which the Fifth Air Force medium bombers did their work. The light and highly-manoeuvrable Japanese fighters made dog-fighting taboo for any Allied type and the diving pass had become the advised method of attack. The contrast in weight between the Thunderbolt and Japanese fighters such as the famed Mitsubishi A6M Zero was particularly significant and in a loaded state one P-47 could gross the equivalent of three adversaries. Only in top speed and dive performance did the Thunderbolt have real advantage and the Fifth Air Force considered that, overall, its shortcomings would make it quite unsuitable for combat in their war zone.

Nevertheless, the pilots of the 348th Fighter Group, the lone Thunderbolt unit based in New Guinea, had confidence in the aircraft and this grew when they found that they could usually come out on top in mock dog-fights with P-38 Lightnings. The Group became operational in late July 1943 and was soon encountering enemy fighters during sweeps over Japanese bases along the northern coast of New Guinea. As in Europe, the excellent stability of the Thunderbolt and its tremendous firepower were decisive factors in combat. The lightweight Japanese interceptors, with little protection for pilot or fuel tanks, rarely survived a well-directed burst of fire from the Thunderbolt's eight heavy machine guns. High-speed diving attacks and the avoidance of turning fights were tactics which resulted in the big American fighter enjoying similar success to that achieved in Europe.

The commander of the 348th Fighter Group, Colonel Neel Kearby, was particularly successful and he was credited with 22 air victories in Thunderbolts. On 11 October 1943 Kearby was leading a squadron on an offensive sweep when large numbers of Japanese fighters were encountered. During the ensuing *mêlée* Kearby alone shot down six of the enemy and for his conduct that day was later awarded the Medal of Honour, the United States' top decoration for bravery. Sadly, Kearby was himself shot down and killed in March 1944. Second-ranking Thunderbolt ace in the South-west Pacific was Major William D. Dunham, who commanded a squadron in the

Right: a P-47D armed with 10 in high-velocity air rockets (HVARs) on zero-length launchers, one of several ordnance loads which made the Thunderbolt a formidable ground attack aircraft. Above far right: the 348th Fighter Group, US Fifth Air Force operated the P-47 in the South-west Pacific Theatre

348th Fighter Group. He scored 14 confirmed victories while flying the P-47.

Two other Thunderbolt-equipped groups were established in New Guinea at the end of 1943 and early in 1944. Range was still the principal objection to the Thunderbolt and two of the groups converted to the North American P-51 Mustang before the end of the war. The other group had by then switched to ground-attack work, like most of the remaining Thunderbolt units in action over occupied Europe.

Ground-attack potential

Surprisingly, this large fighter, which had been developed specifically for high altitude interception, was to achieve its most creditable reputation as a tactical attack aircraft in support of ground forces. The three racks installed on the Thunderbolt to carry external fuel tanks could also be utilised for bombs, as in fact they were bomb shackles. The two wing racks could each take a 1,000lb bomb and the under-fuselage 'belly' rack a 500lb bomb, which was a very useful load for an aircraft of that day. The effect of the Thunderbolt's gun armament in strafing ground targets was also considerable. Consequently, with the improvements in low-altitude performance shown by latter P-47D models, it was decided that the Thunderbolt would make an excellent ground attack aircraft.

The Ninth Air Force, the tactical air arm supporting American ground forces for the invasion of western Europe, had 15 of its fighter-bomber groups equipped with P-47s. Additional firepower was added with the introduction of air-to-ground rockets, initially tube-

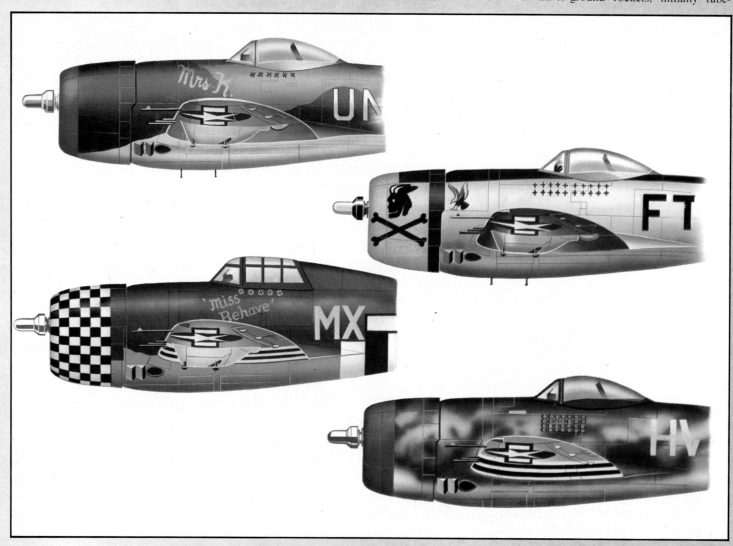

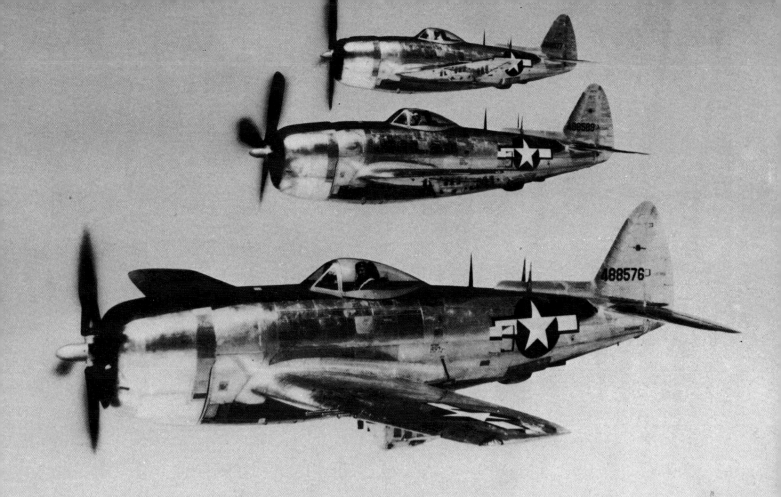

launched 4·5 in missiles similar to the infantry bazooka. A cluster of three tubes was carried under the wing on both sides of the fuselage, but the weapon was difficult to aim accurately and many pilots considered the tubes had an adverse effect on performance and control. A later development, the so-called 'zero-length' or 'railless' missiles with 5 in warheads were far more satisfactory. They only saw limited use in Europe, as hostilities were drawing to a close when the first P-47D models equipped to carry these rockets arrived in the war theatre. The racks under wings and fuselage were utilised for delivering other forms of ordnance, including anti-personnel bomb clusters and incendiary weapons. A frequent practice against some targets was to carry old drop tanks filled with oil, which would be ignited by strafing after release.

The Ninth Air Force Thunderbolts were used for regular offensive patrols in support of advancing armoured columns during the land campaigns in western Europe. Usually operating at flight strength of four or eight aircraft, pilots were in direct radio communication with forward ground controllers, who would vector the aircraft in to attack enemy strong points encountered. P-47s were also used with telling effect against enemy road and rail transportation, where strafing attacks alone could destroy trains or vehicles. Low-altitude patrols brought the heaviest losses of Thunderbolts to enemy aircraft, which would surprise the P-47s when heavily loaded and operating in their low-speed range.

Low-level ground attack work was notoriously dangerous, as aircraft at an altitude of 15 m (50 ft) to 30 m (100 ft) were very vulnerable to small-arms fire. The Thunderbolt, however, possessed advantages in this work which it is doubtful if Kartveli and his team considered when the design was conceived. The radial engine was particularly hardy and could sustain an extraordinary amount of damage, yet continue to function. The great weakness of

liquid-cooled engines was the vulnerability of their cooling systems, where a hit on a coolant line and loss of fluid could quickly cause the engine to overheat and seize up. The other advantage which the Thunderbolt had over its contemporaries in ground attack work was the protection afforded the pilot by the extensive ducting to and from the turbo-supercharger which ran under and around the cockpit. Not only did this absorb low-velocity missiles, but, in the event of a crash-landing, it protected the pilot's legs and feet. Indeed, the Thunderbolt was such a substantially-made aircraft that it could sustain a tremendous amount of punishment and continue to fly. In the event of a crash, its rugged structure frequently permitted the pilot to escape unharmed. Many experienced pilots said that they never felt safer in combat than when flying a Thunderbolt, a fact often reflected in their scores.

The bubble canopy
One of the most notable changes made to the Thunderbolt during the course of production was the installation of a 360 degree, all-round view cockpit canopy. This was achieved by removing the rear decking, or so-called 'razorback' and installing an electrically operated clear-view canopy not unlike that fitted to the British Hawker Typhoon. This improvement was originally effected on a P-47D taken from the production line and modified under the designation XP-47K. A further development prototype, the XP-47L—also a modified P-47D—featured the new canopy, as well as an enlarged main fuel tank and an increased oxygen supply, giving the aircraft further high-altitude endurance.

Originally it was intended to introduce these improvements with a new model designated P-47L, but in the event it was decided to continue the P-47D series and the introductions were made with the P-47D-25 from Farmingdale and the P-47D-26 from Evansville. The loss of the rear fuselage spine affected the lateral stability of the Thunderbolt and eventually a modification had to be introduced to rectify matters. This took the form of a small extension to the lower part of the fin. Kartveli had been against the removal of the original spine decking and he was proved correct in his prophesy that this would have a detrimental effect on control. The 'bubble' canopy was so advantageous in the visibility afforded the pilot, however, that it was introduced into production despite misgivings about changes in flight characteristics.

The Thunderbolt's phenomenal diving speed could take it into the realms of compressibility, where recovery could often be difficult. The P-47D-30 model introduced blunt-nosed ailerons and electrically operated dive-flaps to make dives from high altitude less hazardous. The dive-flaps were positioned under each wing forward of the undercarriage stowage and could be lowered during a steep dive to put a brake on the aircraft's descent. The P-47D-30 was built in larger numbers–a total of 2,600 by both factories–than any other D-series model. The last of the D-series, built only at Evansville, was the P-47D-40 which introduced a gyro gunsight, based on a British design, and installation points for 10 'zero-length' rocket launchers under the wing.

The various additions and modifications made to production Thunderbolts had resulted in a gradual decline in performance and in 1944 Republic began experimenting with a new high-power version of the R-2800 engine known as the C-type. This had originally been developed for the US Navy and had a power rating of 2,100 hp, against 2,000 hp for the B-type engine fitted to the P-47D. This was for normal operation, but with the use of water injection the power rating was 2,800 hp, as against 2,300 hp for the B-type. The new engine made an impressive difference in performance to the Thunderbolt and it was initially used in 130 P-47Ms, which were basically D airframes fitted with the new engine. All P-47Ms were shipped to England, where they were used by the 56th Fighter Group–the only Thunderbolt-equipped fighter group in the Eighth Air Force which did not eventually convert to the P-51 Mustang.

The P-47M was the fastest of all production Thunderbolts, with a top speed of 761 km/h (473 mph) at 9,150 m (30,000 ft). At first considerable trouble was experienced with the engines of the P-47M in England and several aircraft were lost in crashes from this cause. A number of factors were involved, but principally it resulted from corrosion through poor protective measures during shipment to the United Kingdom. Eventually all engines had to be changed, delaying the M model's introduction to combat. During the final weeks of the war, P-47Ms were responsible for shooting down a number of Messerschmitt Me 262 jets which they caught in fast diving attacks.

Experimental variants

Several experimental Thunderbolts were built or converted by Republic during the war years. Many were private ventures to try new equipment or components and made on the P-47B, C or D models retained for test-flying at Farmingdale. These received no special distinguishing designations. On the other hand, military-funded prototypes were built under a new model designation. The XP-47E was a P-47B airframe modified to include a pressurised cabin. With the Thunderbolt's high-altitude performance, a pressure cabin would have been beneficial to pilot comfort on long-range flights through eliminating the wearing of an oxygen mask. The development of this feature ran into several problems and, though these were

eventually overcome, the pressure cabin was not entirely successful. In any case, development took so long that there was little point in introducing the pressure cabin on production aircraft.

The XP-47F featured a completely new wing, using the laminar-flow aerofoil which had been adopted by North American for the P-51 Mustang. The aerofoil had very low drag properties and was thought to offer a means of obtaining more speed from the Thunderbolt without a power increase. The wing shape featured straight trailing and leading edges, with rounded tips. Tests proved disappointing in that XP-47F was found to have no substantial performance improvement over a standard P-47C and had some undesirable flight characteristics. Experimental flights continued for some months until the XP-47F crashed, killing the pilot. XP-47H was the designation given to two P-47D-15s used as test beds for the 16-cylinder, liquid-cooled Chrysler engine. There were no plans to put this version into production, for the Thunderbolt had been selected purely as the most suitable substantial airframe for this large 2,500 hp engine. The

first XP-47H did not fly until July 1945 and the second flew after the end of hostilities. By then any future for such an engine was bleak in view of the power potential of jet propulsion, so testing of the XP-47H was soon abandoned by Republic.

All aircraft manufacturers of the day were faced with the problem of increased weight on production models as military equipment was added. In the case of the Thunderbolt, this amounted to nearly a 450 kg (1,000 lb) advance between the empty weight of the XP-47B and that of the later P-47D. The XP-47J was an attempt to completely revise the basic design and reduce airframe weight wherever possible. As it happened, only some 180 kg (400 lb)

Top left: a Thunderbolt of the CAF representing a P-47D of the US Ninth Air Force.
Above: a P-47N armed with two 1,000 lb bombs and ten 5 in HVARs. The long-range P-47N was the final version of Thunderbolt to see action in World War II, flying a few missions over Japan in the closing weeks of the war

was saved on the empty weight, but, by reducing internal fuel tankage and a rigorous pruning of war equipment, 900 kg (2,000 lb) was saved on the gross weight. The XP-47J also featured the new C-series R-2800 engine and a redesigned, more restricted cowling. A fan was fitted at the front of the cowling to ensure adequate cooling. Several other refinements were incorporated, including a new model supercharger and extra glazing to improve visibility from the cockpit. The XP-47J first flew in November 1943 and exhibited a far superior performance to standard Thunderbolts. During the following year it was claimed that this aircraft exceeded 804 km/h (500 mph) in level flight, a record for a propeller-driven aircraft at that time. In spite of this experimental model's excellent performance it was not introduced into production, because the redesign of the airframe would have entailed an extensive factory re-tooling and caused a stem in the flow of Thunderbolts for some weeks. Another reason was that the economies made in war equipment were not acceptable to the USAAF and much of the performance advantage would be lost through reinstating the items deleted to save weight.

In any case, the XP-47J had been eclipsed by another advanced project which made use of the Pratt & Whitney R-4360 Wasp Major engine rated at over 3,000 hp. The installation of this new 28-cylinder radial brought the new model designation XP-72, although this aircraft was certainly a Thunderbolt development, using much of the P-47D airframe. Contra-rotating propellers were to be installed to absorb the new engine's full power output, although, when the first of the two prototypes ordered

Above left: preserved at Lackland AFB, Texas, this P-47D represents the aircraft flown by Major Francis Gabreski, the US Eighth Air Force's top-scoring ace.
Left: P-47Ds of the 27th FG, US Twelfth Air Force seen over the Italian Appenine Mountains, engaged on ground-attack duties in support of the US Fifth Army

flew in February 1944, it was fitted with a special 4·5m (15ft) diameter, four-blade unit. A top speed in excess of 804km/h (500mph) was expected when a mechanical supercharger was installed, but this was apparently never carried out and the top speed of 789km/h (490mph), though creditable, was nowhere near the potential of the design. A top speed of 885km/h (550mph) was anticipated from the fully-developed engine. Although 100 P-72s were ordered from Republic, the success of the jet fighter saw the contract cancelled before any of these 'Super Thunderbolts' were produced.

The long-range wing

The XP-47N was the official USAAF prototype testing what came to be known as the 'long-range wing'. There had, however, been at least two unofficial prototype long-range wings previously flown on modified Republic test aircraft. From the early days of the Thunderbolt's introduction into service, Republic had been aware of its endurance limitations and demands for increased range were continually being aired by the USAAF. Many attempts were made to solve this problem and it was apparent by early 1944 that a substantial increase in internal tankage would only be achieved by enlarging the airframe. The USAAF was firmly resolved that any interruption of production should be kept to a minimum, but to introduce a major change inevitably meant some production loss. Republic engineers eventually arrived at a solution which provided the extra fuel capacity and could be incorporated in production with little disruption. A 46cm (18in) wide section was devised which could be added between each mainplane and its root. The section contained space to enable fuel cells with around 423 litres (93 gallons) capacity to be installed. The wingspan was increased through this addition, although the curved wingtips were deleted—thus providing the long-range wing and XP-47N with its most prominent recognition feature. The undercarriage track was also 1m (3ft) wider than that of previous models.

Empty, the XP-47N weighed over 410kg (900lb) more than a production P-47D and with a full load could gross the then-extraordinary figure for a single-engine, single-

Top right and above far right: the Texas-based Confederate Air Force maintains several airworthy Thunderbolts.
Top far right: French P-47Ds seen at Basle in mid-1945.
Centre right: a preserved ex-Brazilian Thunderbolt.
Above right: seven French escadrilles were flying the P-47 by 1945. The French used the type until 1960.
Below: Yugoslavia equipped its air force with 150 P-47Ds under the Mutual Assistance Pact of 1950 with the USA

bolt pilots usually inflicted heavy losses on the enemy. The greatest hazard to these operations was the long over-water flight, where, if mechanical trouble was encountered, the chances of rescue were not very great. Happily, the reliability of the R-2800 C-series engine was such that few aircraft were lost. Two external fuel tanks were carried on the flights to Japan to obtain maximum endurance and, with a full fuel and armament load, the P-47N often weighed 9,525 kg (21,000 lb) at take-off. Such overloads required very long take-off runs to gain sufficient airspeed and it was policy for pilots to use the complete length of the 2·4 km (1·5 mile) runways. Tyre failure was under-standably a common occurrence in such circumstances, particularly when temperatures were very high. More P-47N aircraft were to have equipped fighter groups transferred from Europe had the war in the Pacific continued into 1946, but when Japan surrendered pro-duction contracts were cut and no further units equipped.

Foreign users
Apart from extensive use by the US Eighth and Ninth Air Forces in north-west Europe, Thunderbolts were also employed in a tactical role by the Twelfth Air Force in Italy. Six fighter groups converted to the type during 1944 and engaged in operations in support of land forces. It was on this front that the only other Medal of Honour award was gained by a Thunderbolt pilot. Lt Raymond Knight of the 350th Fighter Group was involved in a series of strafing attacks on heavily defended airfields in northern Italy on 24 April 1945, during which he shot up and destroyed 20 aircraft. On his last pass, Knight's P-47D was badly damaged by flak; he subsequently crashed into a mountain and was killed while trying to nurse the crippled aircraft back to base. The French air force also operated Thunderbolts on the Italian front and later in southern France and Germany. All told six French squadrons became operational and flew the same type of combat sorties as their American counterparts.

Thunderbolts were also operated in China and Burma. The USAAF sent two groups to China to protect the B-29 Superfortress bases in the spring of 1944. The type was not popular, as its hefty appetite aggravated the constant shortage of fuel – all of which had to be flown in from India. One group was subsequently withdrawn and the other went over to the ground-attack role. At one period in 1944 the US Tenth Air Force in Burma had 10 squadrons equipped with the P-47D operating in support of British forces. However, the major Thunderbolt force in this theatre of war was operated by the Royal Air Force, who commenced the re-equipment of their fighter-bomber squadrons with the Thunderbolt in the summer of 1944; 16 different squadrons had used the Republic heavyweight by the time combat on the Burmese front terminated.

Both 'razorback' and 'bubble' canopy versions of the P-47D were used, known as Thunderbolt Mk I and II respectively. Combat sorties were, with few exceptions, in support of the ground forces and little contact was made with Japanese fighters. RAF pilots held a very high opinion of the Thunderbolt's ruggedness and reliability and it is said that it had the lowest combat loss rate of any aircraft flown by the RAF during World War II. In 1946 RAF Thunderbolt squadrons supported the Dutch during the conflict which erupted in Indonesia.

Other nations operating the Thunderbolt during World War II included the Soviet Union, which received over 200 P-47Ds. How these aircraft were employed has never been revealed and even Republic were told little after the delivery was made. Brazil had a single squadron operating

seat fighter of 9,070 kg (20,000 lb). With a moderate loading, test pilots reported that the XP-47N handled favourably with no vices. The location of the additional internal fuel cells in the wing root area meant that the aircraft's centre of gravity was not affected by additional weight at this point. The XP-47N also featured the R-2800 C-series engine, a new turbo-supercharger and a number of automatic devices to ease the pilot's workload.

To meet requirements for the long-range escort fighter to accompany the Boeing B-29 Superfortress raids on Japan, the XP-47N was put into production, with the first P-47N models appearing late in 1944. These had a top speed of 740 km/h (460 mph) at 9,750 m (32,000 ft) and also featured an autopilot to ease the pilot's task over long distances. Both Republic factories built the P-47N, although the Evansville line did not start until the spring of 1945 and only 149 were delivered before production was terminated in September. The P-47N equipped one fighter group flying from the island of Iwo Jima and three groups operating from Ie Shima near Okinawa, the former some 1,130 km (700 miles) from the nearest point in Japan and the latter about 530 km (330 miles).

Despite its size and weight, the P-47N acquitted itself well in the relatively few encounters with Japanese fighters. Using the well-proven diving tactics, the Thunder-

alongside USAAF Thunderbolt units during the last year of hostilities, while Mexico also had a single squadron attached to a USAAF group engaged in the final operations in clearing Japanese forces from the Philippines.

Other uses were found for Thunderbolts in addition to the offensive fighter role. In England and Italy they were used by bomber commanders to marshal formations before a raid. In the same theatre, a few P-47Ds were modified to carry special air-sea rescue equipment. They were operated in patrolling near the enemy coastline to aid any flyers forced down in the sea. Away from the war fronts, many were used for target-towing in gunnery practice. As high-speed trainers, with the oxygen equipment behind the pilot removed enabling a second cockpit to be fashioned, many P-47s operated in several parts of the world. Curtiss carried out a special modification on two P-47G aircraft, where a second cockpit was placed in front of the first. These two-seat types were considered for production, but the idea was dropped when Curtiss ceased Thunderbolt manufacture in the spring of 1944.

Only 354 P-47G aircraft were produced by Curtiss, due to various problems and, with Evansville in full production, the third source of Thunderbolts was no longer required. Evansville had built a total of 6,242 P-47D and N aircraft by September 1945 and Farmingdale–which did not make final deliveries until near the end of the year–built 9,087. Total production from all plants was 15,683–more than any other American fighter of World War II.

Postwar service

Thunderbolts were soon replaced in first-line USAF (as the USAAF became in 1947) fighter groups by jet types, the last to re-equip being the 86th Fighter Group in Germany in 1950. Some second-line USAF P-47 units existed until 1952 and the Air National Guard, a part-time, State-administered organisation, flew examples of the P-47D and P-47N until 1955. In postwar years the United States Government supplied Thunderbolts to several foreign air forces, notably those in South America

and Latin America, where a few were still in squadron service as late as 1967. Others were supplied as defence aid or sold to Yugoslavia, Greece, Turkey, Italy, Portugal and Iran. The French made extensive use of the Thunderbolt in their early postwar air force and formed a special ground-attack unit equipped with P-47Ds for use in the Algerian war. The last French Thunderbolts were withdrawn in 1960. At the end of World War II 150 P-47Ds were given to the Chinese Nationalists, who used them for three years in attacks on the Communist forces. When driven from the mainland, the Nationalist forces continued to operate several Thunderbolt units and later received P-47Ns to re-equip their units. Over 2,000 surplus Thunderbolts were supplied to foreign nations by the United States between 1945 and 1956.

Although the most numerous of American wartime fighter types, very few Thunderbolts were to be found anywhere by the 1970s. Some have been rescued from breakers' yards and others rebuilt from abandoned wrecks. The best examples still flying are six originally purchased by an American dealer from the Peruvian government shortly before they were due to be scrapped. Apart from these and three other airworthy examples in the United States, all other surviving Thunderbolts are static examples, mostly in museums, the representatives of one of the most dependable fighter aircraft ever built.

The XP-47J resulted from studies made in 1942 for a high-speed, lightweight P-47. The single prototype was evaluated at Wright Field in 1944 and proved superior to standard Thunderbolts reaching 813 km/h (505 mph)

LEADING US ARMY AIR FORCE REPUBLIC P-47 ACES AND THEIR VICTORIES	
Maj Francis S. Gabreski	28
Maj Robert S. Johnson	28
Lt Col David C. Schilling	$22\frac{1}{2}$
Col Neel Kearby	22
Lt Frederick Christensen	$21\frac{1}{2}$
Maj Walker M. Mahurin	21
Maj Thomas J. Lynch	20
Lt Col Glenn E. Duncan	19

BACKBONE OF NATO

American-supplied Republic F-84s served with many Western air arms through the 1950s

Republic Aviation's Farmingdale plant in 1944 was the scene of great activity; among the projects in hand were the simultaneous flight development of eleven piston-engined fighters stemming from – or variants of – the P-47D Thunderbolt, and urgent studies of how best to move into the new age of jet propulsion. Republic had taken the piston-engined fighter about as far as anyone, the XP-47H and XP-72 reaching 789 km/h (490 mph) and the XP-47J a remarkable 812 km/h (504 mph). With the poor thrust and many problems of early jets, this at least offered some hope of postponing the plunge into the unknown, but chief designer Alexander Kartveli was noted for bold design. Like his former employer, Major Alexander Seversky, Kartveli was an *émigré* Russian from the city of Tiflis, and he had become the vice-president engineering after designing several notable fighters.

Thunderbolt developments

There was ample evidence that the P-47 wing, especially in slightly modified forms, could reach speeds well above 800 km/h (500 mph) with jet propulsion; the basic P-47 itself appeared a possible candidate for conversion to jet propulsion. Various studies took place in early 1944 in collaboration with General Electric, whose TG-180 axial turbojet was the only engine considered, and the USAAF

Below right: most examples of the F-84B and G Thunderjet carried 32 5 in rocket projectiles in eight retractable underwing launchers in addition to six 0·5 in machine guns.
Below: the P-84B/F-84B was the first operational Thunderjet, 226 being built. Deliveries began in mid-1947, the 14th Fighter Group being the first unit to convert to the type

Air Research and Development Command and Air Materiel Command. At this stage the fighter looked remarkably like a P-47, despite having a TG-180 in the mid-fuselage fed by a nose inlet and exhausting at the tail. It was with reluctance that the decision was taken to begin again in September 1944 with a completely fresh, uncompromised design, and in November 1944 the studies of 'Jet-Jugs' were abandoned.

Republic agreed with Air Materiel Command to adhere

Right: the F-84F Thunderstreak was the principal fighter-bomber of NATO air forces for over a decade. A Belgian F-84F is illustrated.

Below right: the first of the three swept-wing YF-84Fs is preserved at the US Air Force Museum, Wright-Patterson AFB.

Opposite below: an F-84G propelled from a Martin Matador guided missile launching platform by a jettisonable rocket pod during experiments at Edwards AFB, California.

Opposite centre: an F-84G preserved at Chanute AFB, Illinois, in the colours of the Thunderbirds, the USAF's aerobatic team.

Opposite bottom: the RF-84F Thunderflash had wing-root intakes and cameras in a redesigned nose section.

Below: the swept-wing F-84F Thunderstreak entered US Air Force service in 1954, equipping units of both Tactical and Strategic Air Commands

to the straight-through duct configuration, which it was thought would make possible the highest performance, surpassing that of the earlier Lockheed XP-80 with centrifugal engine and cheek inlets. On the other hand the arrangement left little room for fuel, except in shallow tanks in the thin wing, which also had to accommodate the rather large main landing gears. One of the main changes in the all-new design was to adopt a nosewheel landing gear, the result being a most elegant fighter but one rather short on range and stowage space. It was assigned the designation XP-84 and was logically named Thunderjet.

The engineering design was virtually complete by late February 1945, by which time detail manufacture had started on the first two prototypes. The vital TG-180 engine had run at Schenectady on 23 April 1944 and later in the year had become the J35, with pre-production manufacturing assigned to Chevrolet. One of the major puzzles of early jet history is why the J35 was never flown in 1945, as were other engines slung under Boeing B-17s or in other test-bed aircraft. As it was, the power plant's first flight took place in the prototype XP-84, which was completed at Farmingdale in December 1945. It was subjected to ground systems testing and then partly dismantled for the flight in a prototype Boeing XC-97 to Muroc AFB, California, where the aircraft's first flight took place on 28 February 1946. From the start the performance was extremely good, so that the USAAF considered an attempt on the world absolute speed record. When the second aircraft flew with the more powerful 1,814kg (4,000lb) thrust J35 in place of the 1,700kg (3,750lb) YJ35 in August 1946, it was quickly groomed for the record. On 7 September it set a national record at 983km/h (611mph) but on the same day Grp Capt E. M. Donaldson reached a higher speed with his specially-modified Gloster Meteor.

Cold War protagonist
Throughout 1946–47 Republic toiled to turn the XP-84 into a fighter, using 15 pre-production and service-test YP-84A aircraft, of which no two were exactly alike. Most aircraft had the J35-15 engine, which by this time had been assigned to Allison instead of Chevrolet, becoming that General Motors division's Model 450, produced in a rapidly growing variety of models at

Indianapolis. Soon the J35 was to become rather poor in thrust/weight ratio, but it remained the engine of the first 4,457 aircraft of the F-84 family. These aircraft were not outstanding performers and, as time wore on, became less competitive because of their lack of thrust. They were, however, tough and serviceable and were not only progressively improved in systems, ordnance and capability but were produced quickly enough to make a tremendous difference to the defence posture of NATO in the crucial days of the Cold War in the late 1940s and early 1950s when the Soviet Union had blocked Berlin and war had broken out in Korea. Most European industries were weak, and it was upon the F-84 that most NATO fighter-bomber squadrons relied in the difficult first half of the 1950s. The designation was changed from P-84 to F-84 in June 1948.

Throughout 1947 the A-series development aircraft flew at Edwards, Farmingdale, Eglin and many other airfields proving the newly-added armament of six 0·5in M-2 guns, four above the inlet duct in the nose and two in the wing roots. Other features introduced progressively included underwing hard-points for bombs or tanks, attachments and piping for 865 litre (192 gallon) tip tanks, a rather primitive ejection seat and a pressurised and air-conditioned cockpit. All the improvements were incorporated into the first production model, the F-84B. The USAAF (USAF from September 1947) ordered 500, but the 86th aircraft introduced retractable zero-length rocket launchers under the wing.

All aircraft from the 227th had the new designation of F-84C with the A-13 engine and slightly shorter jetpipe, pitot head relocated on the inlet splitter in the nose and a sequencer for multiple loads of bombs or rockets. This batch was again cut short at airframe number 191 to make way for the greatly improved D model, with 2,270 kg (5,000 lb) A-17 engine, restressed wing for heavier loads and many other changes including simpler telescoping main undercarriage legs. From the 154th Thunderjet the designation was again changed, the F-84E being restressed throughout with only a very small penalty in structure weight. This variant was to fly without combat limitations at weights over a ton heavier than previously, and could operate with JATO (jet-assisted take-off rockets) at 10,886 kg (24,000 lb) with four drop tanks.

Altitude/range trade-off

Curiously, compared with the old Thunderbolt, all Thunderjets had a lower service ceiling yet a greater combat range – quite the reverse of what one might expect. In fact, for the kind of missions flown in the Korean War from autumn 1950, long endurance with attack loads was far more important than ceiling. Like most jets, the F-84 found life hard in Korea where the need was for ordnance, short field length, serviceability and long mission endurance. The F-84D and E were at least effective, although on a hot day the field length required for take-off was excessive even with JATO when a maximum weapon load was carried. This was later to become an enduring problem with air forces in Europe and many hotter places. At no time was the straight-wing Thunderjet considered a top-line air-superiority fighter, and in Korea the MiG-15 was best left to the North American F-86 Sabre.

A useful run of 843 of the E model was followed by no fewer than 3,025 of the F-84G, ending in July 1953. This had the 2,540 kg (5,600 lb) J35-29 engine, but no attempt was made to increase gross weight – indeed there was nowhere to put extra fuel or weapons. Instead the G responded to the new requirement for rapid global

mobility and theatre reinforcement by incorporating an autopilot and provision for in-flight refuelling. Extensive trials took place in England in 1950 with the Flight Refuelling company's probe/drogue method, but it was Boeing's 'flying boom' system which was selected, the receptacle being located in the leading edge of the port wing where it disrupted local lift and made the pilot fly with his control column offset to the right. Subsequently, however, many Tactical Air and Air Defence Command aircraft adopted the probe method. Externally the F-84G was immediately distinguishable by its multi-framed canopy, which was also retrofitted to a number of E models.

Total production of straight or 'plank-wing' Thunderjets was 4,457. Although numerous examples were later bought second-hand by many nations, the major exports were 100 F-84E and 1,936 F-84G fighters assigned with Mutual Aid Program funds to Belgium, Denmark, France, Greece, Italy, the Netherlands, Norway, Portugal and Turkey, with further batches supplied under different aid programmes to Iran, Yugoslavia, Taiwan and Thailand. Yugoslavia used ex-NATO aircraft, not replacing them until 1970–74. The last NATO user was Portugal, which kept a squadron operational at Luanda almost until the final withdrawal from Angola in 1975.

Parasites and rockets

Naturally, Kartveli had closely watched swept wings in the late 1940s and also became involved in numerous surprising research programmes. One of the latter was the scheme for 'parasiting' fighters by hanging them on to bombers, either for the latter's protection or to carry the fighters close to hostile surface targets for runs with bombs or cameras. Neither idea was new, but Republic took it furthest with the F-84; there were numerous schemes in 1946–53 for parasiting straight and swept-wing F-84s on the wingtips or in the weapon bay of the Convair B-36. Less well-known were the wingtip multiple schemes which at one time promised to surround each B-36 by its own fighter squadron.

The strangest Republic fighter was surely the XF-91, first flown on 9 May 1949. Despite severe financial constraints, Republic managed to obtain funding for this curious beast which had little commonality with the F-84 apart from some sections of fuselage and cockpit. The engine was a General Electric J47 with afterburner giving 3,175 kg (7,000 lb) thrust, augmented by a Reaction Motors XLR11-RM-9 rocket engine with two chambers above the main jetpipe and two below. The wing was incredible, with variable incidence and inverse taper as well as sweepback. The structural problems were severe, though the large tips provided room for the outward-retracting tandem-wheel landing gears and had slats to avoid tip stall. In December 1952 this oddity became the first US fighter to exceed Mach 1 in level flight.

More logical was Kartveli's January 1949 proposal for an F-84E with swept wing and tail. The funding appeared so modest that USAF approval was given and on 3 June 1950 the YF-96A made its first flight. Originally the 209th F-84E, it had roughly 60 per cent commonality with the original but featured all-swept flying surfaces. The engine was a J35-25 of 2,360 kg (5,200 lb) thrust. The YF-96 offered increased range as well as speed, because the new wing accommodated much more fuel. While being tested, the YF-96 confirmed the great further increase in performance which would result from a more powerful engine; when, 22 days after first flight, war broke out in Korea, money was no longer in short supply and a programme began to redesign the YF-96 into a completely

new aircraft which, for political reasons, reverted to the old number. Ultimately there were two new aircraft, the F-84F Thunderstreak and RF-84F Thunderflash, both powered by the Wright J65, the Armstrong Siddeley Sapphire built under licence by Curtiss-Wright. This far more powerful engine necessitated a new fuselage with 178 mm (7 in) added to the depth, giving an oval nose inlet to handle the airflow. The structure was redesigned with heavy-press forgings, the canopy was changed to open upwards on parallel links and perforated airbrakes were added to the rear fuselage.

Swept-wing Thunderstreak

The first YF-84F flew on 14 February 1951 with a mainly British engine, the first production machine following on 22 November 1952. Unexpected problems delayed Wright's Americanisation of the previously reliable engine, and during 1952–53 Farmingdale was packed with rows of F-84Fs awaiting the emergence of the J65-1 rated at 3,275 kg (7,220 lb). Buick came in to help produce engines, and by 1954 aircraft with J65-3 engines were flowing to Tactical Air Command, plus a few with nuclear capability to Strategic Air Command. In 1955 delivery began to NATO air forces which soon included the reborn Luftwaffe; Thunderstreaks eventually became the chief fighter-bomber of the air forces of Belgium, Denmark, France, West Germany, Greece, Italy, the Netherlands,

Below: an RF-84K reconnaissance aircraft. A prototype and 25 RF-84Ks were converted from RF-84Fs for the FICON (Fighter Conveyor) project, with nose pick-up hooks and tailplane anhedral to clear the bomb-bay of the B-36 mother-ship.
Below right: the two XF-91 Thunderceptors had rocket motors in the tail to supplement the primary J47 jet and a variable-incidence swept wing with a unique inverse taper. With combined power, the XF-91 sustained speeds over Mach 1 and reached 15,250 m (50,000 ft) in under six minutes

Norway, Taiwan and Turkey. Total production was 2,474 by Republic plus 237 by General Motors at the former North American B-25 plant at Kansas City. The F-84F was a big, heavy attack aircraft, landing at over 250 km/h (155 mph), but later blocks with a slab tailplane were adequate for most missions and many survived (especially in Greek and Turkish units) into the 1970s.

Back in 1951 the second J65 prototype had flown with wing-root inlets, but these resulted in loss of thrust. Despite this, the need for a reconnaissance aircraft with camera-filled nose resulted in this installation being chosen for the RF-84F, the first of which flew in February 1952. Gradually the performance of this model was brought very close to that of the F-84F and by 1958 Republic had delivered 715 of these useful aircraft to TAC, SAC and all the recipients of the F-84F. The nose accommodated up

Republic F-84F Thunderstreak Wing, Belgian Air Force

of No 10 Fighter

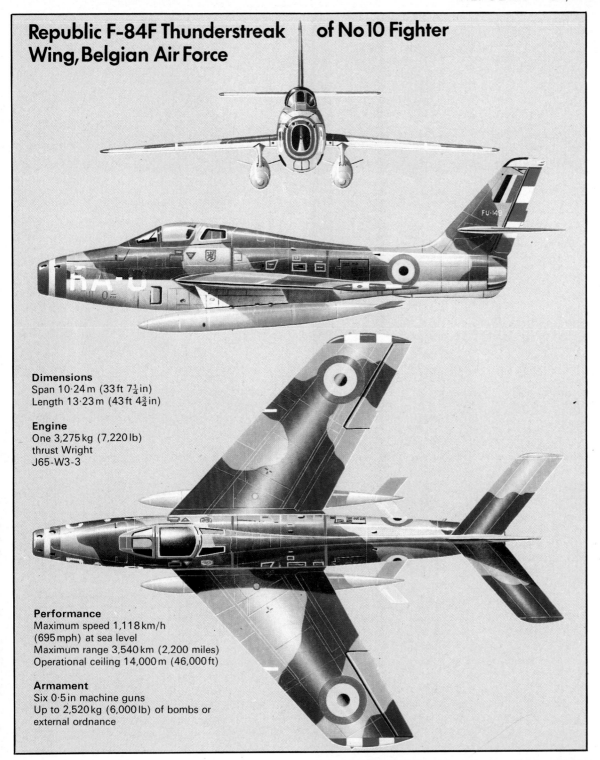

Dimensions
Span 10·24 m (33 ft 7¼ in)
Length 13·23 m (43 ft 4¾ in)

Engine
One 3,275 kg (7,220 lb)
thrust Wright
J65-W3-3

Performance
Maximum speed 1,118 km/h
(695 mph) at sea level
Maximum range 3,540 km (2,200 miles)
Operational ceiling 14,000 m (46,000 ft)

Armament
Six 0·5 in machine guns
Up to 2,520 kg (6,000 lb) of bombs or
external ordnance

to six cameras with advanced sighting and control systems for low and high-level photography. Four M-3 guns were accommodated in the outer part of the wing inlet structure, while the wing carried four large fences.

In 1954 two YF-84J aircraft were flown with the General Electric J73-3 and -7 engines, while in 1955 no fewer than 25 Thunderflashes were fitted with trapeze hooks for trials with the GRB-36. Subsequently these were restored for normal use but because of numerous non-standard features were designated RF-84K. The final variant was the XF-84H, built for testing the 5,332 hp Allison XT40 coupled turboprop. This aircraft had wing-root inlets, a T-tail, a vortex-inducing dorsal fin and many other modifications which assisted the XF-84H to reach the speed of 1,078 km/h (670 mph), which was practically as fast as the all-jet F-84F.

The Thunderchief

Though planned more than 25 years ago, the F-105 Thunderchief set standards of flight performance, ordnance capability, electronic capability and, many would argue, all-round mission capability which can only just be exceeded in the late 1970s. Called 'The Thud', 'Lead Sled' or 'Mighty Iron Hardware' by its pilots, it was in all respects a most impressive aircraft which falls short of more modern counterparts only in a few basic respects, such as the length of runway needed and the thirst of its afterburning straight-jet engine. The F-105 took 26 engineering hours for every hour needed to build previous Republic jet aircraft. Overall, more than five million engineering man-hours and some 10,000 engineering drawings went into its creation. More than 65,000 different items went into the production of each F-105. Designed under the integrated weapons system concept, it carried more electronics than any contemporary aircraft of comparable size and one third of its cost covered electronic 'brains' and computers. The F-105 was the last programme created under Kartveli, and also the last by Republic before the company became a part of Fairchild Hiller (later retitled Fairchild Industries).

Supersonic fighter-bomber

Like the North American F-100 Super Sabre, the F-105 project began as a company initiative to supplement or replace an existing product. Kartveli planned his AP-63 project around the Pratt & Whitney JT4 afterburning turbojet, a scaled-up JT3 (J57) planned to give over 10,886 kg (24,000 lb) with afterburner. This appeared sufficient for a Mach number of 1·5 to be attained by a large fighter-bomber with an internal bay for a nuclear weapon, while retaining considerable capability in the conventional attack role with external stores or as a fighter. No fewer than 108 configurations were examined before the concept gelled in 1954 and was formally funded as Weapon System 306A. The USAF subsequently ordered 15 development aircraft designated F-105.

Two things then happened which deeply affected the programme. The first was adverse: delay with the development of the JT4 into the military J75 engine resulted in the first two F-105 prototypes being redesigned to fly with the smaller, but readily-available J57. The second was positive: NACA aerodynamicists led by Richard Whitcomb had discovered the Area Rule for shaping aircraft for minimum transonic or supersonic drag; when this was applied to the F-105 the maximum speed attainable with the J75 rose to over Mach 2. The first YF-105A flew at Edwards Air Force Base in the hands of Rusty M. Roth on 22 October 1955, with a J57-25 engine fed by inlets similar to enlarged versions of those of the RF-84F. It exceeded Mach 1 on the first flight. This aircraft was almost unique in being kept secret from the public for two years, the first illustration of the type being a heavily-retouched ground view published unofficially in Japan.

Though similar in side view, the F-105B, with the J75-P-3 engine rated at 10,433 kg (23,000 lb), was actually redesigned from nose to tail. The main change was to Area Rule the fuselage by increasing the width at front and rear and reducing it in the centre. The vertical tail was increased in height. Another unique feature was that, because of the Mach 2 performance, the inlets were redesigned to have sharp lips and oblique-shock aerodynamics. Most aircraft achieved this by using a centre-body or wedge with the outer lip further back; Kartveli did the opposite and generated the oblique shock by the outer lip which, in the form of a forward extension of the leading edge of the wing, resulted in a plan view unique among fighters and a variable-inlet system which matched well with the large and powerful engine. Fuselage boundary-layer air was diverted by a splitter plate and dumped through upper and lower nozzles projecting above

the root of the wing. This gave laminar subsonic flow in the inlet ducts and minimised turbulence over the low-mounted, one-piece, fully manoeuvrable tailplane, called a stabilator, which proved increased longitudinal efficiency and stability at supersonic speeds. A pilot-operated drag parachute slowed the F-105 during landings to reduce the length of runway required. A ram air intake at the base of the vertical fin captured more air to cool the after end of the aircraft and supplied additional overall thrust.

The mid/high-mounted wing, with the bomb bay beneath it, had slight anhedral, no de-icing, and conical-camber leading-edge flaps over the whole span outboard of the inlets. The tip ailerons were used only at low speeds; at higher speeds they were locked centrally and the Thunderchief rolled by five sections of hydraulic spoiler above each wing. At the rear was a ventral fin with tail bumper, irreversible tail controls and a unique four-petal airbrake, made of titanium and stainless steel, which was powerful and smooth in operation. The geometry of the inlet duct left enough depth at the wing root for the main landing gears, which were certainly among the longest and strongest fitted to any fighter. This method of retraction freed more of the fuselage for the F-105's payload. Fuel capacity presented problems as the three main fuselage cells added up to only 2,915 litres (641 gallons), but there was provision for an additional tank in the bomb-bay and for 5,870 litres (1,291 gallons) in three drop tanks.

The first of these great F-105B Thunderchiefs flew on 26 May 1956. The first of the remaining 12 on the original contract, it proved outstandingly successful and production began within a year. Three of this batch were

Left: an F-105D carrying the type's maximum external weapons load—sixteen 750lb bombs. Below left: the Thunderchief's warload included combinations of nuclear weapons, high-explosive or incendiary bombs, rockets, missiles and fuel tanks. Below: the 507th Tactical Fighter Group of the US Air Force Reserve has flown F-105s since 1972, an F-105D being shown. Bottom: the 4th Tactical Fighter Wing was the first USAF unit to equip with the F-105B Thunderchief

A 'Thud', as the Thunderchief was nicknamed by its crews during the Vietnam War, flies to its target. This F-105D, from the 355th TFW, carries fuse extenders on part of its bomb-load. These ensured that the bombs exploded before burying themselves in the ground to achieve maximum effectiveness against enemy personnel

designated RF-105B and had camera and IR/radar sensors for advanced reconnaissance missions. Before completion of a single such example, this role was dropped and the aircraft were subsequently flown as special-test platforms in 1957 with designation JF-105B. Production F-105B models totalled 75, deliveries being made from 27 May 1958 to the 4th Tactical Fighter Wing (335 Tactical Fighter Squadron, followed by 334 and 336 TFS) at Eglin AFB, Florida. Like the very limited Lockheed F-104 Starfighter they carried the General Electric M61 Vulcan six-barrel 20mm gun, with a large ammunition tank housing 1,029 rounds which, with a rate of fire of 6,000 rounds per minute, allowed 10 seconds' fire. This phenomenal rate of fire was attained partly because the M-61's six barrels were revolved in front of the cannon's single breech, on the Gatling principle, thus avoiding the cooling problems of single fixed barrel guns. It remains one of the most powerful aircraft guns in the world and can be used in air-to-air combat as effectively as against ground targets. F-105s were able to carry up to 5,443 kg (12,000 lb) of external and internal stores, including the Sidewinder AIM-9B and virtually every non-strategic air-to-ground store in the USAF. The Thunderchief was also unusual in being equipped for flight refuelling by both the probe/drogue and the 'flying boom' systems. A radar-ranging sight was carried in the nose, but the B model did not have all-weather capability.

One-man air forces

This situation was changed by the switch on the production line to the F-105D, the first of which flew on 9 June 1959. Though structurally similar to the B, the F-105D had dramatically upgraded mission capability. This was partly due to the J75-19W engine with maximum thrust of 12,020 kg (26,500 lb), but the main change was the General Electric FC-5 autopilot and flight-control system, Autonetics NASARR R-14A monopulse radar and APN-131 doppler navigation radar. Visually identifiable by the pointed black nose radome, this integrated series of new avionics transformed the Thunderchief into an outstanding all-weather attack aircraft.

Republic made a straight run of 610 F-105D models in production blocks which all introduced refinements. By 1963 these aircraft, popularly known as 'one-man air forces', equipped seven USAF Tactical Fighter Wings, plus the 4520th Combat Crew Training Group at Nellis AFB. After 1966 nearly the entire force was rotated on combat duty in South-East Asia, where they not only flew all kinds of attack missions but also served as the

Republic F-105D of the 4th TFW, U

Dimensions
Span 10·63 m (34 ft 11 in)
Length 19·5 m (64 ft)

Engine
One Pratt & Whitney J75-P-19W turbojet

Performance
Maximum speed 2,236 km/h (1,390 mph)
Tactical radius 1,450 km (900 miles)

Armament
One General Electric M-61 20 mm Vulcan cannon
6,350 kg (14,000 lb) of external stores

chief electronic-warfare aircraft able to penetrate defended airspace. Throughout the production run of the F-105D, emphasis swung ever more strongly from nuclear to conventional warfare and all were eventually fitted with 17 stores pylons and attachment points. The internal bay was invariably occupied by the tailored fuel tank, leaving the main centreline external fitting and four chief wing pylons. The centreline was generally occupied by an MER (Multiple Ejector Rack) for six Mark 83 bombs or similar stores, while the outer pylons were often occupied by AIM-9B Sidewinders for self-defence or various ECM (electronic countermeasure) pods. A further important modification introduced progressively in the field was an airfield arrestor hook.

Two-seat tactical trainer

The final batches of new-build aircraft were two-seaters. The original F-105C trainer had been cancelled at the mock-up stage, but the F-105F was a dual-control mission trainer with full tactical capability; the first flew on 11 June 1963. This suffered very little penalty in performance and, thanks to a body stretch to 21·23 m (69 ft 7½ in), accommodated the new cockpit without loss in fuel capacity. The extra side area was countered by an even taller vertical tail. A total of 143 F-105F models were built, the last in 1964. The Air National Guard received its first F-105B and D aircraft in the same year.

Most of the F-105F aircraft were fitted out as Wild Weasel electronic-warfare platforms, fitted with comprehensive navigation, communications and ECM equipment. Basic fits included the Westinghouse ALQ-105 jammer pod split into two conformal pallets mounted flush against the fuselage beside the weapon bay, as well as the Hallicrafters ALQ-59 data-link jammer and the advanced Westinghouse ALQ-131 wing pod with Loral reprogrammable-software computer to respond instantly

*Right: F-105s continue in
service with the USAF
Reserve and the Air
National Guard,
Thunderchiefs of the
Reserve 301st TFW being
illustrated.*
*Below: two Thunderchiefs
from the 355th TFW
operating from Takhli in
Thailand during the
Vietnam War. The nearest
aircraft is an F-105D
armed with Bullpup air-to-
surface missiles and the
two-seat F-105F carries
Shrike anti-radiation
missiles to attack surface-
to-air missile sites.
Opposite below: the 23rd
TFW was the last regular
USAF wing to fly F-105s.
Opposite bottom: two
Thunderchief wings served
in Germany in the all-
weather fighter-bomber
role. The 36th TFW, one of
whose F-105Ds is pictured,
was based at Bitburg and
the 49th TFW flew from
Spangdahlem*

to changed threats. The wing outer pylon could carry the
General Electric ALQ-87 active pod with nose 'windmill'
and two down-pointing ventral aerials.

Later F-105D aircraft and all F models were built
with an improved ASG-19 fire-control system called the
Thunderstick, with modified NASARR, GE lead-comput-
ing sight, toss-bombing computer and associated equipment. Between 1969 and 1975 about 350 D models in
three blocks were rebuilt by Fairchild Republic with a
further improved system named Thunderstick II, in
which 14 new boxes or other units were installed along the
top of the fuselage in a fat 'saddleback' fairing extending
to the cooling-air inlet at the base of the fin. Yet another
major rebuild programme was the conversion of 48
F models into F-105G missile-suppression platforms.
These had much of the Wild Weasel systems installed,
plus eight new subsystems and a new kit of external
stores: the 2,459 litre (541 gallon) centreline tank with
its own small 'tailplane' and the AGM-45 Shrike or
AGM-78 Standard ARM anti-radar homing missiles on
the wing pylons. The first F-105G flew on 7 August 1967,
but this series was continually being updated in South-
East Asia and in 1974 began to acquire the capability to
operate against CW (continuous-wave) missile sites.

Vindication in Vietnam
The F-105 was initially criticised in operational service
because it was considered to be too big, too fast and too
complex for the conventional weapons fighter-bomber
role. The Vietnam War, however, showed that a successful
fighter-bomber depended upon speed to penetrate and

escape defences, sophisticated electronics to strike
accurately and evade interception, and a heavy and
flexible warload in order to strike effectively first time
around and thereby reduce the overall number of missions
required. The McDonnell Douglas F-4 Phantom, the
F-105's successor, proved the maxim in being even
heavier, more complex and much more expensive.

Although primarily designed as a nuclear strike
aircraft, the F-105 was successfully adapted to deliver
conventional weapons. The primary purpose of air attacks
on North Vietnam was to slow the supplies of men and
matériel from North to South, achieved in large part by
repeatedly attacking points on communications and
supply routes which, if blocked, would result in bottle-
necks. In this, the F-105 took a leading part.

In addition to bombs, the F-105 could carry a wide

range of missiles, a capability which the Vietnam experience
emphasised, of which the AGM-12 Bullpup, the AGM-45
Shrike and AGM-78 Standard were representative. The
Bullpup was guided by pilot radio command signals to
its target. It had a 250lb warhead and was useful against
strongly-defended positions which it would be hazardous
to attack from the ground or with aerial free-fall bombs.
The Shrike and Standard were carried by Wild Weasel
SAM (surface-to-air missile) suppression F-105Gs. Specifically designed to counter radar sets, they locked into
and homed onto enemy radar emissions. In defence
the enemy could only switch off his radar.

The F-105D and F needed sophisticated systems for
the all-weather role. For navigation the Doppler radar
system computed and presented the aircraft's position
to the pilot to within two per cent accuracy on a longi-

tudinal and latitudinal grid, but errors were corrected by setting into the system prominent visual and radar landmarks on the aircraft's designated course. For the attack stage of the mission Thunderstick, the integrated fire control system, linked into the nose-mounted ground-mapping radar and the automatic pilot. It was then able to guide the aircraft to the target and release the bombs automatically. Error was within a 180m (200 yard) radius around the target centre. Although this error was acceptable with a nuclear payload, it was not acceptable with conventional weapons, with effective destruction radii of only half such an error; visual corrections in the target area thus became necessary. The F-105 could not therefore be used satisfactorily for blind attacks with conventional weapons at night or in zero-visibility conditions without external radar control, thus limiting its full all-weather capability to nuclear strike.

Eluding ground defences

North Vietnam was heavily defended by anti-aircraft guns of various calibres and, to a lesser extent, by surface-to-air missiles (SAMs). In Vietnam, the F-105 was forced down to altitudes of below 6,000m (20,000ft) to avoid the SAM defences, but this brought them within range of the anti-aircraft guns. Missiles could, however, be effectively jammed by the type's electronic countermeasures systems, but most kills against F-105s were scored by the anti-aircraft guns; missiles claimed only a one in fifteen overall success ratio against American aircraft. F-105s were occasionally engaged by MiG-17s and MiG-21s but, with the aid of the M-61 cannon and AIM-9 Sidewinder missiles, the F-105 proved surprisingly competent in fighter combat, although its main advantage was its great speed at low level. However, F-4s began to fly top cover to F-105 missions during the course of the conflict.

The F-105 was taking the major part in air strikes against North Vietnam and attrition was high. Losses were reported as only one per cent of total missions flown but, as the units which operated the F-105 over North Vietnam were flying 60 combat hours per aircraft per month, even such a small loss rate resulted in heavy attrition over a period. On 30 June 1966 the US Air Force had 597 F-105s on strength; by 5 May 1967 only 406 remained in service. At the end of 1970 the last operational F-105 attack unit serving in Vietnam was withdrawn to the United States and its aircraft were assigned to Air National Guard units. Attrition, not obsolescence, caused their replacement in front line units.

The 'Thud' was for many years standard equipment of USAF Tactical Fighter Wings in Europe, and Japan/South-East Asia, as well as several independent Tactical Fighter Squadrons flying Wild Weasel missions. In speed, manoeuvrability, firepower versatility and ordnance capability the F-105 qualified for virtually every tactical mission: fighter-bomber for close support of ground forces, air defence interceptor, air interdiction fighter, SAM-suppression platform, long-range thermonuclear bomber and supersonic tanker. The F-105 could fly 3,220km (2,000 miles) non-stop without refuelling, as demonstrated in Operation High Flight in 1961 during the Berlin crisis when F-105 flights to Europe from the USA became a routine deployment feature. With mid-air refuelling the F-105 could fly anywhere on the globe and pinpoint a nuclear bomb-load from a base in the United States. There is little point in comparing this battleship of the sky with the older F-100 or newer F-4, because all were great in their day and all were equally good at several types of mission.

KNIGHTS UNDER THE BLAC

Manfred von Richthofen and his brother
Lothar scored 120 aerial victories between them

Manfred was commissioned in the autumn of 1912 and was deployed with the Uhlan Regiment No 1 in eastern Germany when World War I began on 1 August 1914. Encamped along the Russian border, the Uhlans were among the first German troops to march into Czarist territory. The main concern of German military planners at this time was the Western Front, so before the war was a month old, Manfred von Richthofen's unit was heading for France. There, the long and dismal prospects of protracted ground warfare became immediately clear to von Richthofen. His early interest in cavalry activities grew out of the knowledge that those mounted troops were always assigned the exciting missions of reconnnoitring enemy lines through a series of fast dashes past bewildered infantrymen. However, the growing network of trench fortifications was particularly frustrating to cavalry elements on both sides of the lines.

To circumvent the long line of trenches and obtain badly-needed intelligence information, military planners designated their military aircraft the 'cavalry of the clouds'. Sensing this development was the way to end the boredom of life behind the lines, Manfred von Richthofen applied for transfer to the German Fliegertruppe, as the flying service was then known.

The von Richthofen family was long prominent in eastern German government and economic affairs and in 1741 .was elevated to baronial status in the Kingdom of Prussia. It was not until the 19th Century, however, that the family produced its first career military officer, Major Albrecht Freiherr von Richthofen. In turn, he became the father of two of the most prominent German fighter aces of World War I, Manfred and Lothar von Richthofen, whose combined combat score totalled 120 enemy aircraft.

Disciplined upbringing
Both sons were born in Breslau, Germany before the era of powered flight began, Manfred on 2 May 1892 and Lothar on 27 September 1894. Their father's military career was cut short when he developed an ear infection after plunging into a stream to rescue a member of his dragoon regiment. The elder von Richthofen could no longer serve on active duty and was granted a disability pension. Although a *freiherr*–the lineal title of the von Richthofens–was just half a step below a baron in the German nobility, it generally carried with it a sizeable estate. It was to this estate in Schweidnitz, in the province of Silesia (now part of Poland) that Major von Richthofen and his family retired.

There, young Manfred and Lothar spent their formative years, learning the duties and obligations of their station in life. Manfred, a natural horseman and athlete, wanted only to spend his days on the playing fields of Schweidnitz. His father had other ideas, however, and at the age of 11 Manfred was sent to the Cadet Academy at Wahlstatt. He spent six years in the Cadet Corps and two years in the military School in Lichterfelde before taking and passing his army officer's examination in 1911.

Observer training
On 10 June 1915, Leutnant Manfred von Richthofen reported to Fliegerersatzabteilung 6 at Grossenhain in Saxony to begin his training as an aviation observer. At the time it was customary to train enlisted men as pilots–making them literally aerial chauffeurs–and placing officer observers in charge of the aircraft. Hence, it was in keeping with von Richthofen's status to train him initially as an observer. Accepting all of this, von Richthofen was quite surprised when he was quickly posted to Feldfliegerabteilung 69 and assigned a pilot senior in rank to him, Oberleutnant Georg Zeumer. The two men fast became friends, but Manfred von Richthofen was to serve for less than two months with Feldfliegerabteilung 69 on the Eastern Front. In the third week of August 1915, he headed west again for an assignment with a unit in Flanders, where he would see aerial combat.

Leutnant von Richthofen was assigned to a squadron with the curious name of Brieftauben Abteilung Ostende (Carrier Pigeon Unit, Ostend), this being a code-name to conceal the unit's mission. This posting introduced von Richthofen to the first generation of large, multi-engined German bombers. Reunited with his friend Oberleutnant Zeumer, Manfred von Richthofen was in one of the unit's AEG GI bombers when he shed his first drop of blood for the fatherland. Assigned to drop bombs over the side of the fuselage, von Richthofen leaned too far on one occasion and nicked a finger on one of the propellers moving the twin-engined pusher aircraft. He subsequently wore his blood-stained glove like a badge of honour.

Zeumer and von Richthofen were flying a morning reconnaissance patrol on 1 September 1915 when they spotted a Farman biplane performing a similar mission.

Above: an Albatros DVa flown by Manfred von Richthofen illustrates his practice of painting his aircraft red. This led to his popular soubriquet of Red Baron.
Below: Albatros DIII and DV and Fokker Dr I scouts of the élite Jagdstaffel 11, led by Manfred von Richthofen.
Far left: a portrait in oils of Manfred von Richthofen

A quick nod of agreement between pilot and observer was all that was needed for them to abandon their patrol and undertake their first aerial combat. The two slow and awkward aircraft went around and around, each trying to gain the advantage. When the battle appeared inconclusive, the Farman pilot slipped away, leaving Zeumer and von Richthofen frustrated at the lack of a conclusion to what they had imagined to be a glorious event.

During the Battle of the Champagne in the autumn of 1915, Manfred von Richthofen chanced to meet the celebrated German air ace Oberleutnant Oswald Boelcke. Eager to learn the secrets of successful aerial combat, von Richthofen blurted out: 'Tell me honestly, how do you really do it?' Boelcke laughed at the directness of the question and then answered: 'It is really quite simple. I fly in as close as I can, take good aim, open fire . . . and then my opponent falls.'

Combat aspirations

Boelcke's simple piece of advice was enough to convince Manfred von Richthofen that he could never make a significant contribution to the war effort sitting in the back seat of a bomber or reconnaissance aircraft. To correct that situation he prevailed upon Zeumer to teach him how to fly. Less than a week later, on 10 October 1915, von Richthofen made his first solo flight, which would have been perfect if his over-eagerness had not caused the plane to turn over on landing.

After further, more formal training at Döberitz and a visit to the Fokker aircraft factory at Schwerin, Manfred von Richthofen was assigned to Kampfstaffel 2, a unit which used a variety of aircraft. He became involved in an aerial combat south-west of Douaumont on 26 April

1916 and, although the German Army official report mentioned his actions, he did not receive full credit for a Nieuport fighter which he brought down that day.

To add to von Richthofen's frustration, his unit was sent back to the Russian Front, where there would be even less opportunity for aerial combat. A second chance meeting with Oswald Boelcke changed that. Hauptmann Boelcke was charged with assembling one of the first fighter squadrons and was on a tour of various units to select the best pilots. Meeting von Richthofen in Russia, the great ace remembered the zealous young nobleman and subsequently added his name to the list of candidates for the new squadron, officially known as Jagdstaffel 2, Manfred von Richthofen was so pleased to have finally joined a fighter squadron that he urged his younger brother Lothar to apply for aviation duties.

Like his older brother, Lothar had attended the Cadet School and then the Military School. When, in the autumn of 1916, he received Manfred's letter extolling the virtues of the air service, he was already a veteran of cavalry service with Dragoon Regiment No 4 and had learned the frustration of cavalry unable to fulfil its proper role. Lothar was further encouraged when he learned that on 17 September Manfred had scored his first official aerial victory, an FE2b of No 11 Squadron Royal Flying Corps, which he attacked over Villers-Plouich. By the year's end, Manfred would be one of the leading lights of the German air service with 15 victories.

While Manfred von Richthofen was adding to his score, Lothar was undergoing observer's training which culminating in a posting to Kampfstaffel 23 on the Somme in December. He would not remain long in an obscure combat unit. Swiftly-moving events hurled the von Richthofen name into the centre of German military affairs. With the death of Boelcke on 28 October 1916 – less than four months after the death of another great ace, Max Immelmann – the German air service's need for a hero figure was being met by Manfred von Richthofen.

The one battle which confirmed Manfred von Richthofen's place among the luminaries of German combat units took place on 23 November 1916 between Bapaume and Albert. In that fight von Richthofen shot down and killed the celebrated British ace Major Lanoc Hawker VC. Manfred von Richthofen scored his 16th victory on 4 January 1917. Twelve days later he was awarded the coveted Pour le Mérite, the highest Prussian bravery award. Manfred was given command of his own fighter squadron, Jagdstaffel 11 and, like Boelcke before him, was allowed to select many of the members. An early choice was his brother Lothar.

A fruitful month

Within two weeks of his arrival at Jagdstaffel 11, Lothar proved his worth by scoring his first aerial victory. On the afternoon of 28 March, he shot down an FE2b of No 25 Squadron RFC, near Vimy. The following month – made infamous as 'Bloody April' due to the high level of casualties suffered by the Allies – both von Richthofen brothers added significantly to their scores. Manfred shot down another 21 British aircraft, bringing his total to 52, while Lothar shot down 15 British aircraft to raise his score to 16.

Lothar shot down eight more aircraft in May, giving the German propagandists an opportunity to enhance his stature even further. It was subsequently claimed that the British ace, Captain Albert Ball VC, was the 20th victim of Leutnant Lothar von Richthofen. While it is possible that the younger von Richthofen was involved in a fight

with a British triplane, which he claimed to have shot down on 7 May 1917, it is unlikely that he shot down Ball's SE 5 biplane.

Lothar von Richthofen scored his 24th aerial victory late on the morning of 13 May, when he brought down a BE2c near Arleux. In the same fight, however, his red Albatros fighter suffered a number of hits and Lothar barely managed to return to his own airfield. The following day Lothar was awarded the Pour le Mérite, which was presented to him in the hospital bed which he was to occupy for the next few months.

Manfred von Richthofen had been on leave when Lothar was wounded. When he returned to the Front in June, he attacked his adversaries with a vengeful fury, shooting down four enemy aircraft within the space of a week. With 56 kills to his credit, Manfred von Richthofen was the undisputed aerial ace of World War I.

The handsome young nobleman – erroneously referred to as a 'baron' – had a darker side to his nature. Not content merely to shoot down his adversaries, the elder von Richthofen brother often followed his hapless quarry for a distance, watching the crew burn to death or, in the absence of parachutes, leap hopelessly from their burning aircraft. At night, in the quiet of his comfortable quarters, he would write to his mother, telling her how they died.

When the famed Dutch-born aircraft constructor Anthony Fokker produced the first of the successful Dr I triplanes, he made sure that they met with von Richthofen's approval. The great ace went on to score more than 20 of his final victories in Fokker triplanes, his aircraft bearing the overall red finish which won him the soubriquet of 'Red Baron'.

Special distinction

When Manfred von Richthofen was proposed for the special distinction of golden oak leaves for his Pour le Mérite, some members of the German General Staff protested that such an honour should be reserved for a higher-ranking officer who had won a battle. To that the German Army Chief of Staff, General Erich Ludendorff, replied that Manfred von Richthofen, then a *rittmeister* or cavalry captain, 'had done more than win a battle'.

To be sure, Manfred von Richthofen had paid a certain price for his success. He had suffered a slight head wound during a fight in July 1917 and the cumulative effect of it was to cause headaches of increasing intensity. Shortly before his death, he wrote: 'I am in wretched spirits after every aerial battle. But that no doubt is an after-effect of my head wound. When I set foot on the ground again at my airfield after a flight, I go to my quarters and do not want to see anyone or hear anything.'

It was in such a condition that, with 80 confirmed victories to his credit, Rittmeister Manfred Freiherr von Richthofen took off on the morning of 21 April 1918. During an encounter with Sopwith Camels of No 209 Squadron RAF, Manfred von Richthofen was shot down and killed by a single bullet through the heart. There was, however, some controversy over whether he was shot down from behind by Captain Roy Brown, a Canadian of No 209 Squadron, or Australian ground gunners.

Lothar von Richthofen was absent from Jagdstaffel 11 when his brother was killed. Lothar had been wounded in a fight on 13 March and was convalescing at the time of Manfred's death. That was the second time the number 13 had proven unlucky for Lothar von Richthofen. Then, on 13 August 1918, the day after he scored his 40th aerial victory, his wartime career was ended when he was shot down again. In 1922 he died in an air crash.

Leutnant Lothar Frhr. von Richthofen

CJ von Dühren phot.
BERLIN

526
Postkartenvertrieb W.Sanke
BERLIN N.37.
Nachdruck wird gerichtlich verfolgt

Top: Lothar flew under the leadership of his brother in Jagdstaffel 11. Wounded several times, he shot down 40 enemy aircraft and was highly decorated.
Above: serial numbers taken from Manfred von Richthofen's victims, including 5964 from Capt Hawker's DH2, shot down on 23 November 1917.
Top left: a cubist painting by J. A. Turnbull depicting Manfred von Richthofen's Fokker Dr I in his last combat.
Above left: pilots of Jagdstaffel 11, left to right; Festner, Schaffer, Manfred and Lothar von Richthofen and Wolff.
Left: the remains of Manfred von Richthofen's Fokker Dr I on the airfield of No 3 Squadron RAF at Valheureux

Hat in the Ring

The US Army Air Service's leading ace in World War I was Captain Eddie Rickenbacker

The American ace of aces during World War I was born in Columbus, Ohio on 8 October 1890. The son of a German-Swiss father and a French-Swiss mother, his name was originally Edward Reichenbacher. During World War I he changed his family name to the less Germanic-sounding Rickenbacker–an appellation which he was to make famous. He also added the middle name Vernon to add what he considered 'a touch of class'. Rickenbacker's formal education ended at the age of 12. With the death of his father, Eddie had to leave school to help his mother support the other seven children in the family. A succession of menial jobs finally brought him to the Frayer-Miller Automobile Company, where he acquired a great interest in internal combustion engines. That led him to enrol in a correspondence course in mechanical engineering.

Motor racing career

When Lee Frayer, one of the partners in the company, decided to go into business for himself, he took the 16-year-old Rickenbacker with him. Although young in years, Rickenbacker had developed an impressive reputation as an expert mechanic and driver. A self-reliant individual from the beginning, Rickenbacker had taught himself how to drive and never bothered with the formality of obtaining a driver's licence. He would later teach himself how to fly and never feel the need for a pilot's licence.

At that time the best advertising for motor cars was in their success racing on unpaved tracks, a sport then gaining wide popularity. Hence, Lee Frayer provided a new opportunity for Eddie Rickenbacker by making him a driver-salesman, driving in races one day and selling cars the next. Rickenbacker continued this dual career for six years and then, at the age of 22, he devoted all of his energies to racing.

Automobile racing was a dangerous sport, but it taught Eddie Rickenbacker a number of lessons he would later use to good advantage in aerial combat over the Western Front. Many years afterwards he noted: 'You didn't win races because you had more guts. You won because you knew how to take turns and baby your engine. It wasn't all just shut your eyes and grit your teeth.'

Rickenbacker's methodical nature paid off. At Daytona Beach, Florida in 1916 he drove a German-built Benz racer to a new world land speed record of 215·74 km/h (134 mph). By the end of 1916, Rickenbacker's last full year in racing, he had earned 80,000 dollars–a considerable sum of money for a 26-year-old man.

When the United States entered World War I on 6 April 1917, Eddie Rickenbacker was in England trying to obtain engines for his own team of racing cars. America's involvement in the war, however, motivated him to return home to offer his services to the military effort. Rickenbacker first suggested that the US Government create a fighter squadron composed of former racing drivers, whose high-speed skills and mechanical abilities he felt would make them a formidable team.

That idea was politely declined with a counter-proposal that Rickenbacker and other drivers could best serve the nation by enlisting in the US Army as drivers on the staff of General John J. 'Black Jack' Pershing, the supreme American commander in Europe. Although friends protested that Rickenbacker's talents would be demeaned by chauffeur duties, the quick-thinking racer saw an opportunity to use a position on General Pershing's staff to transfer to the new aviation branch of the US Army's Signal Corps.

The odds were against Rickenbacker being selected either for commissioned officer status or pilot training. He did not have the background and college education for the former and, at the age of 26, was considered too old for the latter. Undaunted, he enlisted as a sergeant on 27 May 1917 and sailed for France as General Pershing's chauffeur. Rickenbacker's stream of requests to transfer to the aviation section were continually turned down. Then he had a piece of good luck. During a tour of the Front, Colonel William 'Billy' Mitchell, then senior officer in the fledgling air arm, was in a captured Mercedes touring car which suddenly broke down. When Mitchell's

Left: Rickenbacker flew with the 'Hat-in-the-Ring' 94th Aero Squadron USAAS (emblem above). Right: Rickenbacker with 'Old No 1', the SPAD SXIII in which he scored a number of aerial victories. Centre right: Rickenbacker with a Hannover CL IIIa which he and Lt Reed Chambers, his friend and flying companion, forced down on 2 October 1918. Below right: Rickenbacker (at head of table) with the Boeing B-17 crew with whom he survived 22 days in a raft in the Pacific

driver was unable to get the car started, he was aided by another chauffeur in the entourage, Sergeant Eddie Rickenbacker. The expert mechanic spotted and corrected the malfunction so quickly that he attracted Colonel Mitchell's favourable attention.

Transfer to flying duties

When Mitchell learned of Rickenbacker's racing background and desire to become a fighter pilot, he persuaded General Pershing to release his driver to the air service. Rickenbacker was then transferred to the 3rd Aviation Instruction Centre at Issoudun, France and, in the absence of a more formal programme, almost literally became apprenticed to qualified pilots. While other would-be American pilots underwent long months of ground school in the United States, Rickenbacker concentrated on the practical aspects of flying.

By January 1918 he had been commissioned, becoming a first lieutenant in the US Army Air Service. His engineering background, however, made him too valuable to assign to the Front, so he was appointed Engineering Officer at Issoudun. There he quietly resumed his flight training, logging hours in various fighter aircraft during lulls in the training schedule.

Early in March, Rickenbacker was posted to Villeneuve-les-Vertus, where squadrons of the 1st Pursuit Organisation were forming. Rickenbacker was assigned to the 94th Aero Squadron commanded by Major John F. Huffer, an American who had served in the French air service and scored three aerial victories. Other veterans assigned to the 94th Aero Squadron at that time included the 17-victory Lafayette Escadrille ace Raoul Lufbery (then a major in the US Air Service), James Norman Hall, Kenneth Marr, David Peterson and Alan Winslow.

The experienced combat pilots were to teach their skills to the novices. Hence, on 19 March 1918, Major Lufbery led the first patrol from an American unit to fly over enemy lines. Flying Nieuport 28 scouts each equipped with one machine gun, Major Lufbery and Lieutenants Eddie Rickenbacker and Douglas Campbell drew some anti-aircraft fire, but the trio encountered no German fighter opposition.

Upon returning to the ground, Lufbery asked Rickenbacker and Campbell whether they had observed any aircraft at all during their time in the air; both men shook their heads. Lufbery replied that he had counted half-a-dozen French aircraft from a nearby pursuit squadron and an equal number of German aircraft. The mentor's lesson was quite clear: he who is alert in the air will survive; he who is not will perish.

The honour of becoming the first American-trained fighter pilot to shoot down an enemy aircraft went to Lieutenant Douglas Campbell of the 94th Aero Squadron. On the morning of 14 April, Campbell and Lieutenant Alan Winslow went after an Albatros D Va and a Pfalz D III from Jagdstaffel 64. Both German fighter aircraft were brought down.

Initial combat success

On 29 April, Rickenbacker scored the first of a long line of aerial victories by shooting down an Albatros D Va over Baussant. The day Rickenbacker scored his second victory, the 94th Aero Squadron suffered the loss of Captain James Norman Hall. During a fight over Vierville-en-Haye on 7 May, Leutnant der Reserve Friedrich Hengest of Jagdstaffel 64 shot down Hall, who was wounded and taken prisoner. Meanwhile, Rickenbacker got into position behind Hengest's squadronmate, Leutn-

ant der Reserve Willi Scheerer and fatally wounded him. The events of that encounter, however, were not confirmed until much later.

Rickenbacker shot down another Albatros on 17 May, two days before the legendary Raoul Lufbery was shot down by a German two-seater he attacked in full view of his comrades at Toul. Despite such losses, the work of the 94th Aero Squadron continued. In fact, Rickenbacker and Douglas Campbell were very active. Rickenbacker achieved his third victory (discounting his 7 May victory) on 22 May and Campbell his fourth on 27 May. Campbell's fifth victory, on 31 May, made him the first American-trained fighter ace.

A serious ear infection kept Rickenbacker from operations during June, July and August of 1918. When he returned, however, Rickenbacker made up for his absence in grand style. During the last two weeks of September he shot down four Fokker D VII fighters, a Halberstadt two-seat reconnaissance aircraft and a captive observation balloon. Appointed commanding officer of the 94th Aero Squadron on 25 September 1918, Captain Rickenbacker shot down another 18 aircraft during the remaining 41 days of World War I.

Belated recognition

Eddie Rickenbacker was the recipient of many American and other military decorations, but his achievements as America's leading aerial ace were not fully recognised until a dozen years after the war. Then, on 6 November 1930, President Herbert Hoover bestowed on him the Medal of Honour, the highest US military award. The citation singled out an aerial combat on 25 September 1918 when he attacked five Fokker fighters and two Halberstadt two-seaters, shooting down one of each type.

After the war Eddie Rickenbacker obtained financial backing to form the Rickenbacker Motor Company, which produced a series of automobiles marked both by their technical merit and the distinctive 'Hat in the Ring' insignia of the 94th Aero Squadron on the radiator emblem. Although the company failed in 1927, Rickenbacker himself raised 200,000 dollars to pay off all outstanding debts and a further 700,000 dollars with which he purchased the Indianapolis Motor Speedway. Here he successfully ran and promoted the celebrated Indianapolis 500 motor race until after World War II.

Rickenbacker subsequently headed General Motors' Eastern Air Transport Division, which then jointly owned Eastern Air Lines with North American Aviation. Within three years he turned the business around from a drain on the owners' reserves to a solid profit-maker. Then, when the US Government forced General Motors to divest itself of its airline holdings, Rickenbacker raised the three million dollars needed to buy it. He ran Eastern Air Lines until his retirement in 1963.

Although Eddie Rickenbacker held a reserve colonel's commission, he always said that captain was the highest rank he earned and, hence, the title he preferred to use. During a World War II inspection tour of American bases he demonstrated the indomitable willpower which propelled him to positions of leadership and success. He was being transported in a Boeing B-17 Fortress and, when it crashed into the Pacific, he literally took command of the survivors for the next 22 days, encouraging them to survive and refusing them the opportunity to end their misery by slipping off into a watery death. Rickenbacker's six raftmates had to admit that they owed their lives to his iron will.

Eddie Rickenbacker's fierce pride and resolute spirit made him the centre of controversy throughout his life. When he died at the age of 82 in a Swiss hospital on 23 July 1973, 'Captain Eddie' was to the end a man revered by many, reviled by others, but respected by most.

A SPAD SXIII restored in the markings of Captain Edward V. Rickenbacker's 'Old No 1' for display at the US Air Force Museum. The principal fighter used in France by the US Army Air Service, the SPAD's fine qualities enabled American pilots to make a significant impact on the air war during the seven months in which the Service saw action

Home Defence Hero

William Leefe Robinson won the Victoria Cross defending London from attack by enemy airships

In 1916 William Leefe Robinson became the first recipient of the Victoria Cross awarded for action over the British Isles. This award was to remain unique until World War II when Flt Lt James Nicolson was engaged in similar work to his predecessor, that of defending his country against enemy air attack. Leefe Robinson, the youngest of a family of seven, was born in Tollidetta, South Coorg, India on 14 July 1895, and when the family moved back to England 14 years later, the youngster enrolled at St Bees, Cumberland. He graduated from Sandhurst, serving in the Worcester Regiment at the start of World War I, and, by 1915, was an observer with the RFC.

Home Defence duties

Wounded and sent back to Britain, Leefe Robinson took up pilot training and was eventually posted to No 39 (Home Defence) Squadron at Suttons Farm, Essex. The unit was one of several squadrons hastily-formed to help combat the ever-growing threat of the German Zeppelin airships which frequently raided London. The Squadron was equipped with converted BE2c aircraft with upward-firing machine guns and, although they were vulnerable on the Western Front, they proved to be ideal for attacking Zeppelins. However, for many months the failure of the gun crews stationed around London, and the seeming invulnerability of the Zeppelins weighed heavily.

On the evening of 2/3 September 1916, the German army and navy airship divisions joined forces to mount a mammoth raid on London; 12 dirigibles headed for the capital that night and one would never return. It was 2308 hours when Suttons Farm learned that Zepplins had been sighted, and Leefe Robinson and other Home Defence pilots were soon in the air to meet the enemy.

The first airship Leefe Robinson sighted was Ernst Lehmann's LZ98, an army ship. However, the German lost his pursuer in heavy cloud and after fifteen minutes the British pilot gave up the chase. Flying towards sweeping searchlights Leefe Robinson found another airship and, although two other pilots dived on the vessel, he was first to the action. Despite having anti-aircraft fire bracketing the ship, Robinson pressed home his attack, diving underneath and emptying a whole drum of ammunition into the hull. When this had no effect, he made a second run with another drum of ammunition, meeting with a similar result. Changing to his final drum of ammunition the British pilot tried another tactic and poured the entire contents into one area beneath the huge tail fins. The trail of tracer bullets disappeared into the airship's fabric and the Lewis gun fell silent. Suddenly a dull pinkish glow appeared deep inside the airship and in seconds the whole tail was ablaze with flames which towered a hundred feet high.

.Below left: Robinson was awarded the Victoria Cross for the destruction of SL11, but his subsequent combat career was brief.
Below: the crew of the German Schutte Lanz SL11 airship which Leefe Robinson shot down on the night of 2/3 September 1916. The airship's commander, Hptm Wilhelm Schramm, is seated second from the left.
Bottom: Robinson seated in his BE2c night fighter a few days after shooting down SL11. In the engagement fire from the aircraft's upward-firing machine gun damaged the upper wing centre section, (displayed in foreground).

Ball of fire

The doomed airship was seen by Londoners as a ball of fire which grew bigger and exploded with a brilliant flare. The civilians watched the blazing hulk, 3,500 m (11,500 ft) above, hang motionless for several seconds before it finally slid out of the sky to fall at Cuffley in Hertfordshire; it burned for over two hours. After a flight of over three hours Leefe Robinson had very little petrol left and following his return to Suttons Farm, he scribbled a report and collapsed into a sleep which remained unbroken until his fellow pilots woke him on Sunday morning and drove him over to the wreck.

Already the area was seething with police, army personnel, and civilians; all the pilots could see was a high tangle of wire, charred fragments of the wooden hull and four burned-out engines strewn over a wide area. These pathetic remnants were all that remained of the German Army's recently-commissioned Schutte Lanz SL11: the first airship to fall over England was not a Zeppelin as many people still claim. In a corner of the field a green tarpaulin covered the charred bodies of thirty-year-old London-born Hauptmann Wilhelm Schramm and his crew of 15 who were later buried with full military honours at Potters Bar. As a result of his victory Lt William Leefe Robinson received the Victoria Cross, monetary gifts from noted individuals and the adoration of thousands.

Operational command

However, when more Zepplins fell to the Home Defence pilots and the menace slowly receded, Leefe Robinson VC was promoted to captain and posted to France commanding No 48 Squadron at La Bellevue. The Squadron was equipped with a new aircraft, the Bristol F2a, which evolved into the famous F2b Fighter.

On 5 April 1917, Robinson led five F2a aircraft on their first operational sortie over the lines with the fixed plan that, if attacked, the group was to adopt a tight circle, each gunner protecting the aircraft behind it with his field of fire. These were fine tactics for lumbering FE2b pushers but not for such a new fighting machine. Thus the stage was set for disaster. Robinson's flight encountered five of the best pilots on the Western Front. Manfred von Richthofen led four red-painted Albatros Scouts into a battle which lasted barely ten minutes, after which four of the Bristols, including Robinson's, lay smashed on the earth below: the VC's vanquisher was Vizefeldwebel Sebastian Festner.

Captain Robinson was captured alive and was transferred from prison camp to prison camp where his escape attempts ended in failure each time. At the Holzminden Camp, Robinson was reputedly singled out by the notorious Hauptmann Karl Niemeyer who swore to make the British pilot suffer for causing the death of Wilhelm Schramm whom, he claimed, had been a personal friend. In 1918 when the war was over Robinson was repatriated and returned to England, weak and sick. In this condition he was not fit enough to resist the influenza which was sweeping the world at the time and was one of the 150,000 in England alone who died.

Lieut. W. L. Robinson, V.C. and Lieut. F. Sowrey D.S.O.

Above: Leefe Robinson in the driver's seat of his car with Lt F. Sowrey DSO, who shot down the Zeppelin L32.
Left: Schutte Lanz SL13, sister to the ill-fated SL11, hangared in the Wittmund Shed in 1916

First Englishman to Fly

A.V. Roe, founder of the Avro company, was the first Englishman to fly an aeroplane

Alliot Verdon Roe was born in 1877, the fourth child of a Manchester doctor. After a varied career surveying, tree-planting, fishing and running a post office in British Columbia, Canada, Roe returned to England as an apprentice with the Lancashire and Yorkshire Railway Works before turning to marine engineering. While sailing between England and South Africa he became fascinated with the albatross which wheeled above his ship and later he began experimenting with paper gliders which he flew from the top windows of the family home.

Scepticism and encouragement

The Times thought little of Roe's efforts when he wrote to that prestigious newspaper in 1906 urging Britain to take the lead in the development of powered flight. 'It is not to be supposed that we in any way adopt the writer's estimate of his undertaking,' commented the editor, 'being of the opinion, indeed, that all attempts at artificial aviation on the basis he describes are not only dangerous but foredoomed to failure from the engineering standpoint.'

The *Daily Mail*, however, was more encouraging. In April 1907 the newspaper organised a model aircraft exhibition at the Agricultural Hall, Islington which attracted 130 entries, among them three rubber-band-powered pusher biplanes built by Roe. The Honourable Charles Rolls adjudged Roe's lattice-framed models to be 'the most tried and perfected in the show', but awarded the prize to a display of spliced rope and basketwork for balloons. A week later flying trials for the modellers were held at the Crystal Palace; less than one quarter of the original entrants attended, but Roe, undiscouraged, brought his three biplanes and on his second attempt flew one model the length of the hall. The 8,000 spectators, who had paid one shilling each to watch, rose to their feet, applauding. All three oil-paper-covered models made excellent flights in the open air afterwards and the judges awarded Roe £75 – claiming, however, that no model had merited the full £150 on offer.

With this prize-money Roe was able to finance his first full-size man-carrying machine, which he began building in stables behind his doctor brother's surgery in Putney. The aeroplane was a scaled-up version of his front-elevator Crystal Palace models, powered by a 9 hp JAP engine. In the summer of 1907 Roe moved the machine to Brooklands racetrack in Surrey, whose proprietors were offering £2,500 for the first aeroplane flight around the course. That year a total of £17,500 was waiting to be won for flying and Alliot Verdon Roe desperately needed more money to continue his vital development work.

Roe's biplane was substantially complete by September 1907, but the track manager at Brooklands, a redoubtable Austro-Pole named Rodakowski, was less than helpful. He insisted that the would-be aviator should build his workshop/hangar in a position from which it would have

Below: the Avro 504, developed from the Type G, was designed in 1913 by A. V. Roe (above). An immediate success, it proved to be entirely viceless to fly and established Roe's reputation. The type served in World War I as a fighter, bomber, reconnaissance aircraft and trainer and until the 1930s as a military and civil trainer and tourer

to be moved when flying commenced, and would not allow Roe to sleep there at night. Roe thus made a grand exit each evening, bidding goodnight to the gatekeeper, then crept back under cover of darkness to bed down alongside his machine. Times were hard. The *Daily Mail* prize money was running out and he was forced to subsist on a meagre five shillings a week for food.

Escape from eviction

Despite the efforts of the more co-operative racing drivers, who attempted to tow the biplane into the air on occasions, Roe's machine refused to fly with the tiny JAP engine. He thus arranged to borrow a 24 hp Antoinette engine, but the end of the year came before it arrived; Brooklands' management withdrew their offer and gave Roe notice to quit.

He persuaded Rodakowski to let him stay, but had to move the workshop outside the track's perimeter fence. Each time Roe wanted to make a flight attempt he had to manhandle the biplane over the fence. Finally he made a detachable section in the fencing, through which he took the aeroplane before dawn. At length he was rewarded; on 8 June 1908 the biplane became airborne during taxying tests and hopped some 46 m (150 ft). Though not officially recognised, Roe's 'hop' (and several subsequent trials that month) were the first flights by an Englishman.

In that summer of 1908 Roe left Brooklands and moved to a disused railway arch on desolate Lea Marshes, where he built a triplane weighing less than 90 kg (200 lb) which was again powered by a 9 hp JAP, this time driving a geared tractor propeller. The triplane was named 'Bulls-Eye Avroplane' and made its first flight in July 1909 – the first powered flight in Britain by an all-British machine – covering a distance of 275 m (300 yards).

Inspired improvisation

Roe soon realised that lack of power was hindering further progress. Moving from Lea to Wembley Park, he substituted a 35 hp Green engine and in August 1910 set out again for Blackpool for the August Bank Holiday flying meeting. Roe arrived four days before the start; his triplane arrived in ashes. He had sent it by rail, and sparks from the locomotive had set fire to the tarpaulin covering its wagon. Determined not to disappoint his native Lancashire crowd again, Roe rushed to Manchester and there assembled another triplane in three days.

He flew several circuits of the field at Blackpool, had three crashes, but took away a £75 consolation prize and an invitation to take part in the Boston-Harvard Aviation

Meeting in America that September. Roe sailed to America with Claude Grahame-White, who thrilled the crowds with his daily triumphs. Roe, dogged with bad luck as ever, crashed three times and won over the crowds with his good-humoured persistence.

On his return from America Roe returned again to Brooklands while establishing the A. V. Roe Company (later Avro) in his home town of Manchester. The triplane configuration, which Roe had pioneered, gave way to the tractor biplane with his 1911 Type D, which retained many features from his early aircraft and was the first step towards the immortal Avro 504 trainer, which Alliot Verdon Roe designed with perhaps half a dozen orders in mind. More than 10,000 were built, and the aircraft became the archetypal training aeroplane of the 1920s. Alliot Verdon-Roe (he had changed his surname by then) left the Avro company in 1929, the year in which he was knighted. He died on 4 January 1958.

Below: Roe's first full-size aircraft was a canard pusher biplane. The machine was underpowered and could only make short 'hops' into the air.
Centre: the first of three triplanes built by Roe before turning with greater success to biplanes.
Bottom: Roe's company was flourishing by 1918 and continued to prosper after the war. Works were established at Birmingham and Hamble, Avro 504K floatplanes at the latter being illustrated

Sharks of the Air

The Roland fighters of World War I were unpopular with their pilots

The success of the Wright brothers in Europe brought about the formation in Germany in 1909 of the Flugmaschine Wright Gesellschaft to manufacture Wright biplanes. The non-recognition of the Wright patents by the German authorities, however, forced the company into liquidation. Its assets were bought by Luftfahrzeug-Gesellschaft (LFG), a company which had existed since 1908 and had been formed to build Parseval non-rigid airships. Using the Wright sheds at Johannisthal, LFG initially investigated the construction of aircraft which would be suitable for service in Germany's African colonies. Steel tube featured in the construction of these machines and both biplanes and monoplanes were produced. Success came when Bruno Langer broke the world's endurance record on 3 February 1914 when he remained airborne for 14 hours and 6 minutes, flying a Roland Pfeil (Arrow) biplane.

Shortly after the outbreak of war, Roland (a trade name adopted by LFG to prevent confusion with the already well-known aircraft manufacturer LVG) began work on two large *kampfflugzeuge* or battleplanes. The first of these, the Rol III was later given the military designation G I. It was powered by a large single engine of 240hp in the fuselage which drove outrigger twin pusher propellers in a fashion similar to the Wright biplane. The Rol IV, designated G II, was more conventional in that it was powered by two 220hp engines.

In the meantime LFG began to build Albatros B II and B III two-seater machines under licence, and the Albatros C I was later licence-built as the LFG C I. While engaged in this production programme, Roland's Chief Engineer, Dipl Ing Tantzen and his design staff, began to look at ways of reducing the high parasite drag of the average two-seat aeroplane. The fuselage in particular came in for a lot of attention; following wind-tunnel testing, a deep oval-section fish-shaped fuselage resulted. This completely filled the gap between the top and bottom wings, eliminating centre section struts. A light wooden framework of stringers and fretted bulkheads was covered with diagonal strips of plywood, resulting in a semi-monocoque structure which possessed great strength, was light in weight and had an efficient aerodynamic shape. This

Left: the design of the Roland C II reduced drag to a minimum and provided the crew with an unparalleled view. The type began to equip units in early 1916 for general purpose and reconnaissance duties. The unarmed prototype is illustrated. Below left: the sole Roland G I was powered by a single 240hp Maybach Mb VI engine buried in the fuselage, driving two pusher propellers through a system of geared shafts

fuselage was embodied in a small two-seater with a span of only 10·3 m (33 ft 9 in), powered by the 160 hp Mercedes D III 6-cylinder water-cooled engine and designated Roland C II Wahlfisch (Whale).

When the Wahlfisch emerged early in 1916, it was one of the fastest aircraft at the Front, being as fast as Allied single-seaters. With full war load it could climb to 1,000 m (3,280 ft) in seven minutes and, with a top speed of 165 km/h (103 mph), was ideal equipment for the *kampfstaffeln*, with their dual roles of bombing and fighting. The speed element was made good use of by assigning single examples to some of the *feldfliegerabteilungen* who used them for rapid reconnaissance work. The machine however, had its failings; the forward view from the pilot's cockpit was poor, the aircraft had a high wing-loading and inexperienced pilots were often troubled when trying to land the Wahlfisch on the small rough operational aerodromes. The lack of dihedral made the machine unstable in badly-flown turns and many accidents resulted. After some 12 months of front-line use, the machine was gradually relegated to training duties. Over 200 aircraft of this type were built in 1916, some of these being licence-built by Linke-Hoffmann.

The streamlined Shark

During the production of this two-seater, a single-seat version, designated Roland D I Haifisch (Shark), was evolved and 100 machines of the type ordered. The value of careful streamlining made itself immediately apparent; the machine's performance was exceptional, with a climb to 3,000 m (9,840 ft) in 13½ minutes and a top speed of 180 km/h (112 mph). The Roland works at Adlershof was destroyed by fire during the night of 6 September 1916. Although some aircraft were destroyed including the Roland C III prototype, which was a two-bay wing version of the Wahlfisch, sufficient tooling was salvaged to enable production to be resumed within a few days at the Automobile Exhibition Buildings in Berlin.

Despite this disruption, the first production Roland D I reached the Front in October 1916. Unfortunately it had inherited some of the shortcomings of the Wahlfisch, including the poor forward view from the cockpit. Later models embodied different top wing centre-sections, revised radiator layouts and reductions in forward fuselage cross-section to improve the pilot's view. The D II used the same engine as the D I, but the D IIa was fitted with the higher-powered Argus engine of 180 hp.

In spite of the attractive appearance of these aircraft, however, aerodynamic faults had been introduced by some of the modifications mentioned. At altitude the D II and D IIa were not as manoeuvrable as had been expected; nevertheless, 550 machines of these types had been ordered by March 1917, 120 of them being licence-built by Pfalz Flugzeugwerke. Their tenure as operational machines was short and units on the Western Front which received the Roland D II and D IIa experienced very low serviceability rates; by mid-1917, most of these units had re-equipped with Albatros single-seaters. On the Eastern Front and in Macedonia Roland fighters were no more popular; however, due to replacement difficulties, they served in these theatres for longer periods.

Boat-like construction method

The Roland D III was basically a D IIa with centre-section struts supporting the top wing in place of the wing pylon previously used, in order that the pilot's view might be improved; only a small number was built. A further attempt was made to improve this basic design with the

Roland D V, but this remained a prototype. The fuselage construction of these Roland fighters was similar to the Wahlfisch in concept and was time-consuming to fabricate. The company made a change at this time to *klinkerrumpf* fuselage construction, where horizontal planking was used in clinker fashion as was the practice on small boat hulls. This form of fuselage was used on a triplane prototype designated D IV, produced during the latter half of 1917, and also on the prototype of the Roland D VI, reputedly the thousandth aeroplane built by the Roland company. The *klinkerrumpf* manner of planking the fuselage structure was to remain the hallmark of Roland fighter design, only being forsaken late in 1918 on the

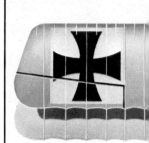

Engine
One 160 hp Mercedes D III

Armament
One flexibly-mounted Parabellum machine gun
One fixed forward-firing Spandau machine gun

last few prototypes built by the company.

Three Roland D VI prototypes were produced; these differed in various ways, mostly in fuselage shape and in the areas and type of balance used on control surfaces. The second prototype was powered by the 185 hp Benz BZ IIIa engine and had a superior performance to the other models fitted with the 160 hp Mercedes D III power plant. In order that the most suitable fighter designs should be produced in quantity, comparison trials were organised at Adlershof aerodrome near Berlin where designs, which in some cases had already been accepted for limited production by the authorities, were flown against each other. Much of this flying was carried out by experienced front-line fighter pilots and great emphasis was placed on their reports.

Fighter competition

The first fighter competition was held in January 1918 and 35 aeroplanes took part, four of these being Roland products. The two D VI prototypes performed well; the Mercedes D III-powered version climbed to 5,000 m (16,405 ft) in 25·2 minutes and had a top speed of 190 km/h (118 mph). The Benz Bz IIIa-engined D VI climbed to the same height in 18·5 minutes and had a maximum speed of 200 km/h (124 mph). The other two Roland machines were not successful; the D VII powered by the Benz Bz IIIb had engine trouble and the D IX, powered by the Siemens Sh III, crashed during the competition.

Production of the Roland D VIa (Mercedes) began in February 1918, and in April the first batch of D VIb

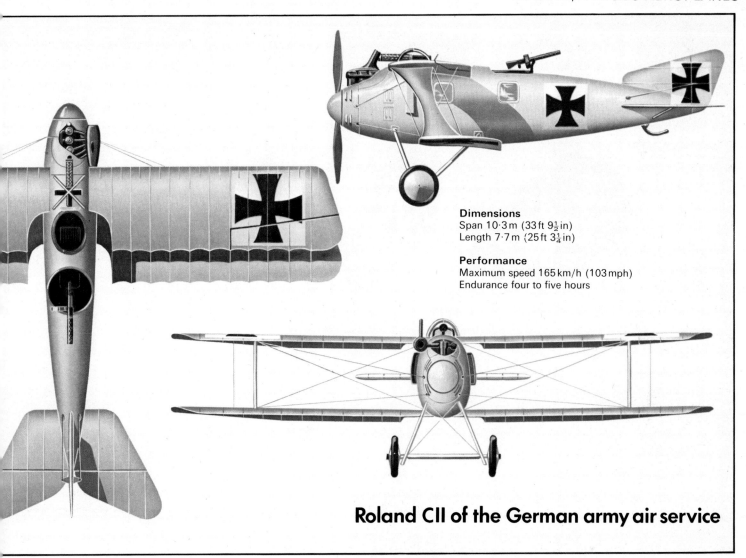

Dimensions
Span 10·3 m (33 ft 9½ in)
Length 7·7 m (25 ft 3¼ in)

Performance
Maximum speed 165 km/h (103 mph)
Endurance four to five hours

Roland CII of the German army air service

(Benz) aircraft was ordered. By the end of the war some 350 machines had been produced and a number of *jagdstaffeln* had been equipped with the type. Operationally, the Roland D VIa was not considered to be much better than the Albatros D Va and Pfalz D IIIa types which it replaced. It was, however, faster and more manoeuvrable, but by its introduction in June 1918, many fighter pilots favoured the excellent Fokker D VII.

Roland continued to develop fighter prototypes and entered these in succeeding fighter competitions, but did not secure production orders. It would appear that the main problem in 1918 was not the technical inferiority of the Roland fighters, but rather the over-long development periods to which they had been subjected by a thorough organisation. Competition was fierce in this field, and although Roland was the fourth-largest German aircraft manufacturer, entries from other well-established companies like Fokker and Rumpler had a better performance than the Roland fighters.

Roland built approximately 3,000 aeroplanes, including some 100 marine aircraft during World War I. The company had a production capacity during the last year of about 100 aircraft per month. By November 1918 some 1,250 workers were employed compared with the 10 employees with which the company had started early in 1914. Following the relaxation of the Armistice restrictions LFG built a number of small flying boats, seaplanes and sporting aircraft in the 1920s; finally, the wheel turned full circle for LFG when the company produced a number of small Parseval type PN airships around 1930.

Opposite: a Roland D VIa serving with Jasta 30. Although the type's manoeuvrability was good, pilots' preference for the Fokker D VII precluded large orders.
Left: D II Haifisch (Shark) fighters of Jasta 25 pictured on Kanatlatsi airfield, Macedonia in early 1917. The D II and D IIa served mainly on the French sector of the Western Front, but did not fully equip any unit

The Factory at Farnborough

Many British warplanes of the World War I era were designed at the Royal Aircraft Factory

Below: a line-up of Royal Aircraft Factory types pictured in front of the airship sheds at Farnborough. They comprise, from right to left: RE7, the two prototype RE8s, two FE2s, SE4a, FE8 and sundry BE2 variants

The Royal Aircraft Factory had its origins in the Balloon Factory established at Aldershot in 1892. Two years later a Man-lifting Kite Section was formed under Captain B. F. S. Baden Powell, brother of the founder of the Boy Scout movement. During the early years of the twentieth century much work was done at Aldershot on balloons and airship design and construction leading, in 1904, to aero engine development. Heavier-than-air craft were first seriously considered in that year by Colonel J. E. Capper, who was directed by the War Office to visit North Carolina, USA, to invite the Wright brothers to continue their experiments in Britain; the British Treasury, however, failed to sanction the expenditure.

Cody's powered kite

The following year the Balloon Factory moved to south Farnborough where, on 11 April 1911, it became the Army Aircraft Factory and, precisely a year later, the Royal Aircraft Factory. By that time another American, Samuel Franklin Cody, had interested the War Office in his man-lifting kites and, in 1907, introduced the military aeroplane in the shape of his first power-driven kite. Soon others were thinking of developing structures of different configuration. During 1911 the Factory Superintendent, Mervyn O'Gorman–now regarded as the founder of Britain's scientific approach to aeronautics–laid down a series of type classifications for pursuing research.

As a design and experimental establishment for the advancement of aeronautics, the Factory had no charter for building aeroplanes. Original designs could only reach fruition within the Factory if they were represented as conversions of existing aircraft, in case Treasury auditors should charge the staff with indulging in work outside their province. It was also against the political tenor of the time for public institutions to engage in construction considered appropriate to industry. These constraints on the talented staff led to subterfuge, so that the stated

meaning of the factory designations bore little resemblance to fact. The famous BE series was a case in point.

A French Voisin biplane was presented by the Duke of Westminster to the War Office in 1911 and sent to Farnborough for overhaul. At that time Frederick M. Green, formerly of the Daimler Company and Geoffrey de Havilland, already a designer and test pilot, had ideas for the production of a tractor biplane. The Voisin presented the opportunity by providing a 60 hp Wolseley engine and the two executives soon had Factory craftsmen constructing a new airframe to their design. This venture, designated BE1 for Blériot Experimental No 1 to accord with O'Gorman's classification, had little in common with a Blériot-type aeroplane. This BE1 was used early in 1912 for wireless telegraphy by Captain H. P. T. Lefroy of the Royal Engineers, with Geoffrey de Havilland piloting.

A young mathematician from Cambridge, Edward Teshmaker Busk, who was to influence the BE series, joined the Factory in June 1912, the same month that an improved tractor design, the BE2, attained an altitude of 3,000 m (10,000 ft). This was during trials at Larkhill, Salisbury Plain, where the following month the Military Aeroplane Competition was being held under War Office arrangements to find the most practical military aircraft type. There were 31 entrants including such names as Avro, Blériot, Breguet, Cody, Farman, Handley Page, Hanriot and Vickers. Only five aircraft, however, were British throughout – all others had French engines.

In spite of suspicions being voiced in the Press that the Factory was competing with industry, the Superintendent was so impressed with the BE2 that he had it demonstrated at the competition. Although Cody's pusher biplane was the official winner, the BE2's unofficial demonstration of superiority could not be ignored and it was the Factory design which was ordered in preference, the manufacture being contracted out to industry. Meanwhile development continued at the Factory and contracts were revised for a BE2a version with an improved fuel system and later the BE2b with deepened fuselage coamings.

The Admiralty also ordered the BE for its air arm and the War Office increased orders for the expanding Royal Flying Corps. When King George V visited Laffan's Plain at the end of Army manoeuvres on 5 June 1913, four BEs joined airships in the first ever Royal Flypast. Two months later a BE2a was given an overload test with weighted sandbags to assess its structural strength, thus pioneering the static testing of airframes.

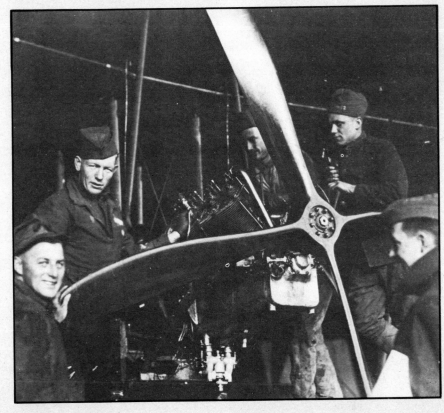

Stable reconnaissance platform

By November 1913, as a result of experiments, the BE2c appeared. Apart from having a 70 hp Renault engine, the wings were staggered and the shape of their tips were changed; the tailplane was modified and a triangular fin added. By these means Busk produced an aircraft which was inherently stable and, since reconnaissance was then the prime role of military aircraft, it provided a useful observation platform. The pilot even had the back seat to give the observer the best forward view.

As the official history put it in retrospect, the BE2c represented 'the embodiment of British aerodynamic knowledge of the period'. The infant aircraft industry, however, was not impressed. There were allegations that the Factory undermined the prospects of private constructors and it was suggested that they were pirating the ideas of private individuals. Factory spokesmen retorted that private firms were not fulfilling Service requirements – a need which became more acute in August 1914 when war

Above: the 90 hp RAF1a engine installed in later BE2c airframes greatly improved the aircraft's performance.
Opposite above: the original BE2 was evolved from the BE1. The BE2a was widely used for reconnaissance in France early in World War I.
Opposite: the BE2e of 1916 had new wings and a modified fuselage

was declared. Only a single BE2c then existed, but drawings were soon available for distribution. Among the companies participating were the armament firms of Armstrong Whitworth and Vickers and the leading aircraft firms of the day such as Blackburn, Grahame-White, Handley Page and Martinsyde. Unhappily, Busk was killed while testing a BE2c on 5 November 1914.

When the Expeditionary Force went to France at the outset of World War I the BE2a/b types were the mainstay of the RFC element, equipping two of the four squadrons, while the other two had Blériot monoplanes, Henry Farman biplanes and a few Avro and BE8 aircraft. The last-named were the result of several prototypes, designated BE3 to BE7, to adapt a rotary engine to the BE. Nicknamed the 'Bloater', by virtue of the streamlined cowling of its 80 hp Gnome engine giving it a fish-like appearance, it went into limited production but proved unsatisfactory in service.

After replacing the 70 hp Renault with a 90 hp RAF1A engine of Factory design, the Royal Flying Corps standardised on the BE2c for reconnaissance, artillery spotting and bombing. During 1915–16 there were more BE2c aircraft on the Western Front than any other type in British service. The RNAS used BEs for coastal patrol and both air arms for home defence. Five enemy airships, four Zeppelins and a Schütte-Lanz, fell to attack by BE2c home defence aircraft. During 1915 the BE2d version, with an external gravity feed fuel tank under the port upper wing and dual control, was introduced. This was followed in 1916 by the BE2e, which featured a revised wing shape, a top wing of greater span than the lower and a modified fuselage. Two other BE types resulted from this change-over on large-scale production: BE2c and BE2d fuselages fitted with new BE2e style wings became the BE2f and BE2g respectively.

A campaign to discredit Factory designs in general and the BE2c in particular led to an enquiry into general RFC administration. The RE8, another Factory design, replaced the BEs on operations at the Front but the latter remained in service until the end of World War I.

The first Reconnaissance Experimental type (RE1) was a biplane, not unlike the early BEs, built with a steel-tube fuselage early in 1913. It was later mounted on floats and tested on Fleet and Frensham Ponds as the HRE2 (H for hydro). The following RE3 crashed soon after building and the RE4 project was abandoned. The RE5, powered by a 120 hp Austro-Daimler engine, showed promise and the Factory opened their first production line, manufacturing 24 during 1914–15 for the RFC in France. Passing over the RE6 project to produce an improved RE5, the RE7 was evolved with the capacity to carry a bomb-load of up to 150 kg (336 lb).

The first RE7 unit, No 21 Squadron, reached the Western Front in June 1916 and quickly suffered at the hands of Fokker monoplane pilots. The observer/gunner,

placed in the front cockpit, had a poor field of defensive fire, and the Squadron was re-equipped with the BE12. This was basically a BE2c (later BE2e) airframe converted to single-seat configuration and powered by a 150 hp RAF4A engine. Intended as a fighter, it failed in this role after reaching France in August 1916 with No 19 Squadron. Relegated to the minor theatres and home defence as a fighter, it continued in use by Nos 19 and 21 Squadrons on the Western Front for a period as a bomber.

Workhorse of the RFC
Finally, the Factory came up with a successful reconnaissance aircraft design in spite of initial setbacks. The RE8 used the basic configuration of the BE2e and the power unit of the BE12, but had the position of pilot and observer reversed so that the latter, at the back, could have a good field of defensive fire with a Lewis gun mounted on a Scarff gun-ring. Its speed of 163 km/h (102 mph) at 2,000 m (6,500 ft) was not impressive and its tendency to spin, before rectifying modifications were carried out, led to the usual spate of criticism of Factory products. No 52 Squadron reached the Front on 16 November 1916 with the first RE8s and suffered severe losses, as did all Corps squadrons up to May 1917. The new RFC fighters, among them the Factory's SE5, did much, however, to permit the RE8s to carry out their artillery spotting and reconnaissance tasks unmolested.

From mid-1917 the RE8 was the workhorse of the RFC. Large contracts were placed, chiefly with motor car producers Austin, Daimler, Napier, Siddeley-Deasy and Standard, plus the Coventry Ordnance Works. Over 4,000 were built, including 45 early deliveries from Farnborough. At the end of the war 16 squadrons on the Western Front and eight overseas units were equipped with the RE8. A Government-sponsored concern had succeeded where private industry had apparently failed – but the success of Army Corps aircraft relied largely on fighter protection and this was another sphere of activity

Top: a squadron of RE8s serving in France. Nicknamed 'Harry Tate', the RE8 was developed in late 1915 as a reconnaissance aircraft. It was later used for bombing and army co-operation.
Above: an FE2d, final production model of the FE series, seen at Farnborough in 1916. The FE2d appeared in mid-1916, serving until spring of the following year.
Left: the BE1, seen as originally built, was designed by Geoffrey de Havilland and F. M. Green. It first flew on 1 January 1912, the BE2 flying a month later

of vital concern to the Factory.

The FE1 was the very first of the Factory aeroplanes. This so-called Farman Experimental had originated privately as the second aircraft built by Geoffrey de Havilland, who had also designed its 45hp Iris engine. The aircraft was purchased by the Factory in December 1910 and de Havilland had joined the staff to further its design and carry out testing. After crashing through engine failure, the FE1 was reconstructed with a 50hp Gnome rotary engine as the FE2.

Development of the FE series was slow, partly because the pusher configuration was becoming outmoded. It was 1913 before a further version appeared, this time with a neat streamlined nacelle for pilot and observer; this aircraft, however, soon crashed. When war came 12 of a new version, already conceived, was ordered as the FE2a, designed as a fighter, and thereafter the FE designation came to mean Fighting Experimental. The 100hp Gnome engine of the early machines was replaced by a 120hp Beardmore and the FE2b, the first true fighting aeroplane, resulted. Contracts were placed for large-scale production and the first reached the Front on 20 May 1915. The impact of the 'Fees', as they were colloquially known, was not felt until 1916, however, when fully-equipped squadrons reached the Front.

The FE2 in combat
The RFC in the field in 1916 was composed mainly of Factory-designed aeroplanes of the BE and FE types. The latter soon made a name for themselves; their observers in the nose, acting as gunners, had an excellent field of fire including backwards over the wings. Realising their vulnerable area, the Germans soon attacked from below and behind; this was countered by the tactic of flying in a close circle when attacked, with each FE2 protecting each other's tail and massing their fire-power. Daily they battled their way over the enemy lines, escorting BEs or engaging in photo-reconnaissance and bombing.

The 120hp Beardmore was soon replaced by a 160hp version. A new FE2d model appeared with a 250hp Rolls-Royce Eagle engine; unfortunately the first delivery to France flew directly into German hands due to a navigational error. By mid-1917 the FEs were outclassed as fighters, but remained in squadron service as night bombers. During August 1917, the FE2bs of No 100 Squadron made night attacks on Marcke airfield where von Richthofen, who had shot down 12 FEs, had his base. At home, the FE2b was used for defence and anti-submarine patrols. It continued to serve as a night bomber in the Independent Force in 1918 and remained in production in Scotland until the Armistice.

The FE2d had been phased out earlier, as the Rolls-Royce engines were required to power more promising designs from industry; none of the other FE designs survived the war. The FE3 pusher biplane was unsuccessful, while an FE4 twin-engined 3-seat biplane bomber, built to carry a Coventry Ordnance Works gun, reached only the prototype stage. The FE5 drawings were never completed and the FE6 and 7 remained respectively bomber and fighter projects only. The FE8 single-seat pusher fighter did go into production, however, in 1915 to serve in four squadrons on the Western Front between July 1916 and July 1917. The FE9, intended as an FE2b replacement, failed trials and the next two designs were abandoned. Finally, the FE12, planned to clear the home skies of enemy raiders by carrying both searchlight and rocket gun, was never completed.

In late 1918 all FEs were declared obsolete for Service

SE5A of No 32 Squadron RAF

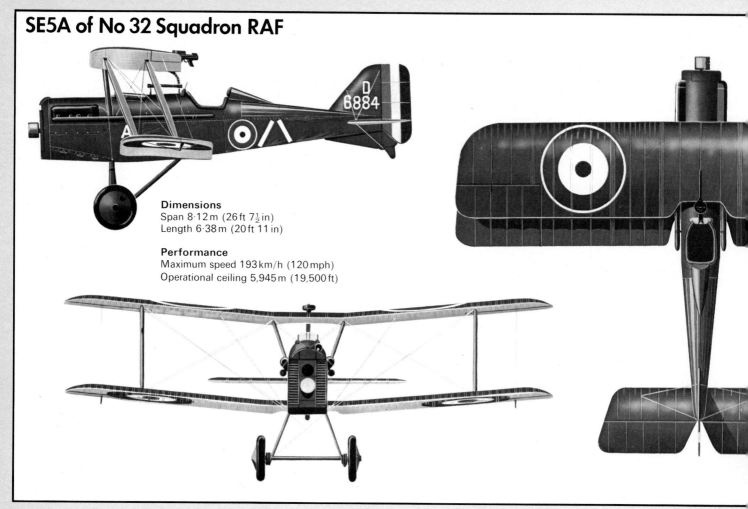

Dimensions
Span 8·12 m (26 ft 7½ in)
Length 6·38 m (20 ft 11 in)

Performance
Maximum speed 193 km/h (120 mph)
Operational ceiling 5,945 m (19,500 ft)

purposes. A single FE2b became a civil aircraft and survived until the 1920s. That was the last seen of the FEs for, unlike the other major design series of the Factory, not one is preserved.

Like other Factory aircraft, the origins of the SE series were almost the antithesis of its developed form. A Blériot monoplane, whose uncertain flying characteristics had earned it the nickname of 'Mankiller', was accepted at the Factory for repair in December 1910. Its 60hp ENV engine provided the means of powering a canard-type biplane which was designed by F. M. Green and Geoffrey de Havilland. It was given the designation SE for Santos Experimental after Santos Dumont, designer of the canard, or tail-first, aeroplane. Unfortunately it crashed and killed Lieutenant T. Ridge, the Assistant Superintendent, on 18 August 1911.

Another design in which Geoffrey de Havilland had played a major part was the first ever single-seat scout, the BS1 for Blériot Scout No 1. This was another example of the perverse designation system, for this conventional biplane had little in common with monoplane Blériots. After crashing in March 1913 it was rebuilt as the BS2, with an 80hp Gnome engine replacing its previous 100hp power plant. Later, re-designated SE2, it represented the first formula for a high-speed scout.

By this time the SE4 with a 160hp Gnome had arrived, designed by H. P. Folland. This was the first aeroplane to have variable-camber wings and its celluloid-covered cockpit was an innovation. In the hands of Norman Spratt it attained a level speed of 209·6km/h (131mph), an unofficial world record, but the engine proved unsatisfactory for service.

A completely new design was presented by Folland in

1916 in conjunction with J. Kenworthy and F. W. Goodden; the SE5 conformed to the basic single-seat tractor biplane configuration and incorporated the first use of tail-trimming and seat-adjusting gear. The SE5 showed promise simultaneously with the RE8 at a time when the Factory was under attack by politicians and the industry. Grave allegations were made by Mr Pemberton Billing in the House of Commons that the officials responsible for deciding types of aircraft failed, either by ignorance, intrigue or incompetence, to provide the best the industry could offer.

After a lengthy enquiry on the administration of the RFC and the Factory, it was recommended that the latter should more strictly observe its Terms of Reference. While fostering research and development, it should not engage in production, not even of prototypes. It was also recommended that the Superintendent should have

Engine
One 200 hp Wolseley
W.4A Viper

Armament
One 0·303 in Vickers
machine gun
One 0·303 in Lewis
machine gun

*Below and bottom left: the SE5A rebuilt by the Royal
Aircraft Establishment (successor to the Royal Aircraft
Factory) was originally built by Wolseley Motors. It was
used for skywriting after World War I.
Below left: an SE5A modified for aerial advertising.
Below far left: the SE5As of No 29 Squadron pictured at
their base at Oudezeele on 18 August 1918*

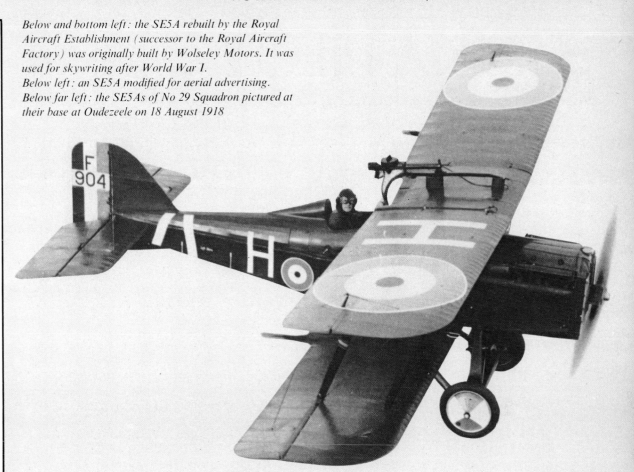

special business experience and on 2 September 1916 Henry Fowler, formerly the Midland Railway's chief engineer, took over from Colonel Mervyn O'Gorman who had held office for five years. Under Fowler, however, both SE5 and RE8 designs were pressed forward and although large contracts were placed with private firms, both types were also built within the Factory.

The prototype SE5 first flew on 22 November 1916 and was flown next day by Captain Albert Ball, then the leading RFC air ace. Unfortunately the second prototype broke up in the air the following January, killing Major Frank W. Goodden, the Factory's chief test pilot. Improvements tried out on early models included shorter-span wings and replacing the 150 hp Hispano-Suiza by a 200 hp engine. Large contracts were then placed with Austin, Vickers, Martinsyde, Air Navigation and Wolseley to this new standard as the SE5A. Initial deliveries of the SE5 were to No 56 Squadron in March 1917 for the unit's move to France the following month. The Squadron had the aircraft's original semi-enclosed cockpit replaced by a conventional windscreen.

From June onwards the SE5A replaced the SE5 and No 56 became the most formidable squadron on the Western Front. As production increased, with a Wolseley-built Hispano known as the Viper, so the SE5A took its place, with the Sopwith Camel, as one of the most effective fighters of World War I. By 1918, the SE5A equipped 15 Royal Air Force squadrons and the 25th and 148th Aero Squadrons of the US Air Service on the Western Front, together with units in Macedonia, Mesopotamia and Palestine. Unlike the Camel, which had twin Vickers machine guns, the SE5A had a single Vickers gun firing forward through the propeller arc and a Lewis gun on a

Foster mounting on the top wing which could be angled to fire forward or upward. In a ground strafing role the SE5A could carry four 20 lb bombs.

The American Expeditionary Force bought a number of SE5As from Britain and the Curtiss factory was tooling up for SE5A production when the war ended. The American Eberhardt company built 50 aircraft, designated SE5E and fitted with a 180 hp Wright-Hispano engine, for the US Army Air Corps.

The Royal Aircraft Factory changed its name to Royal Aircraft Establishment after 1 April 1918 to avoid confusion when the Royal Air Force was formed. In the last year of the war the Factory built 104 SE5A fighters and helped with the building of 24 Handley Page 0/400s and a few Vickers Vimy bombers. Full-scale experimental work included radio-controlled aerial bomb carriers and two prototype CE1 (Coastal Experimental No 1) flying boats. In all the Factory built 533 aircraft of 28 different types up to 1919 when full-scale construction work ceased.

The contribution made by the Factory in those years to the general advance of aeronautics, and to the aircraft industry, included the introduction of the protective PC10 dope and the aircraft general standard (AGS) system of common items in use throughout the industry today. There were also significant advances made in aero engine design and development. As evidence of the advanced thinking of the scientific staff a wind tunnel was installed in 1907, ground-to-air wireless experiments started in 1908 and helicopter development and radio control in 1916. Although aircraft are no longer built at Farnborough, design and development work continues there today; the airfield is thus a fitting venue for the Society of British Aerospace Constructors' exhibition.

STUKA PILOT

Hans-Ulrich Rudel's astounding combat career was recognised by the unique award of the Golden Oakleaves

The bitterness of the fighting which raged between Germany and Russia from mid-1941 until the end of World War II was unmatched on any front. The numbers of men and machines involved – and the casualties suffered – staggers the imagination, as does the vastness of the terrain covered. Inevitably the four-year campaign was punctuated by a succession of set-piece battles involving massed guns, tanks and aircraft, and it was just this type of warfare that the Wehrmacht and Luftwaffe had been evolved to fight.

With the prolonged continuity of combat service which was a feature of a career in the Luftwaffe, it was not surprising that a number of pilots registered outstanding personal achievements. Among the German fighter pilots were men like Hartmann and Barkhorn whose tally of air victories far exceeded those of any other air force's pilots, while one man, Hans-Ulrich Rudel, was to emerge head-and-shoulders above all others with his extraordinary score of enemy ships and vehicles destroyed from the air. To say that luck and survival throughout the long campaign played a major part in this remarkable success would be to detract from the man's unquestioned skill and supreme courage.

Pilot and observer

Rudel was born the son of a Protestant priest at Konradswaldau in Silesia on 2 July 1916; he attended school until 1936 and excelled at numerous sports. On reaching his twentieth birthday he applied to join the new Luftwaffe and succeeded in passing the entrance exams. After a couple of months with the Reichsarbeitsdienst (State Labour Service) he joined the Luftwaffe as a *fahnenjunker*

on 4 December 1936, and the following June started his flying training at the Berlin-Werder Luftkriegsschule. In June 1938 he was posted to I Gruppe, Stukageschwader 168 for dive bomber training along with men like Dietrich Peltz, Walter Sigel and Hans-Karl Stepp, all of whom were later to become outstanding Stuka pilots during World War II.

Then, inexplicably, Rudel was transferred away from the dive bombing arm in December that year to re-train as an observer with a reconnaissance unit, attending the Aufklärerschule at Hildesheim. This was possibly fortunate for Rudel as his old Stukagruppe (nicknamed the Grazer Gruppe) suffered tragedy when, during a training exercise on 15 August 1939, 13 crew members were killed in crashes when a sudden fog obliterated their bombing target at Neuhammer. Nevertheless, the posting away from Stukas was a bitter disappointment to Rudel.

On 1 January 1939 Rudel was promoted *leutnant* and exactly five months later he completed his training as a reconnaissance observer and was posted to 2 Staffel, Fernaufklärungsgruppe 121, based at Prenzlau; it was with this unit that he participated in the Polish Campaign of September. When he was awarded the Iron Cross Second Class on 10 November Hans-Ulrich Rudel embarked on a campaign to secure his return to Stukas, but his applications were constantly refused.

His constant requests to return to dive bombers eventually bore fruit, however, and at the end of the Battle of France he was returned to the Grazer Gruppe (now designated I/StG 3), then based at Caen in northern France, although he did not fly any combat missions during the Battle of Britain. Promotion to *oberleutnant*

Right: virtually all of Rudel's fighting career was spent flying the Junkers Ju 87 with Stukageschwader 2 'Immelmann' (badge above). Joining the unit as an oberleutnant in April 1941, he was appointed Geschwaderkommodore in September 1944.
Below: Rudel's Ju 87D about to lead a dive-bombing mission over the Eastern Front

during his first attack, and sinking a cruiser and a destroyer later in the day. On 8 December he received the German Cross in Gold; in that month Rudel flew his 400th combat sortie and on 6 January 1942 he was awarded the Knight's Cross before being given a short spell off operations as a staff pilot with the Stuka-Ergänzungsstaffel, which was moved to the Crimea during the summer of 1942.

On 15 August 1942 Rudel returned to operations with the appointment as Staffelkapitän of 9 Staffel, Stukageschwader 2, now flying the Junkers Ju 87D on combat sorties over the Black Sea and Caucasus. On 24 September he flew his 500th mission.

After a brief spell in hospital at Rostov-on-Don with hepatitis, he was given the leadership of 1 Staffel, StG 2 and continued to fly numerous sorties over the Southern Sector of the Eastern Front, becoming the first pilot in the world to pass 1,000 missions on 10 February 1943. On 1 April he was promoted *hauptmann*, the promotion being backdated a whole year in recognition of his outstanding operational service.

At about this time Rudel started flying the Junkers Ju 87G ground-attack aircraft armed with two 37mm anti-tank guns under the wing. His introduction to this aircraft was somewhat exploratory and he was allowed to fly a number of trial combat sorties, but after he had destroyed 70 Russian landing craft at the Kuban bridge-head in a period of little over a week this version of the Stuka came to be fairly widely adopted and Rudel henceforth flew most of his missions in the anti-tank role. On 14 April he was awarded the Oakleaves to the Knight's Cross for his record of 1,000 missions.

Rapidly-mounting score

In the holocaust of Kursk Rudel ran riot with his Stuka; in his first sortie over the battlefield on 5 July 1943 he knocked out four Russian T-34 tanks and, before that first day of the battle was over his score of these formidable vehicles had reached 12. On 12 August Rudel flew his 1,300th mission, while his radio operator, Oberfeldwebel Erwin Hentschel, reached the 1,000 mark – the first crew member to do so. On 30 October the Stuka pilot destroyed his 100th Russian tank while flying the Ju 87G, an achievement signalled by the award of the Swords to the Knight's Cross on 25 November; the citation mentions that by that date his mission tally had reached 1,600.

In the critical tank battle which erupted at Kirovograd during the second week of 1944, I/StG 2 was in action against the Russian 67th Armoured Brigade and Rudel was credited with the destruction of 17 tanks and seven self-propelled guns in four days. His score of tanks destroyed reached 150 during this bloody battle. Promotion to *major*, announced on 1 March, was backdated 17 months and he was appointed Gruppenkommodore, III Gruppe, Schlachtfliegergeschwader 2 (as his Geschwader was now re-designated).

The last 14 months of fighting in the East witnessed a succession of withdrawals, stands and bloody counter-attacks by the doomed German armies. On 20 March Rudel and Hentschel were returning from an attack on the Yampol bridge over the Dneister river when the pilot spotted a Stuka which had been forced to land in enemy-held territory. Landing nearby to pick up the stranded crew, Rudel was prevented from taking off by water-logged ground. Seeing Russian soldiers approaching, the Germans made off under heavy rifle fire, Rudel being hit in the shoulder. Both men managed to reach the Dneister and the pilot succeeded in swimming it to regain the German lines 50 km (30 miles) away; the gallant Hentschel,

followed on 1 September, but there is evidence to suggest that his ability as an operational pilot was still in question.

Immelmann Geschwader

After a brief posting to the Stuka flying training school at Graz-Thalerhof early in 1941, Rudel was transferred to I Gruppe, Stukageschwader 2 'Immelmann', which was based in Greece in April that year. He was to remain with this famous Geschwader throughout the remainder of his illustrious combat career.

In June almost the entire Stuka force was concentrated in the East in readiness for the great German attack on Russia, Rudel being initially listed as a line pilot with his Geschwader's 2 Staffel. On the opening day of the campaign he flew his first four combat sorties against Russian armour in support of the advancing ground forces near Grodno. Within a month he had flown almost 100 missions and, with the award of the Iron Cross First Class, was appointed Technical Officer of the Geschwader's III Gruppe on 18 July. He also received the Mission Clasp in Gold.

On 23 September, flying from Tyrkowo, III Gruppe attacked the Soviet fleet in Kronstadt harbour. Rudel flew three sorties that day, scoring a direct hit on and sinking the 23,600 ton battleship *Marat* with a 1,000 kg bomb

veteran of 1,490 combat missions and holder of the Knight's Cross, drowned in the icy waters of the Dneister near Volfanivka, after swimming almost half a mile.

Notwithstanding his shoulder wound, Rudel continued flying throughout the week following his escape, and on 29 March was awarded the Diamonds to the Knight's Cross – then the highest German gallantry award. By that date he had flown 1,800 missions and destroyed 202 tanks. On 1 June he destroyed his 301st tank, of which 78 had been knocked out using bombs and 223 with the 37mm cannon. Two days later he was presented by Goering with the Pilot's Medal in Gold with Diamonds and the Mission Clasp in Gold with Diamonds for reaching 2,000 missions.

On 19 August he was shot down by flak over Kurland, escaping with a forced landing among the German front-line outposts; this time he suffered a wounded leg, but his new radio operator, Dr Ernst Gadermann, escaped unhurt. Following promotion to *oberstleutnant* on 1 September, Rudel was appointed Geschwaderkommodore of SG 2 a month later. Six weeks afterwards, while flying over Hungary, he was hit in the left thigh by ground fire and made an emergency landing on Budapest airfield.

Golden Oakleaves award

Three days before the last Christmas of the war Rudel flew his 2,400th combat sortie, and the following day destroyed his 463rd Russian tank. One week later he was summoned to the Führerhauptquartier Adlerhorst in the Taunus mountains where, in the presence of Goering, Grossadmiral Dönitz and the entire Supreme Staff, Rudel was presented with the Golden Oakleaves by Hitler himself, and promoted *oberst*. The award of this decoration was unique in the German armed services.

Still his combat career continued. A score of seven tanks in two days at the end of January 1945 brought his score to 505, and was followed by seven more on 2 February alone. A further miraculous escape occurred on 8 February – a day on which Rudel destroyed no fewer than 12 enemy tanks – when his aircraft was struck by 40mm flak near Lebus, and he was badly hit in the right foot. Putting his Ju 87G down behind German lines, he was only saved from bleeding to death by the efforts of his crew member, Dr Gadermann. Rudel was rushed to the Waffen SS hospital near Küstrin where his right foot was amputated above the ankle.

Despite his wound, Rudel returned to his Geschwader

on 25 March with a new radio operator, war correspondent Hauptmann Niermann, and went on to destroy 26 more Russian tanks before surrendering to American forces at Kitzingen/Main airfield on 8 May. Eleven months in hospital followed before he was eventually released.

Hans-Ulrich Rudel's final score—achieved during 2,530 operational missions—included at least 519 tanks destroyed, one battleship, one cruiser, one destroyer and 70 assault craft sunk, more than 800 other vehicles, 150 self-propelled guns and four armoured trains destroyed. His air victories included seven Russian fighters and two Ilyushin Il-2 assault aircraft shot down. He was himself shot down by ground fire no fewer than 30 times, was wounded five times and rescued six stranded aircrews from enemy territory.

Left: the Junkers Ju 87G, the tank-busting version of the Stuka, was flown by Rudel with great success and by the end of the war he had destroyed more than 500 Russian tanks.
Below: mechanics at work on the engine of Rudel's Ju 87D dive bomber. Rudel's greatest triumph as a bomber pilot was the sinking of the Russian battleship Marat in the naval base at Kronstadt on 23 September 1941.
Right: the Stuka's radio operator/gunner was armed with twin 7·9mm machine guns for rearward defence.
Below right: Rudel's regular radio operator, Oberfeldwebel Erwin Hentschel (right), received the Knight's Cross in November 1943. Hentschel was killed in the following March

GERMANY'S HIGH FLYERS

Edmund Rumpler specialised in high-altitude reconnaissance aircraft during World War I

Had the morning reconnaissance crew from Fliegerabteilung (A) 253 not been flying in a Rumpler C VII on 28 May 1918, they would surely have been another 'kill' in a long string logged by RAF fighter ace Major William A. Bishop, VC. As it turned out, however, when observer Leutnant der Reserve Hanns-Gerd Rabe spotted Bishop's SE5A climbing toward the Rumpler, he ordered his pilot, Vizefeldwebel Peter Johannes, to make use of the aircraft's best defence – its superior altitude.

The Rumpler C VII was the highest-flying aircraft of World War I, capable of reaching a maximum ceiling of over 7,000 m (23,000 ft). Hence, while Bishop applied full power to his fast fighter, in the hope of catching the two-seater, the German pilot called upon the 240 hp Maybach engine and steadily climbed away from his adversary. Bishop stalled while trying to get within firing range and was eventually forced to give up the chase, even though he was angrily challenged by the cheery wave from Leutnant Rabe, who knew that the Rumpler's ability to outclimb all other aircraft was his margin of safety when operating over enemy territory.

Developing the Dove

The high-flying C VII was the culmination of an aircraft series which had begun less than ten years earlier. Dr Edmund Rumpler, an Austrian-born engineer who had

been working in Germany as production chief for the Adler Automobile Company, announced on 24 November 1908 that he was forming an aircraft design and production facility at Berlin's Johannisthal airfield. Although his company was short-lived, Dr Rumpler's talent for improving existing designs influenced a generation of German aircraft engineers.

Following several attempts to produce successfully the Austrian Etrich-Wels glider, Rumpler looked for a better adaptation of the bird-like design which characterised the type. He found it in Etrich's Taube (Dove) monoplane, with its gracefully sweeping wings and fanned tail. Rumpler was one of a number of German and French manufacturers to purchase production rights to the Taube design. Rumpler's modification was clearly marked by a deeper forward fuselage and his Taube's had more fully-developed rear stabilisers.

Tannenberg reconnaissance

With the outbreak of World War I on 1 August 1914, production of Rumpler Taube and other aircraft was diverted to the German Fliegertruppe. Before the month was out a two-seat Taube of Feldfliegerabteilung 14 had alerted the German 8th Army that a Russian force was massing to attack it near Tannenberg Forest. That early application of aerial reconnaissance led to an impressive early victory for the German Army and a greater awareness of the value of military air power by the German General Staff.

Even before the outbreak of war, however, Rumpler's basic 4C monoplane became the source of three additional designs designated 4A 13, 4A 14 and 4A. All had fuselages and empennages similar to the 4C, but the 4A two-place biplane was the design selected for full production, being designated the Rumpler B I by the German Army. Floatplane versions of the 4A design were also produced for the

German Navy and these were designated 4B1 and 4B2. These – and succeeding designs, culminating in the 6B1 – were produced for maritime activities, but never in the quantities enjoyed by Rumpler designs for the Army.

The B I was the antecedent of Rumpler's successful Army aircraft. The two-bay biplane was marked by the sweeping top wing which was inherited from the graceful Taube design. The span of the top wing was 13m (42ft 7in) and the bottom wing 11m (36ft 1in). The 8·38m ((27ft 6in) fuselage housed a 100hp Mercedes engine capable of attaining speeds near 120km/h (70mph).

Configuration changes

Demand for the Rumpler B I was such that licence-built variants were produced by the Pfalz Flugzeugwerke. Success of the B I, in which the pilot sat behind the observer, led to the development of the Rumpler C I design. Better suited to defence in the air, the C I allowed the observer to occupy the rear cockpit, from whence he could operate a ring-mounted machine gun to fend off attackers. In addition to production at Rumpler's Johannisthal facilities, the C I was also built under licence by the Brandenburg, Germania, MFW (Märkische Flugzeugwerke) and Pfalz companies, as well as Rumpler's Bavarian subsidiary, Bayru (Bayerische Rumpler Werke). Rumpler C I aircraft powered by the 160hp Mercedes engine and C Ia types equipped with the 180hp Argus were so good that the 1915 design was still used by a few front-line units early in 1918.

The development and subsequent expansion of German day and night bombing operations created a need for more G-type large, twin-engine bomber aircraft. The Edmund Rumpler-Flugzeugwerke joined the AEG, Friedrichshafen and Gotha concerns in 1915 with the introduction of the Rumpler G I (5A 15). A three-seat biplane powered by two fully-enclosed Benz 150hp engines, the G I saw limited service until August 1916. The G II (5A 16), introduced in mid-1916, was similar to the G I, except for its 220hp Benz engines. The ultimate design in the series was the G III (6G 2), which was produced for front-line units and was so close in configuration to the Gotha G V that it was often mistakenly identified as a Gotha machine by Allied fighter pilots.

Rumpler introduced the C III reconnaissance aircraft in 1916 and with it a style of streamlining which made the firm's future aircraft distinctive. A semi-circular radiator mounted above the engine, on the leading edge of the top wing, and a tall, so-called 'rhinoceros horn' exhaust pipe characterised the type. The 220hp engine in the C III was replaced by a 260hp Mercedes for the C IV, which was noted for exceptionally good performance and the ability to attain altitudes as high as 6,400m (21,000ft). Indeed, the C IV design coupled with the 'super-compressed' Maybach 240hp engine were the elements of the C VII, which was also known at the Rubild (Rumpler photographic) aircraft. Although the Rumpler firm was less successful with its development of fighter aircraft, it is noteworthy that the prototype D I could attain altitudes of 8,000m (26,200ft).

Under the conditions of the 11 November 1918 Armistice which ended World War I, factories were required to cease production of all military aircraft. Accordingly, Dr Edmund Rumpler tried to convert his two-seat reconnaissance aircraft into enclosed-cockpit commercial aircraft. Towards that end, he opened a subsidiary named Rumpler-Luftverkehrs (Rumpler Air Service) which, along with his aircraft production facilities, did not survive the chaotic fluctuations which marked the German economy of the immediate postwar years.

Top left: the Rumpler B I served in quantity with the German air arms as a reconnaissance and training aircraft from 1914.
Above left: a Rumpler C IV (right) and a Fokker D II seen in Dutch service after World War I.
Left: the Rumpler C I was one of the most popular of the first armed two-seat C-type aircraft, seeing wide service on the Western Front and elsewhere.
Right: the 260hp Mercedes-powered Rumpler C IV was met with enthusiasm by crews when it entered service in 1917. Its good rate of climb and high ceiling enabled it to escape most Allied scouts

Sportsmen's Airplanes

The builders of Lindbergh's Spirit of St Louis aimed to cater for the sport flying market

Although it is well-known that Charles Lindbergh was the first man to fly solo across the Atlantic Ocean and that his aeroplane was named *Spirit of St Louis*, the company which built it—the Ryan Airplane Company—remains more obscure. Its history began ten years before Lindbergh's epic trip when Tubal Claude Ryan learned to fly at a dusty US Army airfield near Los Angeles in 1917. Five years later, with a little money, more experience and unlimited ambition, Ryan arrived in San Diego and spent his four hundred dollars on a war-surplus Curtiss Jenny. He then set up in the aerial sightseeing business from a landing strip at the foot of San Diego's Broadway.

Enterprise and expansion

Ryan lived cheaply at the YMCA, advertising himself by scattering leaflets from the Jenny. On Army Day a young Army major named 'Hap' Arnold allowed him to carry passengers from Rockwell Field for five dollars a head. Ryan would also assemble and test-fly a Jenny or Standard for an inexperienced buyer at a cost of thirty-five dollars. Business was scarcely booming, but he soon had enough in the bank to arrange a loan for two more Jennies, and the Ryan Flying Company moved to new premises on the former Marine base at Dutch Flats. Here Ryan arranged for drivers of sightseeing buses from Los Angeles to stop so that he could entice tourists to see San

Diego from the air: the drivers received one dollar of each fare for their trouble. Two surplus Standard J-1s were acquired in 1925 and Ryan hired Hawley Bowlus, a former flying school mechanic, to redesign them to carry four passengers; the Jennies carried only one. The Standards were used on a twice-daily service from San Diego to Los Angeles, the first year-round airline service in the United States. The return fare was twenty-two dollars and fifty cents, with a five dollar rebate if the aircraft force-landed, as they frequently did.

A touch of class was added to the Ryan Airlines fleet when Claude Ryan acquired Donald Douglas' Cloudster, built for an attempt at a non-stop crossing of the USA, and modified it to carry ten passengers in an enclosed cabin. It was the forerunner of modern airliners and was used to carry many famous passengers, including General 'Billy' Mitchell and a number of Hollywood film stars. Ryan also used the Cloudster to haul beer from Mexico to America until it eventually crashed on a beach at Mexicali.

Profitable first design
In 1926 Ryan Airlines carried 5,000 passengers and made a profit. With the source of war-surplus aircraft dwindling, Ryan and Bowlus took a bold step and designed and built their own machine, a three-seat high-wing monoplane called the Ryan M-1. The aircraft appeared at an opportune moment: the US Government was contracting private companies to take over its airmail routes and the compact, speedy M-1, with its excellent short-field capability, was ideal for mail-carrying. Ryan surveyed the airmail route between San Diego and Seattle with his first customer Vern Gorst, founder of Pacific Air Transport which later became United Air Lines. Consequently, Ryan soon had a backlog of orders for 'The Plane that Pays a Profit'.

To provide manufacturing space to meet orders for the M-1 he leased the upper floor of an abandoned fish factory and by late 1926 was offering the improved M-2 Bluebird, which had a fully-enclosed cabin for the pilot and four passengers. Relationships with his business partner Franklin Mahoney had deteriorated, however, and in January 1927 Ryan sold out for 25,000 dollars, handing over the Ryan Airlines name, plus all rights to the M-1, M-2 and designs for a new B-1 monoplane, to Mahoney.

On 3 February 1927 a young ex-barnstormer and airmail pilot named Charles Lindbergh cabled Ryan Airlines in San Diego: 'Can you construct Whirlwind engine plane capable flying nonstop between New York and Paris? If so please state cost and delivery date.' Back came the reply: 'Can build plane similar M-1 but larger wings capable of making flight. Cost about six thousand dollars without motor and instruments, delivery about three months.' After a further exchange of telegrams Lindbergh arrived at Ryan's dilapidated premises on 23 February

Above and above right: over 1,000 examples of the Kinner-engined PT-22 served with civilian-operated flying training schools from 1941. Above far right: powered by a 145 hp Warner engine, the SCW three-seat tourer was produced in limited numbers during the period 1939–40. Right: first flown in 1934, the Ryan S-T open-cockpit sports and training monoplane proved highly popular. Later developments included the S-T-A and S-T-A Special. Left: a replica of Ryan's most famous aircraft, the NYP. Lindbergh's epic transatlantic flight in 1927 elicited many orders for a similar aircraft, known as the B-1 Brougham

and met Mahoney, Bowlus and the company's chief engineer Donald Hall, who had already done some preliminary design work. Lindbergh gave Hall his requirements for the transatlantic aeroplane and, after a trip to San Diego Public Library–to measure the distance from New York to Paris by stretching a piece of string around a globe–the engineer confirmed that he could redesign the M-1/M-2 airframe to accommodate the necessary fuel. The total cost of the aeroplane was agreed at 10,580 dollars with a Wright J-5 engine and Mahoney promised delivery within two months.

Spirit of St Louis–officially dubbed Ryan NYP (New York-Paris)–was flown on 28 April 1927, and on 21 May Lindbergh set off from Roosevelt Field, New York in the heavily-overloaded monoplane on his epic solo endurance flight, which ended $33\frac{1}{2}$ hours later with a tumultuous welcome at Le Bourget, Paris.

Best-selling Brougham

The effect of Lindbergh's success on Ryan was tremendous. The little company could not meet the demand for its B-1 Brougham, which was basically similar to the *Spirit*, but with a five-place cabin and a choice of Hisso or Wright Whirlwind engines. Production of the Brougham, which sold for 9,700 dollars, was soon running at three per week and the model ran through seven variants before the renamed Mahoney-Ryan Aircraft Corporation merged with the Detroit Aircraft Corporation, becoming a victim of the Great Depression in 1931.

T. Claude Ryan meanwhile had been distributing German Siemens radial aero-engines; after the Wall Street crash, he went back to his old business of flight instruction with the Ryan Flying School at what was to become Lindbergh Field in San Diego. Ryan offered private, commercial and transport pilots courses with Great Lakes Trainer biplanes and Ryan Broughams, giving especially thorough training in cross-country and formation flying. The Ryan School of Aeronautics gained an enviable reputation for the quality of its pilot training, but Ryan still wanted to build his own aeroplanes.

Not surprisingly in view of his background, the next Ryan aeroplane was a trainer, the Ryan S-T (Sport Trainer), which first flew on 8 June 1934. The S-T was an open cockpit, tandem two-seat low-wing monoplane of exquisitely clean design, powered by a 95 hp Menasco Pirate engine. More power was added later, with a 125 hp unit in the S-T-A and 150 hp in the 1936 S-T-A Special. The 'Sportsman's Airplane' was an immediate success, and was sold both in basic form and in a package including a complete training course to Airline Transport Rating standard. Naturally, the Ryan School of Aeronautics employed the all-metal lightplane in its fleet; orders also came for the export version of the S-T-M from the air forces of China, Guatemala, Honduras, Mexico, the Netherlands East Indies and South Africa.

Pilot training school

In June 1939, as the possibility of war began to figure in US strategic thinking, Ryan was awarded a US Army contract for 16 YPT-16 military trainer versions of the S-T-A, powered by 125 hp Menasco engines. Ryan School of Aeronautics at Lindbergh Field became the first of many Civilian Pilot Training (CPT) schools operated for the US military during World War II. The basic S-T-A/PT-16 design evolved through the similar PT-20 to the 132 hp Kinner radial-engined PT-21 and the PT-22, which had a 160 hp Kinner with exposed cylinders, a slightly swept-back wing and unfaired landing gear. It was a much less elegant aircraft than the beautiful S-T-A, but was numerically the most successful of Ryan's designs, 1,023 being built in the peak year of 1941 for the CPT programme. Production of the S-T series terminated in 1942 and Ryan was contracted to build a new trainer from non-strategic materials. The resultant S-T-4/YPT-25 was made almost entirely of plastic-bonded wood, but no production order was received.

With the cancellation of military contracts in peacetime, Ryan's payroll shrank from nearly 8,000 employees to 600. He turned briefly to the manufacture of metal coffins: 'Whether you're flyin' or dyin', rely on Ryan' his competitors quipped. Claude soon came back to aviation, buying the rights to North American's Navion four-seat lightplane in 1947. The US Army ordered 158 Navions from Ryan in 1948 as L-17B liaison aircraft, while the basic design was further refined into the early 1950s as the Super Navion 260. Ryan eventually disposed of the Navion rights to the Navion Rangemaster Corporation, which updated the aircraft and marketed it sporadically throughout the 1960s and early 1970s.

Thereafter the Ryan company undertook component manufacturing for Boeing, building fuselages for KC-97 tankers and early 707s. Two experimental vertical take-off and landing aircraft–the X-13 Vertijet and XV-5A Vertifan–were pioneered by Ryan, which also built the first air-to-air guided missile used by the United States Air Force and the first jet-propelled target drone, the Ryan Firebee, which is still widely used throughout the world.

Having sold out his business interests to Teledyne Incorporated–who retained the Ryan name–T. Claude Ryan has returned to lightplanes, building the Ryson ST Cloudster with his son Jerry. At 80 years of age he still flies the elegant, T-tailed, powered sailplane over San Diego, where he first went into business from a packing-case office more than half a century ago.

Originally developed by North American Aviation, the Navion was acquired by Ryan in 1947. The design was the subject of considerable refinement and, with a 260 hp Continental engine, became the five-seat Super Navion (bottom). This aircraft was later marketed by the Navion Rangemaster Corporation, to which the design rights were sold

Since 1937 Saab aircraft have contributed to the defence of Swedish neutrality

The name of Saab is today so synonymous with virtually every major product of the Swedish aircraft and automotive industries that the casual observer might be forgiven for supposing that this had always been so. In fact, Saab (or, since 1968, Saab-Scania) was preceded by no fewer than 15 different aircraft manufacturing organisations in Sweden, the earliest of which was founded in 1909. Five of these, of which the best-known was the AB Thulinverken, were defunct by 1919, and in the postwar period the production of military aircraft was chiefly in the hands of the Royal Swedish Air Force maintenance depots at Malmslätt and Västerås.

Saab's origins

Of four private-industry aircraft companies to emerge during the 1930s, two joined forces on the eve of World War II to form the Saab company, the name of which was an abbreviation of Svenska Aeroplan Aktiebolaget (Swedish Aircraft Company). The original bearer of the Saab name–Saab-T, as it was at first known–had set up its factories and offices at Trollhättan in April 1937. Its 1939 partner, and the only other aircraft company in Sweden comparable in size and output ability, was the Svenska Järnvägsverkstädernas Aeroplanavdelning (ASJA). This company, formed in 1930, had built the best-known Swedish fighter of that period, the J 6 Jaktfalk, designed originally by Svenska Aero AB. It was natural, therefore, that, with the impending prospect of hostilities in Europe at that time, ASJA and Saab-T should eventually amalgamate in April 1939. Before this the two companies had worked together briefly under the auspices of the Royal Swedish Air Force (Flygvapnet, or FV), sharing the responsibility for producing British, German and American aircraft under licence for that service. Aircraft were also built for commercial use under the title of Aktiebolaget Förenade Flygverkstäder. Upon the merg-ing of the two companies the main factory and workshops were moved to Linköping, with offices and a planning department remaining at Trollhättan.

The Saab-T company's first product was the Junkers Ju 86, at first assembled from German-built components in 1937. The maiden flight of the first fully Swedish-built aircraft, designated Ju 86K-13, took place in August 1939. The Flygvapnet had ordered 80 examples in July-August 1938, but the order was later reduced by half and, due to the onset of World War II, only 16 were delivered. With the FV designations B 3C and B 3D, they served as bomber and reconnaissance aircraft until 1956, some having been converted to transports by that time. Another pre-war type, which ASJA began building under licence in 1938, was the North American NA-16-A tandem-seat trainer. A total of 76 were ordered by the FV in three batches, the last of which were delivered during late 1941 and early 1942. They were given the Swedish Air Force designation Sk 14 or Sk 14A, powered by a 455hp Wright Whirlwind or 525hp Piaggio P VIIc radial engine respectively. In February 1942 a further 60 aircraft were

Below: the unusual pusher configuration of the J 21A resulted from a desire to improve the pilot's view, utilise a nosewheel undercarriage and concentrate a heavy armament in the nose of a single-engined fighter. The type was employed in the fighter and attack roles. Bottom: the B 18A bomber appeared in 1942, entering service two years later. The Pratt & Whitney radials of the A model were replaced by Daimler Benz DB 605 engines in the B 18B, thus increasing performance. The type served until 1953

ordered from the Saab factory, delivery of these finishing in 1944. Production was also undertaken of the Northrop 8A-1 dive bomber, 64 of which had been ordered in 1938–39 and given the FV designation B 5B. These were built jointly by ASJA and Saab; after the two companies had amalgamated, a further 39 were ordered from Saab. The aircraft, known as B 5Cs, had all been delivered by the middle of 1941.

Bomber production

Saab's first aircraft of its own design was originally known as the Saab L 10. Begun at Förenade Flygverkstäder, it was a development of an even earlier sesquiplane design. American technicians were employed by the company to give the Saab engineers some assistance with the all-metal construction envisaged for the new prototypes, two of which were ordered in late 1938 as the Saab-17. However, the US advisers left towards the end of 1939, and Saab had to continue on its own. Models were tested in wind tunnels in Sweden and the USA to evaluate the main features of the design, which included a fully-retractable undercarriage. The first flight, on 18 May 1940 at Linköping was undertaken with the landing gear locked down; the long glazed canopy was torn off during this flight, however, and extensive testing followed. This resulted in the addition of an anti-spin strake fairing under the tail. The Saab-17 was designed originally for reconnaissance duties; with the addition of an advanced bomb-sight built by Saab, the aircraft could also be employed as a dive bomber, since the large fairings over the mainwheel legs would serve a very useful secondary purpose as dive-brakes.

Several variants of the basic aircraft were built, designated according to function and the type of engine installed. First was the Saab-17A dive bomber (FV designation B 17A), with a Swedish-built 1,065 hp Pratt & Whitney Twin Wasp SC3-G. The Saab-17B, powered by a Swedish-built 980 hp Bristol Mercury XXIV, was designated B 17B (dive bomber), S 17B (reconnaissance) and S 17BS in floatplane form by the Flygvapnet. The final model, the Saab-17C, was solely a dive bomber, powered by a 1,020 hp Piaggio P IXbis RC40D engine and given the military designation B 17C; 77 of these were completed, the last being delivered in 1944. A total of 323 Saab-17 aircraft was built. After their useful service life with the

Flygvapnet ended in 1948, about 60 were sold to Ethiopia, where they were still in use at least 15 years later.

Approximately a year after the Saab-17 series was mooted, the first drawing-board designs appeared for the L 11, a twin-engined, mid-wing monoplane bomber and reconnaissance aircraft. The influence of the American engineers was apparent in the initial stages, but after 1939 the Swedes took over the design completely. When the first of two Saab-18 prototypes flew initially on 19 June 1942 it bore more than a passing resemblance to the German Dornier Do 217. The first production batch of 60 Saab-18As did not start to be delivered until June 1944. They were powered by two 1,065 hp licence-built Pratt & Whitney SC3-G Twin Wasps, and were designated B 18A and S 18A according to the duties they were to perform. The S 18A was a reconnaissance model, equipped with Ska 5 and Ska 13 cameras; radar equipment was later installed in a pod under the nose.

The B 18A bomber variant was found to be underpowered for its intended operational role and was superseded by the B 18B with two licence-built 1,475 hp Daimler Benz DB 605 engines. Better performance was achieved with this power plant, the maximum speed being increased by about 65 km/h (40 mph). A total of 120 B 18B aircraft was produced and one was used as a prototype for the final variant, the T 18B heavy attack or torpedo bomber, 62 of which were completed. The T 18B had accommodation for a two-man crew, with an armament comprising two 20 mm cannon and, on some examples, an additional 57 mm cannon under the nose. Production of the Saab-18 series ended in 1949; the last was phased out of service with the Flygvapnet around 1951–52.

Top: one of 35 Saab-91D Safirs built for the Finnish air force. The Saab-91D was the last of four basic Saab-91 models, appearing in 1957. The type served the Swedish air force as a liaison and training aircraft, and was sold to the air arms of Norway, Finland, Austria, Tunisia and Ethiopia.
Above: a Saab-90A-2 Scandia of Aktiebolaget Aerotransport (ABA), the Swedish airline, which bought ten examples. The prototype and the 17 production aircraft were later sold in Brazil

Piston to jet

A projected fighter, the L 12, was designed in 1939, but with the outbreak of war the Swedish government felt that there was no time to develop this. Instead, 60 Republic EP-106s, given the designation J 9 by the Flygvapnet, were purchased from the USA and 60 Reggiane Re 2000s, designated J 20, from Italy. The Saab-19, as the L 12 would have become, was similar in appearance to the J 22 fighter later produced by the FFVS (Flygförvaltningens Flygverkstad, the FV's own factory), but it was not built and in any case would probably have been underpowered. Saab was, however, involved with one other modern fighter at about this time: the Brewster B-239 Buffalo, 44 of which were sold to Finland by the USA for use in resisting the Soviet invasion. These were assembled by Saab at Trollhättan and delivered to Finland by Swedish pilots. During the war many aircraft from different nations entered neutral Sweden either deliberately or by chance, and were interned for the duration. Among these were 68 Boeing B-17 Flying Fortresses, a few of which were converted by Saab in 1945 as stop-gap postwar civil transports for the domestic airline ABA (Aktiebolaget Aerotransport) and the Danish operator DDL (now part of SAS).

The next Saab fighter design, however, was destined to remain in production for six years. The only twin-boom piston-engined 'pusher' fighter to be built in series anywhere at this time, this was the Saab-21A, the first prototype of which flew on 30 July 1943. Two further prototypes appeared, the second of which crashed during tests. The company produced a further 296 aircraft. Perhaps the most interesting feature of the

Saab-21A, besides its unusual layout, was the ejection seat. The pilot was located in a central nacelle, above the wing leading-edge, on a seat which was installed on a gunpowder-actuated catapult, which would throw him clear of the propeller once he had jettisoned the canopy. It was primitive, but, after much development, effective. The Trollhättan factory produced three variants between 1943 and 1948, beginning with the J 21A-1, a fighter equipped with one 20mm cannon and four 13·2mm machine guns, of which 55 were built. Next model to appear was the J 21A-2 of which 124 were built. It had the same gun armament as the J 21A-1, but could also be used in the attack role fitted with underwing bomb racks. The final model in the series was the J 21A-3, or A 21A in its attack version. The 119 built had underwing bomb racks and wingtip fuel tanks, and provision under the fuselage

Top: J-29F Tunnans of F3 Wing flying in echelon. The J-29 formed the backbone of the Swedish fighter force during the 1950s. The J-29F was the final version, appearing in 1954 and serving until the mid-1960s.
Above: a J-29F preserved in the markings of F20 Wing of the Swedish air force's Flying Cadet School

known Bü 181 Bestmann. The Safir was a two/three-seat monoplane with a retractable tricycle undercarriage, and it was powered by a 145 hp Gipsy Major 10 engine. The prototype, which first flew in November 1945, and the first 10 Saab-91A production models, went to the Flygvapnet, which gave them the designation Tp 91 and used them as light transport and liaison aircraft. One Saab-91A was fitted with floats, for Arctic service between 1949–52. The Saab-91B, with a 190 hp Lycoming O-435-A engine, appeared in 1949, and suited the Flygvapnet's requirement for a trainer. It purchased 75, which were given the FV designation Sk 50B; these were built by the Dutch De Schelde company, since Saab's Linköping works was completely absorbed by then in the production of the Saab-29 jet fighter. The Saab-91C Safir was a four-seat model of the 91B, having the same engine; 14

for a cluster of eight 13·2 mm machine guns; alternatively, one 250 kg bomb could be carried in that position, and eight Bofors rockets under the wing, or a single under-fuselage 500 kg bomb. All models were powered by a single 1,475 hp licence-built Daimler Benz DB 605B. Although in some respects the J 21A did not come up to the standard of other contemporary foreign fighters, it was popular with its pilots, who found the firepower perfectly adequate. In addition, its layout proved particularly suitable for testing jet engines in the middle and late 1940s.

Designs projected during the war included an improved J 21A, to be designated Saab-21B and be powered by a 2,000 hp Rolls-Royce Griffon engine; the jet version of the Saab-21A rendered this unnecessary, however. The Saab-23 single-seat fighter project, powered by a 1,475 hp Daimler Benz engine, was considered less efficient than the Saab-21 series and was not, therefore, developed. In 1942 an advanced two-seat, twin-engined dive bomber, fighter, night fighter and attack aircraft was proposed, known as the Saab-24. Once again it was realised that these duties could be performed by the Saab-21 series; besides, the Saab-24 would have needed a longer take-off run than most Swedish air bases could then provide. In 1945, when Saab began converting J 21As to jet propulsion, another advanced fighter project was cancelled, that of the Saab-27. Designed to use a 2,000 hp Rolls-Royce Griffon and contra-rotating propellers, it bore some similarity to both the Supermarine Spitfire and the North American Mustang.

Safir trainer

Meanwhile, in 1944, design work had been started on Project CT. This was to emerge as the Saab-90 civil transport, and the first flight took place on 16 November 1946. Named Scandia, it was powered by two 1,450 hp licence-built Pratt & Whitney R-2000 Twin Wasp engines, fitted with a retractable tricycle undercarriage, and could carry 24 to 32 passengers. Only 18 were built, some of them by Fokker in Holland, and in spite of an intensive sales campaign in Europe, all were eventually sold to Brazil, where some remained in service until the mid-1960s. The Saab-90A-2 production model was powered by two 1,650 hp R-2180-E-I Twin Hornets. Developments with higher-powered engines were proposed, but none were produced.

The Scandia was followed rapidly off the drawing-board by the Saab-91 Safir (Sapphire), intended to be used as a trainer or light touring aircraft. It was designed by A. J. Andersson, who had previously worked for the German Bücker company and had designed the well-

Top: an A-32A Lansen attack aircraft of Eskader 1 (Group 1), with a representative ordnance load. By late 1957 all four attack wings of Eskader 1 were Lansen-equipped. Above: Sk-35C two-seat conversion trainers serving with F16 Wing. The unarmed Sk-35C had a redesigned nose section but a similar performance to the J-35A. Opposite above: the J-35F carried Hughes Falcon air-to-air missiles, which were fitted with either infra-red or radar guidance

were ordered by the FV in 1959, by which time Safir production had returned to Sweden, and were designated Sk 50C. Last model in the series, the Saab-91D, originated in 1957: this had a 180 hp Lycoming O-360 flat-four engine and other improvements. Thirty-five, with photographic equipment installed, were bought by the Finnish Air Force in 1960–61, and other export orders came from Austria for 24 and from Tunisia for 15. In all, 320 Safirs were produced, many of them being bought by commercial airlines for pilot training.

Design of the first Saab jet aircraft, designated RX 1, began in 1945. The power plant was to have been a Swedish-developed turbojet, and this was also to have been used in the more highly developed RX 2, which had an inverted vee tail, mounted on twin booms. A more sophisticated project was known as R 101 – but before any construction could take place the Lockheed P-80 Shooting Star appeared in the USA and was so similar in appearance that the Swedes cancelled this project. They decided instead to modify the Saab-21A, which the RX 1 and RX 2 had broadly resembled, for jet propulsion. Four prototypes, designated Saab-21R, were converted from existing J 21As to incorporate the de Havilland Goblin turbojet engine. Other improvements included a more streamlined cockpit canopy, extra fuel tankage, a raised tailplane to be clear of the jet exhaust, and the installation of airbrakes.

First flight was made at Norrköping on 10 March 1947 and 30 Saab-21RA production aircraft were built – the suffix indicating that the engines were built in Britain. Another batch of 30, designated Saab-21RB, was then produced with Swedish licence-built engines. Deliveries to the Flygvapnet began in February 1949. Service designations were J 21RA and J-21RB for the fighter models, and A 21R for the attack model, which was similar but could be equipped with the under-fuselage 13·2 mm gun pack of the piston-engined attack version.

Flying Barrels

Arrangements were made in 1946 for Saab to build the 2,268 kg (5,000 lb) thrust de Havilland Ghost jet engine under licence and this turbojet was chosen by Saab to power its new venture, which had the project number

Saab J 35D Draken of the Royal Swedish Air Force

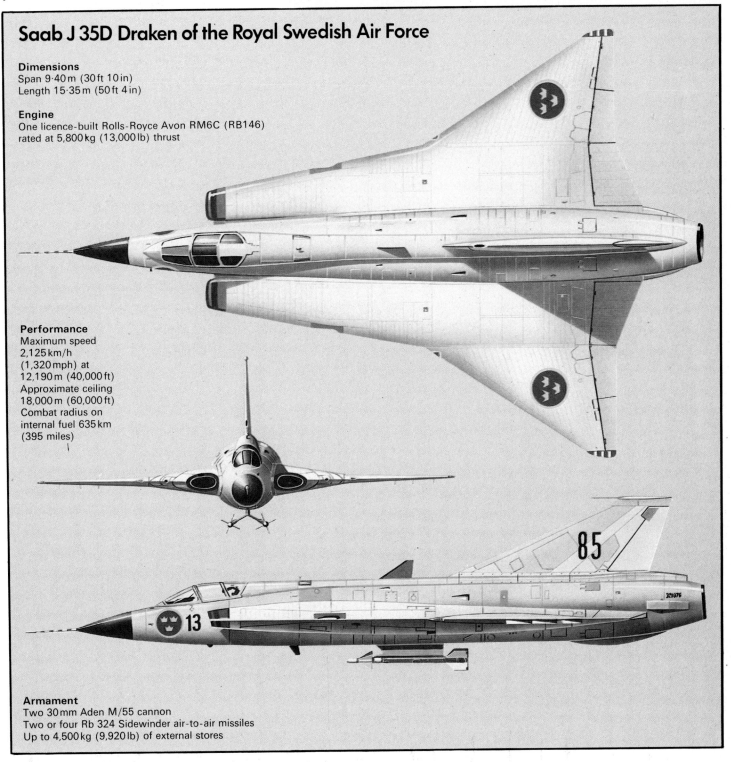

Dimensions
Span 9·40 m (30 ft 10 in)
Length 15·35 m (50 ft 4 in)

Engine
One licence-built Rolls-Royce Avon RM6C (RB146) rated at 5,800 kg (13,000 lb) thrust

Performance
Maximum speed 2,125 km/h (1,320 mph) at 12,190 m (40,000 ft)
Approximate ceiling 18,000 m (60,000 ft)
Combat radius on internal fuel 635 km (395 miles)

Armament
Two 30 mm Aden M/55 cannon
Two or four Rb 324 Sidewinder air-to-air missiles
Up to 4,500 kg (9,920 lb) of external stores

R 1001. After study of some late-war German designs which had become available, Saab gave the R 1001 a 25 degree swept wing, a scaled-down replica of which was flight-tested on a specially-modified Safir, redesignated Saab-201. In its final form, with a pressurised cockpit, the new fighter was known officially as the Saab-29, and less formally as the Tunnan (Flying Barrel). It was the first swept-wing jet aircraft to be produced in quantity in Europe and its eventual production total of some 665 was then the greatest number of any one type built in Sweden.

The first flight by the prototype was made on 1 September 1948. Three further prototypes were built for evaluation, and the specified maximum speed of 1,050 km/h (652 mph) was easily achieved. The first of 224 J 29A production aircraft, with Swedish-built RM2 (Ghost) engines, entered service with F13 Wing at Norrköping in 1951. The next production version, totalling 332, was the Saab-29B, which could be used either as a fighter (J 29B) or attack aircraft (A 29B). A total of 76 Saab-29C (Flygvapnet designation S 29C) reconnaissance versions was built, equipped with six automatic cameras in an under-nose housing. Swedish-designed afterburners were fitted on the few Saab-29Ds, a small number of these being used by the FV as J 29D fighters. The Saab-29E variant, of which 29 were built, introduced new 'dog-tooth' outer wing leading-edges, which improved flight in the transonic speed range, also retrospectively fitted to the J 29C. It was not fitted with an afterburner initially, but in the final Saab-29F form first flown on 20 March 1954 the Tunnan incorporated both the wing improvements of the J 29E and the after-

was powered by the 6,804kg (15,000lb) thrust RM6A (Avon 200), and deliveries to Wings F1 and F12 were made between 1959 and 1960. Armament comprised four 30mm cannon (20mm on the A 32A) and some 1,500kg (3,307lb) of bombs, rockets and Sidewinder or other missiles carried externally. An unarmed photo-reconnaissance version, the Saab-32C, was first flown on 26 March 1957, and this production model entered service with F11 as the S 32C. Production of the Lansen ceased in April 1960, after 450 had been built; the type had a long and useful service life which lasted until mid-1971, when the last A 32As were finally retired and replaced by AJ 37 Viggens.

Double-delta Draken

In 1949, three years after the Lansen project began, work was started on the celebrated supersonic 'double delta' wing fighter design that became the Draken (Dragon). Project R 1250 first materialised as a scaled-down model for flight testing. Known as the Saab-210, it was powered by a single 499kg (1,100lb) thrust Armstrong Siddeley Adder turbojet, and made the first of many hundreds of test flights, on 21 January 1952. Work on the full-size design, allocated the designation Saab-35, began in December 1951, and a speed of Mach 1·7/1·8 was anticipated. Yet this Swedish fighter, in its fully-developed form, was capable of flying at more than twice the speed of sound – a remarkable piece of advanced engineering by designer Erik Bratt and his team at Saab. In August 1953 the Swedish Air Force gave Saab a contract for three prototypes and three pre-production J 35As. The first Draken prototype made its maiden flight on 25 October 1955; the second flew in January 1956 and the third, with full armament, in March of that year. A production order from the Flygvapnet for 65 J 35As followed in August 1956. These were powered by SFA-built 4,990kg (11,000lb) thrust RM6B (Avon 200) engines, giving 6,895kg (15,200lb) with full reheat. Deliveries to the FV began towards the end of 1959, the first recipient being F13 Wing at Norrköping. The Mach 1·8 speed requirement was fulfilled, and armament comprised twin 30mm cannon, and underwing points for two or four Sidewinder air-to-air missiles. The J 35B first flew on 29 November 1959 and went into production at the end of 1961, refinements including a longer rear fuselage and improved cockpit canopy. It also incorporated the Saab S7 collison-course fire-control system and was designed for integration with the STRIL 60 air-defence system. A feature first introduced on the J 35B was a pair of small retractable tailwheels, later fitted to the A model also, to allow it to land at greater angles of attack.

The RM6B (Avon 200) power plant and armament of the J 35A were retained, but the J 35B could also carry packs of 19 75mm Bofors rockets, 12 135mm rockets, 1,000kg (2,205lb) of bombs, or auxiliary fuel tanks. The Saab-35C two-seat combat trainer (FV designation Sk 35C) first flew on 30 December 1959, followed 12 months later by a more powerful fighter version, the Saab-35D (J 35D), with an 8,000kg (17,637lb) thrust RM6C (Avon 300) engine which boosted the top speed to more than Mach 2 and enhanced the sea-level rate of climb by more than 3,050m (10,000ft) per minute to nearly 15,250m (50,000ft) per minute. Based on the J 35D, the Saab-35E (S 35E in service) was built in large numbers for photographic reconnaissance, replacing the S 32C Lansen. The penultimate Draken model, the J 35F, is an improved fighter version of the J 35D with uprated radar and fire control systems and Hughes Falcon

Above left: a Saab 105Ö of the Karo-As aerobatic team, piloted by instructors of the Austrian air force. By 1972 the Saab 105Ö entirely equipped the trainer, fighter and light attack units of the Austrian air force's fixed-wing combat element.
Left: the Saab Viggen was developed to meet a Swedish air force requirement for a supersonic multi-role combat aircraft capable of STOL operations.
Above: the weapons alternatives available to the Viggen include Saab Rb 04E anti-shipping missiles (pictured underwing), air-to-air and air-to-surface missiles, bombs and rockets

burner used on the D model. The A 29F attack variant was armed with 24 75mm Bofors rockets, two 250kg bombs, or other stores. More than 300 Saab-29A, B and E models were eventually modified to Saab-29F standard. Production finished in April 1956 and 30 were exported to Austria, where they remained in service into the late 1960s.

One of Sweden's best-known and most efficient postwar aircraft was the Saab-32 Lansen (Lance), whose specifications originated in 1946. The Swedish Air Board required a successor to the Saab-18B for attack duties, for which Saab evolved a project numbered R 1119, with two DH Ghost engines. When this proved too expensive, the company drew up a revised design for a more easily-constructed, single-engined two-seat all-weather attack aircraft, and in December 1948 was instructed to proceed with its development. It was a low-wing monoplane, with 35 degrees of wing sweep and Fowler flaps. Once again a Safir was used as a testbed (redesignated Saab-202) for the wing configuration: scaled-down wings of the intended design were fitted, and a first flight was made in the summer of 1950. The only major changes made were the use of boundary layer fences instead of wing slots, and replacement of the intended Swedish STAL Dovern engine by an afterburning Rolls-Royce Avon Series 100, to be constructed by Svenska Flygmoto (SFA) as the RM6.

The first Lansen prototype was flown on 3 November 1952, and first production A 32A Lansens began delivery in December 1955. The Flygvapnet's four attack wings (F6, 7, 14 and 17) all had the type in service by the end of 1957. The A 32A was followed by the Saab-32B all-weather fighter version, designated J 32B by the FV. This

infra-red or radar-homing air-to-air missiles in place of the earlier Sidewinders. With Flygvapnet production finished, Saab turned its eyes to the export market, selling 49 Saab-35Xs to Denmark and 12 to Finland, a version based on the Saab-F but with much-enhanced attack capability and greater range. For the three customer countries, a total of more than 600 Drakens was built before production ended in the mid-1970s.

Concurrently with Draken production, Saab was also responsible for another successful product, the all-through jet Saab-105, designed in early 1960 and originally intended to be a private-venture jet successor to the Safir. Although finding no takers as a civil tourer/air taxi, it soon attracted the Flygvapnet, and after the prototype had flown on 29 June 1963, the Swedish Air Force ordered 130 as Sk 60 trainers and 20 more as A 60 light attack aircraft, the former entering service in 1966. With six underwing hardpoints, the A 60 could carry two 30mm gun pods, two 250kg or six 125kg bombs, two air-to-surface missiles, twelve 135mm rockets, ECM equipment or other similar loads. The Saab-105's versatility was improved after entry into service, when the Sk 60s were modified into three sub-variants: the Sk 60A and B, with limited or complete provision to be adapted from a training to an attack role, and the reconnaissance Sk 60C, similar to the B model but with a permanent camera installation in a modified nose. A total of 40 Saab-105XT export models, with two 1,293kg (2,850lb) thrust General Electric J85-17B turbojets replacing the lower-powered Turboméca Aubisque turbofans of the domestic variants, was built for the Austrian Air Force. The Saab-105G multi-role light combat aircraft flew in May 1972.

Current Saab aircraft programmes centre chiefly around three types. In 1968, the year in which Saab broadened its industrial horizons by a merger with the large Scania-Vabis road vehicle manufacturing concern, it also absorbed a small aircraft company known as Malmö Flygindustri (MFI). Previously, MFI had been responsible for licence-building the little Bölkow 208C Junior lightplane, in a version known as the MFI-9 Militrainer. Saab evolved an improved version, known originally as the MFI-17 and currently as the Safari (in civil guise) and Supporter (in military configuration). First flown in July 1969, the Safari/Supporter is a three-seat high-wing monoplane, suitable for primary training, light utility duties, or as a mini-attack aircraft with six underwing attachments for up to 300kg (660lb) of bombs, rockets or gun pods. More than 150 of the two types have been sold, including 32 Supporters to the Danish armed forces, 45 to those of Pakistan, and 20 to Zambia.

Multi-role Viggen

By far the biggest programme to date for Saab has been that for the Viggen (Thunderbolt), begun in 1961 as a multi-purpose combat aircraft, initially to replace the A 32A Lansen for all-weather attack and subsequently the J 35F Draken in the interception role and the S 32C Lansen and S 35E Draken for reconnaissance. Seven prototypes were built, including one two-seater, and the first of these was flown on 8 February 1967, revealing a radical but logical design utilising a large delta main wing, with anhedral, ahead of which are delta-shaped 'canard' foreplanes, creating in effect a variation of the 'double delta' single wing that gave the Draken its excellent STOL (short take-off and landing) performance. In a country whose air bases are relatively few and widely separated, this STOL capability enables Sweden's air defence to operate from any 500m (1,640ft) straight stretch of

motorway; many Flygvapnet aircraft are nowadays stored in hangars hollowed out of cliff faces, and for this reason the Viggen, a large aircraft, has its tail-fin hinged to fold downward for storage. The first production Saab-37 was flown on 23 February 1971 and by 1978 five versions had been ordered for the Flygvapnet: the AJ 37, for attack, of which deliveries began in mid-1971 to replace the Lansen; the Sk 37 two-seat combat trainer; the overland tactical reconnaissance SF 37, to replace the S 32C

Lansen; the maritime reconnaissance SH 37, to replace the S 35E Draken and the JA 37 interceptor, to supplement and eventually replace the J 35F Draken. Orders for the first four versions total 180, and for the JA 37 totalled 149 by late 1978, with possibly another order for 25–30 to follow. Power plant is an 11,800kg (26,015lb) thrust RM8A engine except for the JA 37 which uses the 12,750kg; (28,108lb) thrust RM8B. The RM8 was developed by Volvo Flygmotor from the Pratt & Whitney JT8D-22 civil turbofan and fitted with a Swedish-designed afterburner. A formidable armament of guns, missiles, bombs and rockets can be carried by all models, with computer-based navigation, weapon aiming and other major functions.

In the past 30 of its 40 years, Saab has produced more than 2,000 military jet aircraft. Its Aerospace Division, with some 5,000 employees, is a leading exponent of missiles, electronics and, as a member of the MESH consortium, space technology. Its next major aircraft programme, already in the advanced design stage, will be a new light attack/jet trainer aircraft to replace the Sk 60 in the mid-1980s. Awaiting a full go-ahead from the Swedish government in late 1978, this is the B3LA, a tandem two-seat strike-capable design able to operate from semi-prepared road strips, carry several tonnes of ordnance, and look after itself in a dogfight.

For such a resolutely non-militant country, Sweden has consistently shown itself able to produce high-class military aircraft which are not only eminently suited to its own particular defence needs but are comparable with the best from other nations. First impressions suggest that, with the B3LA, that high standard will be maintained into the next decade.

The Viggen was the first combat aircraft in the world to feature a delta wing with canard foreplanes. The advantages of the configuration are short take-off and landing runs, exceptional stability at all speeds and outstanding manoeuvrability

Winged Samurai

Saburo Sakai scored 64 victories as a fighter pilot with the Imperial Japanese Navy

Saburo Sakai, pictured during his training as a pilot in 1937, was one of the few Japanese enlisted men to be commissioned as a reward for his gallantry

Early on the morning of 8 December 1941, American forces in the Philippines began receiving disconcerting snatches of news indicating a dawn attack on the naval base of Pearl Harbour on the other side of the International Date Line. In anticipation of a similar attack on Luzon, northernmost of the main Philippine islands, fighters were put into the air on patrol; however, nothing developed. Eventually fuel ran low and the pilots were forced to land their Curtiss P-40 Warhawks for refuelling. At that moment unidentified aircraft approached, and within minutes the Luzon airfields were under heavy attack. The Japanese navy air force formation had been delayed by mist over their airfields in Formosa. They had expected the delay to be disastrous, but instead it provided them with an unexpected advantage. One of the few P-40s to claw its way back into the air over Clark Field became the first American casualty of the new war in the Pacific; its victor was an experienced pilot of the Tainan Air Corps' Fighter Group, Naval Air Pilot First Class Saburo Sakai.

Born on 26 August 1916 at Saga on Kyushu island, Sakai was the son of a poor samurai. In May 1933 he joined the navy as an ordinary seaman, undergoing the traditionally tough and rigorous Japanese training before becoming a gunner on the battleship *Kirishima*. Sakai received rapid promotion and, by 1937, was a Petty Officer 3rd Class on the *Haruna*, when he applied for selection as a pilot. More training followed, leading to his graduation as a fighter pilot late the same year.

Ground-support duties

Sakai was not to wait long for action, for in May 1938 he was posted to the land-based 12th Fighter Group which was flying Mitsubishi A5M Claude aircraft at Kiuchang, China. His first sortie, closely watched over by the more experienced pilots in the formation, brought him an initial victory over a Russian-built Polikarpov I-16 fighter during a mission over Hankow. Thereafter, however, few Chinese aircraft were seen and the unit concentrated on ground-support duties. On 3 October 1939 a rare Chinese raid was made by 12 Tupolev SB-2 bombers on Hankow airfield, by then in Japanese hands, creating havoc and resulting in many aircraft being damaged. Sakai was the only pilot able to get into the air and he managed to inflict some damage on one of the fleeing raiders. Shortly afterwards he returned to Japan for a year's home duty, having been ordered to maintain complete silence regarding this incident.

In May 1941 he returned to China as a pilot in the experimental unit operating the first test batch of the superlative new Mitsubishi A6M1 Zero fighter. These swiftly dispatched any remaining Chinese aerial resistance from the skies, although it was some time before Sakai had an opportunity to add to his score. On 11 August 1941, while escorting bombers, he saw two I-16s taxying on an airfield below and dived down to strafe these, destroying both. He then saw a small biplane which he also shot down.

In September 1941 came a posting to the Tainan Air Corps which was forming in Formosa for the forthcoming Pacific War. Here the fighter pilots initially spent many hours learning to coax the maximum cruise range from their fighters. This experience later allowed them to undertake some of the longest-range fighter sorties ever attempted – well beyond what the Allies believed to be viable distances.

Following the initial attacks on the Philippines, the group soon moved to newly-captured airfields between Luzon and Borneo, from which missions could be flown against the Dutch and American fighters defending Eastern Java. The Japanese pilots also came up against the fast, tough and heavily-armed Boeing B-17 Fortress bombers of the US Army Air Force at this time, finding them difficult opponents to bring down. Sakai was to be involved in one of the first such combats, shooting down a bomber flown by Captain Colin Kelly. Several victories against the Allied fighters over Java during February raised Sakai's personal score to 13, but during the next month he was taken ill and hospitalised.

Elite chutai

On recovery he rejoined his unit on the north coast of New Guinea, and it was here that he was really to make his name. At Lae the *chutai* (flight) of the group in which he served was to become the most successful in the IJNAF. The flight included not only himself, but several of the future leading aces of his country, including Hiroyoshi Nishizawa (87 victories), Toshio Ota (34 victories), Toraichi Takatsuka (16 victories) and the unit commander Ltd Cdr Junichi Sasai (27 victories). The Lae fighters enjoyed great success against the American and Australian units defending the Port Moresby area on the other side of the island. Not only did the Japanese pilots possess a marked superiority in experience and training, but their manoeuvrable Zeros outperformed the opposing Bell P-39 Airacobras and Curtiss P-40s on most counts.

By mid-May Sakai's personal tally had reached 27 and by the first week of August 1942 this had increased to 58, making him Japanese top-scorer at this time. It should be noted, however, that this total apparently included a number of shared and probable victories, other sources giving his score at this time as nearer 28. Included among his victims were North American B-25 Mitchells and Martin B-26s, Boeing B-17s, Australian Lockheed Hudsons, P-40s and a considerable number of P-39s, including four in one day on 16 June. American night raids frequently disturbed the sleep of the Lae pilots, however, and on one July night, earth from a bomb burst buried Sakai, who was lucky to escape death by suffocation.

On 8 August 1942 an order was issued for a completely different type of operation. The US Marines had landed on Guadalcanal in the Solomons and air support to bombers and naval vessels retaliating against the Americans was desperately needed. The Lae units took off for the maximum-range mission with some trepidation at the prospect of meeting their opposite numbers, the US Navy fighter pilots. Arriving over Guadalcanal, combat was immediately joined, and Sakai claimed two aircraft – identified as a Grumman F4F Wildcat fighter and a Douglas SBD Dauntless dive bomber – shot down. He then saw eight aircraft which he took to be more Wildcats, and attacked from behind. These turned out to be Grumman TBF Avenger torpedo bombers and, although he believed he had brought two down, return fire from their

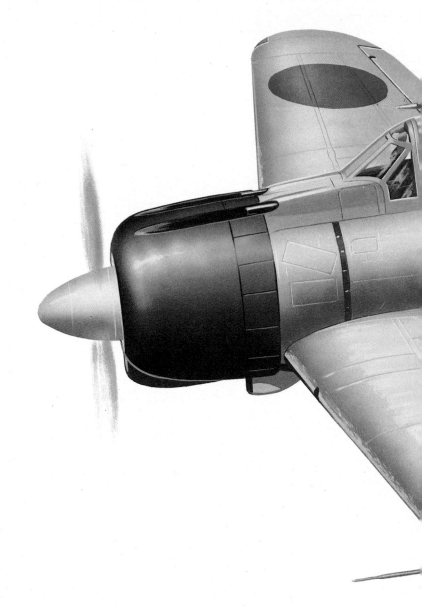

gunners struck his aircraft around the cockpit, inflicting severe injuries to Sakai's eyes and head. In terrible pain and near to fainting, he managed by a sustained effort of will to complete the long flight back to Lae. However, his ordeal was far from over, for on evacuation to Japan it was necessary for the surgeon to operate on his eyes without anaesthetic to remove the remaining shell splinters.

Despite losing the sight in his right eye, Sakai eventually rejoined the Tainan Group, now back in Japan at Togo-hashi having suffered terrible losses over Guadalcanal. Not allowed to fly on operations, he made test flights and undertook training duties until June 1944. Posted to the Yokosuka Group, he flew with this unit to Iwo Jima where he undertook one sortie against US Navy Grumman Hellcats, claiming one shot down. On 3 July the unit was sent on a *kamikaze* mission, escorting bombers; American fighters destroyed all the bombers, so surviving fighters abandoned the mission. The following month the unit returned to its home base at Yokosuka, Japan.

Posted in 1945 to the Matsuyama Group, which was flying the new Kawanishi N1K2-J Shiden-kai fighter, Sakai was again denied permission to fly operationally. However, finally on 13 August 1945 – the day on which the war ended – he and another pilot took off and between them they shot down a Boeing B-29 – by Sakai's reckoning this last success was his 64th victory.

Above: at the start of the Pacific War in December 1941 Sakai flew the Mitsubishi A6M2 Zero with the Tainan Air Corps. The unit, operating at extreme range from its Formosan bases, provided air cover for the Japanese assault on the Philippines and the Dutch East Indies

Above right: by the autumn of 1943 when the A6M5 entered service the Zero was outclassed by such fighters as the Hellcat, which Sakai fought over Iwo Jima. Right: the A6M2 model Zero was in widespread service with Japanese naval fighter units at the end of 1941. Fast and agile, it consistently outfought its American opponents

Chiefs of the Air Staff

John and Geoffrey Salmond both ended their Service careers in the highest RAF appointment

The history of the Royal Air Force includes many examples of a single family providing several brothers and sisters who made outstanding contributions to–or made distinguished careers in–the RAF. Yet none ever matched the unique achievement of the two Salmond brothers, both of whom initially entered the Army, then transferred to the Royal Flying Corps and eventually rose to the very peak of the Royal Air Force, each in his turn being appointed Chief of the Air Staff.

South African Campaign

The son of a regular army soldier, William Geoffrey Hanson Salmond was born in August 1878 and entered the Woolwich Academy prior to regular service in the Royal Artillery, starting in 1898. Serving in the Boer War, he passed through the Camberley Staff College in 1911–12, but then decided to learn to fly and gained Royal Aero Club Certificate No 421 on 18 February 1913. In doing so he had followed the example of his younger brother, John Maitland Salmond. Born in July 1881, John had joined the army and was commissioned in the King's Own Royal Lancashire Regiment in 1901. He too saw service in the South African campaign and, by 1910, had been promoted to captain. Two years later, on 13 August 1912, John obtained Royal Aero Club Certificate No 272, electing

with his brother Geoffrey to transfer to the recently-formed Royal Flying Corps. John became an instructor at the RFC's Central Flying School at Upavon in Wiltshire, while Geoffrey was appointed a staff officer at RFC Headquarters. By August 1914 John had been promoted to major, commanding No 3 Squadron RFC, which he led to France in the same month; Geoffrey, still a captain at RFC HQ, followed suit.

Serving throughout the early months of the air war in 1914, both brothers had been promoted by the following year–John as a colonel commanding an RFC wing and Geoffrey, after commanding No 1 Squadron, also being appointed to command a wing. For his service to date John was, in addition, awarded the Distinguished Service Order. Further promotion soon followed for each brother. As a brigadier-general in 1917, John Salmond became the Director-General of Military Aeronautics in England, while Geoffrey succeeded to the command of the RFC units in the Middle East theatres of operations, as a major-general. In 1918 John was appointed to succeed Hugh Trenchard as General Officer Commanding the RAF in France and, at the end of the war, had been knighted. Geoffrey was also decorated with the DSO and, in 1919, the Salmond brothers were each granted a permanent commission in the peacetime Royal Air Force.

Proponent of air control

A staunch advocate of air power in general and air control in particular, John Salmond was given a unique opportunity to put his theories into practice when he was appointed as the first Air Officer Commanding in Iraq in 1922–24. His post amounted to overall command of all British forces–air and ground–in the country and his task was to quell the series of tribal revolts. Using his meagre air formations as the spearhead, Salmond proved conclusively the practical superiority of aircraft over cumbersome, expensive standing army garrisons for 'police control' over such vast desert areas as Iraq. His success in the Middle East led to the government of the day sending him briefly to India, there to investigate the low state of RAF affairs. In his usual meticulous way, John Salmond presented the Viceroy of India with a highly detailed, 40-page report, which included strong recommendations for the future RAF presence in India.

Promoted to air marshal in 1923, John became AOC-in-C, Air Defence of Great Britain in 1925 but, three years later at the request of the governments of Australia and New Zealand, he visited these countries to advise on the future structure and use of each country's embryo air services. Further promotion to air chief marshal came when, on 1 January 1930, he succeeded Hugh Trenchard as Chief of the Air Staff. Though possessing none of Trenchard's visionary concepts for air power, John Salmond was without contemporary equal in his theories on practical use of the air services. In his three years' tenure in office as CAS, John Salmond faithfully carried out Trenchard's dream of a totally independent RAF.

In the meantime his brother Geoffrey had spent a large proportion of his time in service outside Britain, serving in the Middle East from 1919 to 1922; then, after a tour of staff duty as Air Member for Supply and Personnel at the Air Ministry, he was appointed AOC-in-C, India. Here he was able finally to carry out the various recommendations of his brother's report of August 1922 and bring the RAF in India up to its proper strength and status. Serving in India from 1927 to 1931, Geoffrey returned to England for another staff appointment; then on 1 April 1933, he succeeded John as Chief of the Air Staff. Tragically, his tenure of office was a mere 26 days, for on 27 April Geoffrey Salmond died. His brother John was recalled temporarily from retirement to resume the office until Sir Edward Ellington became CAS.

As a civilian John Salmond accumulated many honours and honorary degrees in recognition of his long and distinguished record of service to the RAF, and was a director of Imperial Airways, forerunner of the present-day British Airways. Continuing to keep in close touch with RAF matters, during his later years in particular, Sir John Maitland Salmond died on 16 April 1968.

Left: King George V meets Major-General John Salmond, commander of the RFC in France, at his headquarters at St Audre on 29 March 1918. Above right: Marshal of the RAF Sir John Salmond (left) pictured with Group Captain Carter (centre) at the presentation of a standard to No 7 Squadron, Bomber Command at RAF Upwood in October 1953. The Squadron had originally been formed under Salmond at Farnborough on 1 May 1914. Right: Air Chief Marshal Sir Geoffrey Salmond was buried with full military honours. He had been appointed Chief of the Air Staff only 26 days before he died

Flying Buccaneer

The swashbuckling Charles Samson was one of the foremost pioneers of naval flying

Born at Cheetham, Lancashire in 1883, Charles Rumney Samson was originally destined for a career in the Royal Navy and joined HMS *Britannia* as a cadet when he was 15 years of age. During the next 12 years Samson saw service with the Fleet in Somaliland and the Persian Gulf, before returning to England for home duties in 1911. Here he found the newborn science of aeronautics emerging and was immediately attracted to flying. In that year the Admiralty was persuaded to permit four naval officers to learn to fly at Eastchurch, Kent, on aircraft supplied free of cost by Mr (later Sir) Francis McClean; Samson was selected as one of the quartet.

Wholly enthusiastic about the future possibilities of naval aviation, Samson persuaded his superiors to purchase McClean's two machines, and to send 12 naval ratings to Eastchurch as the nucleus of a naval flying school. Aided by a fellow officer and flying enthusiast Lt Arthur Longmore (later Air Chief Marshal Sir Arthur Longmore), Samson conducted a series of experiments to adapt aircraft for sea-going operations, and obtained permission to construct in Chatham dockyard a form of ship's platform to be fitted over a ship's deck. This was erected aboard HMS *Africa* at Sheerness and on 10 January 1912 Samson successfully flew a Short biplane off the wooden trackway and then alighted on the sea, his machine having been fitted with flotation air-bags to prevent it sinking.

Right and below: Wing Commander C. R. Samson seen with his two-seat Nieuport before taking off to bomb Turkish positions in the Dardanelles. No 3 Wing, commanded by Samson, received six Nieuports in July 1915, each armed with a 0·303 in Lewis machine gun firing over the propeller arc. He said of his machine that 'it climbed like a witch'

He repeated this take-off procedure from a similar runway aboard HMS *Hibernia*, in a Short S38, while the ship was underway at a speed of 15 knots, on 12 May 1912 in Weymouth bay. By then Samson was a member of the technical subcommittee which prepared a scheme for the formation of the Royal Flying Corps and, in 1912, was appointed as commander of the Eastchurch naval flying school. Samson's duties seldom prevented his continuing energetic experiments into the naval use of aircraft and in June 1912 he successfully tested a wireless set while airborne. During the following two years he conducted a wide variety of trials in night flying and pure armament experiments. The latter consisted of flying at varying heights over explosive charges, detonated in order to determine the effects of aerial bomb-dropping on bomber aircraft. King George V's review of the Fleet at Spithead from 18 to 22 July 1914 saw Samson lead a 'massed formation' of naval aircraft over the assembled naval vessels.

On the outbreak of war in August 1914 the first naval air unit to be dispatched abroad was Samson's Eastchurch Squadron, which moved to France on 27 August, with ten aircraft, an airship and a variety of mechanical transport. Initially responsible for air reconnaissance, Samson's formation was quickly ordered to seek means of preventing German airships from operating. By mid-September Samson had acquired additional motor vehicles, which were then armoured and fitted with machine guns. Leading this tiny 'armoured car' force, Samson then proceeded to harass the German forces in Belgium, attacking cavalry and infantry formations wherever they were encountered. In the air Samson's men undertook many bombing raids against German forces and communications posts, but the gradual retreat of the British Expeditionary Force meant that the Squadron was eventually forced to move to Dunkirk, from where it was withdrawn to England in February 1915.

Samson's Pirates

On his return, Samson was immediately given orders to prepare his squadron for service in the Dardanelles, and on 23 March he arrived at Imbros with his unit. For the remainder of the year 'Samson's Pirates'—a soubriquet acquired during their service in Belgium and enhanced by their leader's stocky, bearded appearance—carried out a continual bombing assault on Turkish forces, interspersed with reconnaissance sorties. During this period, on 19 November, a pilot of No 3 Wing (as Samson's unit had become), Squadron Commander R. B. Davies DSO, earned the Victoria Cross for deliberately landing near Turkish forces and retrieving another pilot of No 3 Wing who had crashed. The Allied evacuation of Suvla and Anzac in December meant the withdrawal of Samson's unit to England, while Samson himself was taken ill and spent several months convalescing in England.

In May 1916 Samson was ordered to take command of HMS *Ben-my-Chree*, with its attendant 'squadron' of two cargo steamers HMS *Anne* and HMS *Raven II*, all based in Port Said, Egypt. In co-operation with both the Army and the Royal Navy, Samson's new command included reconnaissance of Turkish communication lines and general operations in the Red Sea. The *Ben-my-Chree* had been converted to carry floatplanes in a hangar, these being hoisted over the side when needed for operations and flown from the sea. Samson and his crews pursued an air and sea offensive against German and Turkish opponents from May 1916 to January 1917, creating a minor legend for their courage and daring. However, on 9 January, while harboured at Castelorizo, the *Ben-my-Chree* was fatally hit by a Turkish land battery and Samson was forced to abandon ship with the crew. Finally on 13 January the ship sank in the shallow waters.

Arriving in Britain at the end of May 1917, Samson spent six months on staff duties with the Admiralty Air Department, then in November 1917 returned to more active duties when he was appointed commander of the naval air station at Great Yarmouth, home of several operational flying boat units. Here he remained until the formation of the Royal Air Force on 1 April 1918, although his heavy administrative responsibilities as station commander did not prevent him participating in many operational sorties in the Felixstowe flying boats and Sopwith Camels of his command.

With the reorganisation of the (now) single air service in April 1918, Samson left Yarmouth on transfer to Felixstowe, where he was given command of an RAF Group, comprising Felixstowe, Yarmouth, Westgate, Manston and a number of smaller units at Covehithe, Bacton, Holt, Brough Castle, Lowestoft and Shotley.

The paperwork involved in commanding so wide and diverse an organisation did not prevent Samson from flying occasionally.

Seaborne trials

On 30 May, 1918 Samson flew the first trial take-off in a Sopwith Camel from a 9m (30ft) wooden platform being towed at sea and nearly drowned when the Camel toppled into the water. Undeterred, Samson had the platform modified and his labours came to fruition on 31 July when Lt S. D. Culley successfully took off from the platform. On 11 August Culley rose from a similar towed 'runway' in a Camel and an hour later destroyed the airship L53 in flames. Continuing the energetic command of his Group until the Armistice, Samson decided to remain in the RAF at the end of the war, rather than return to the Royal Navy. Awarded the Distinguished Service Order and Air Force Cross, Samson was shortly afterwards promoted to air commodore and given command of RAF Near East.

Samson's deep commitment to aviation, combined with his restless pioneering instincts, saw him authorise and personally lead several experimental long-distance formation flights in the 1920s. In October 1926 Samson led three de Havilland DH9As and two Vickers Victorias on a long reconnaissance over the Kharga and Baharia oases in the Libyan desert. This was mainly to test the Victoria's endurance and reliability under primitive conditions of maintenance, having already flown a Victoria from Cairo to Aden in the previous month and returned safely–a round trip of over 6,400km (4,000 miles). On 30 March 1927 he led four Fairey IIIF two-seaters from Heliopolis, Egypt to Cape Town, South Africa, arriving there on 21 April. Four days later he set out on the return trip, arriving at Cairo on 22 May, having made a round trip of 18,285km (11,362 miles) without encountering any serious problems *en route*. These and other pioneering sorties, were instrumental in founding the air links around what was then the British Empire.

By the end of 1929 Samson had retired from the RAF. After a morning ride on 5 February 1931, however, he complained of feeling unwell and before the local doctor could be called Charles Samson had died from heart failure at his Wiltshire home in Cholderton.

Top: Wing Commander Samson, seen in Tenedos, led No 3 Wing in support of the British Empire forces in the Dardanelles campaign.
Above: Samson (right) inspecting the defences of No 3 Wing's airfield at Tenedos in 1915.
Left: a painting by C. R. Fleming-Williams entitled 'An "OK" bombing of Chikaldir Bridge, 27 August 1916'. The raid was carried out by Wing Commander Samson, Flight Commander England and Flight Lieutenant Clemson

Yachts of the Air

The Saunders Roe company at Cowes were best known for their graceful flying boats

Saunders-Roe Ltd had its roots in a small business established in 1830 at Streatley-on-Thames, to help build weirs and locks on the river. By the 1890s it had been relocated at Goring-on-Thames under the leadership of the founder's grandson, Samuel B. Saunders, who was one of the pioneers of motor boats. To save weight and increase the speed of these craft, Saunders devised his patented Consuta method of construction, which consisted of stitching together very thin diagonal laminated plywood planking with toughened brass or copper wire.

As part of the Saunders Patent Launch Building Syndicate, Sam Saunders built launches both at Goring and later at Cowes in the Isle of Wight where he opened a branch works in 1901. In 1906 his agreement with the syndicate expired and two years later he reorganised his business as a private limited company.

Prize-winning Bat Boat

It was not long before Saunders branched out into aeronautical engineering and in 1909 he contributed to the construction of the French Revaud hydroplane. In 1912, he used his Consuta method to build the cedar wood hull of the Sopwith 'hydro', later to become known as the Bat Boat, which was Britain's first practical flying boat. This little biplane two-seater, with its tail carried on outriggers, first appeared at the 1913 Olympia Aero Show powered by a 90 hp Austro-Daimler engine. Later in the year, as an amphibian with a 100 hp Green engine fitted, it won the £500 Mortimer Singer Prize for the first all-British aircraft to make six consecutive flights between two points eight kilometres (five miles) apart, one of which – marked by a buoy in the Solent – was on water, and one – at Cowes – on land. The pilot, Harry Hawker, was accompanied by Lieutenant Spenser D. A. Grey as official observer. This

Top: the two Windhovers were of unusual configuration.
Right: four RAF squadrons used the London in 1936–41.
Below: the single Saunders Valkyrie seen during tests

first Bat Boat was subsequently purchased by the Admiralty and took part in the Naval Review of 1914. When war broke out it was sent to the RNAS seaplane base at Scapa Flow, whence it flew patrols over the Fleet until late November 1914 when it was wrecked in a gale.

During World War I Saunders' firm built under sub-contract such aircraft as the Avro 504A, the Short 184 seaplane and the Felixstowe F.2A flying boat. The Cowes factory had expanded to both sides of the River Medina by the time of the Armistice, but the wholesale cancellation of Government contracts made the company's future seem very uncertain at first. Fortunately it managed to survive by reconditioning and producing spares for F.2A and F.5 flying boats and manufacturing parts for the de Havilland DH9A 'Nine-Ack' day bomber.

S. E. Saunders Ltd had started to build aircraft of its own design in 1917. The first was the T1, a two-seat biplane intended to operate either as a landplane or floatplane, although it is doubtful if it ever flew in the latter form. Powered by a 150hp Sunbeam engine, it first took to the air at Cowes, but due to the death of its designer, H. H. Thomas, in the 1918 influenza epidemic, it was not developed for quantity production.

Next Saunders type to fly was the twin-engined Kittiwake amphibian of 1920. Accommodating two crew and seven passengers and featuring variable-camber wings, this

biplane was built for the 1920 Air Ministry Commercial Amphibian Competition at Martlesham Heath, but it appeared too late to enter. The leading-edge camber gear came adrift during the machine's maiden flight in September 1920 and in the ensuing forced landing on the sea off Egypt Point, Cowes, the hull was holed by a submerged rock. Nevertheless the Kittiwake was soon repaired and flying again, but it was very underpowered and was scrapped in July 1921.

Metal hull development

Vickers had acquired a fairly large financial stake in the company in 1918 and, from S. E. Saunders Ltd's earliest days, the Wolesley Tool and Motor Car Company had held a small investment. Both these interests were bought out by Sam Saunders in 1921 and two years later an aircraft design office was established at the Cowes works. Its first design to be produced was the Valkyrie biplane flying boat, powered by three Rolls-Royce Condor engines, which was intended for military general-purpose use and first flew in 1927. On 12 August that year it left Felixstowe in company with three other flying boats for a 15,120km (9,400 mile) Baltic cruise. Although it completed

Above left and above: the Princess was designed to a government specification of 1945 for a 220-passenger long-range flying boat. BOAC initially expressed interest but withdrew in 1951, from when the Princess was developed as a military transport. Only one flew, on 22 August 1952. Trials were extensive and successful, but were suspended in 1954 to await more suitable engines. Right: the SR A/1 was the world's first jet fighter flying boat, but no peacetime requirement for the type existed by the time it flew in 1947 and consequently the type saw no RAF service

riveted stringers unnecessary and reduced the weight of the hull by several hundred pounds. This type of construction was later used on many other Saro flying boats of the inter-war period. The first completely Saro-designed flying boat to appear was the Cutty Sark high-wing monoplane civil transport, variously powered by two ADC Hermes, DH Gipsy or Armstrong Siddeley Lynx or Genet Major engines. Carrying three passengers, it was the first British high-wing passenger-carrying monoplane flying boat; the prototype made its first flight at Cowes in July 1929. The Cutty Sark had a wooden wing and an all-metal hull and, although it was at first produced purely as a flying boat, a two-wheel landing gear was subsequently fitted, making it an amphibian. A total of 12 Cutty Sarks was built, the ninth example being to the order of a Japanese pilot for a flight from San Francisco to Japan. Powered by a 240hp Armstrong Siddeley Lynx, this particular machine was the only single-engined version of the Cutty Sark and was specially fitted with long-range fuel tanks and blind flying equipment.

The prototype Cutty Sark did not utilise a corrugated hull as fitted to the A14; the first Saro machine to do so from the outset was the elegant Severn (type number A7) of 1930, which was designed to meet an Air Ministry requirement for a three-engined military flying boat. Powered by Bristol Jupiters, the sole example built boasted many interesting features; the most notable of which was its overload range. This enabled it to make the first non-stop flight from Gibraltar to Plymouth and it would have been capable of flying non-stop across the Atlantic. Although a larger machine, the Severn was the forerunner of the better-known Saro London.

Cloud and Windhover

The year 1930 was altogether a busy one for Saro, for two other new aircraft took to the water and the air for the first time; these were the Cloud and the Windhover. The Cloud was a twin-engined amphibian with a very roomy cabin and appeared in both civil and military forms. The RAF's version was used at Andover, Hants, Calshot, Hants, and Manston, Kent, for navigational training and pilot conversion from landplane to flying boat. As a navigational trainer, it carried a number of pupils in the cabin, with the blinds drawn. Each pupil had his own instruments and was expected to plot the Cloud's course.

The Windhover, also an amphibian, was approximately halfway between the Cutty Sark and the Cloud in size. Six passengers were carried in each of the two examples built and the power arrangement was unusual, consisting of three DH Gipsy engines mounted on struts above the mainplane, with an auxiliary aerofoil above the engine. The second Windhover eventually had its land undercarriage removed and fuel tankage increased for an attempt upon the world's endurance record by the use of in-flight refuelling. It took off on 9 August 1932, landing on 11 August with an airborne time of 54 hours 13 minutes, having been refuelled in flight by a civilianised Bristol Fighter. Unfortunately it did not gain the record and was later reconverted to amphibian configuration and used until 1938 by Jersey Airways.

Meanwhile, in 1928, Saro had produced a prototype of an aircraft far removed from a flying boat. The dainty little A10 was designed to a 1927 Air Ministry specification for a multi-gun, high-altitude single-seat interceptor fighter. Powered by a 490hp Rolls-Royce F.XIS inline engine and armed with four fuselage-mounted machine guns, the A10 first flew in January 1929, but it was not ordered into production.

this without incident and underwent further test flying, it was not ordered into production. The field of large flying boats was dominated by Shorts, Blackburns and Supermarines at that time and when Saunders followed the Valkyrie with another all-wooden flying boat, the Medina, for potential civil use by Imperial Airways, this too was left on the shelf. It was now obvious that time had come for change; the day of the wooden-hulled flying boat had passed and with it the major application of Sam Saunders' Consuta patent to aircraft construction.

Considerable capital for new equipment was required to facilitate the change-over to metal construction. This was eventually provided in 1928, when a controlling interest was acquired by Sir Alliott Verdon-Roe—who had broken with the firm of Avro of which he had been the creator—John Lord and H. E. Broadsmith. Other parties also subscribed large sums and the company was renamed Saunders-Roe Ltd, usually abbreviated to Saro.

Aviation was Saro's main preoccupation, however, and its first venture was a metal hull which was married to a Supermarine Southampton flying boat superstructure to form the Saro A14. A special feature of this hull was its embodiment of longitudinal corrugation, which rendered

The twin Bristol Pegasus-engined London biplane flying boat won an immediate production order in 1934 as part of the RAF Expansion Scheme. The type became standard Service equipment, being used for patrol and reconnaissance and saw wartime use in the early days of World War II in the hands of Coastal Command. The experimental A33, built to the same Air Ministry specification as the Short Sunderland, flew in 1938 and was unusual in being a parasol monoplane equipped with stub wings or sponsons. The 29m (95ft) span Monospar wing with its four 830hp Bristol Perseus engines was carried over the hull by massive 'N' struts based on the sponsons. This wing failed when the A33 made a heavy impact with the water during high-speed taxying trials in the Solent and the machine suffered such serious damage that it was deemed a write-off. Saro then concentrated on production of the twin Bristol Hercules-engined Lerwick high-wing monoplane flying boat for the RAF; but only 21 were completed, however, as the type proved unsatisfactory during its Service life and was withdrawn in May 1941.

The company's south of England establishments built large numbers of Supermarine Walrus and Sea Otter air/sea rescue amphibians for the Royal Navy and RAF during World War II. Work continued on flying boat development at Beaumaris on the Menai Straits, producing the Shetland in conjunction with Short Brothers, its designers. Saro also serviced and, where necessary, modified American flying boats at Beaumaris.

Postwar jet fighter

Saro's first postwar product was the little SR A/1, the world's first jet fighter flying boat which, powered by two Metrovick Beryl turbojets, attained 830km/h (516mph). First flown in July 1947, the SR A/1 was of wartime origin, being originally intended for use in the Pacific against the Japanese. Armament consisted of four 20mm Hispano cannon mounted in the decking above the oval nose air intake, but the type was not put into production. A similarly sad fate befell Saro's magnificent giant transatlantic civil flying boat the Princess, three of which were ordered for the British Overseas Airways Corporation in 1946. Spanning 66·7m (219ft) and powered by ten Bristol Proteus turboprops, the Princess was the largest flying boat in the world when she first flew in 1952, but was grossly underpowered. The second and third Princesses never flew, the entire programme was cancelled and all three boats were consigned to store.

In 1956 de Havilland Holdings acquired an interest in Saro. The SR53 interceptor, of which two prototypes were built and flown, had a DH Spectre rocket motor and an Armstrong Siddeley Viper turbojet and was armed with two wingtip-mounted DH Firestreak missiles. The production version was to have been the SR177, for which Government funding was not forthcoming. Thereafter, Saro chiefly concentrated on helicopter development and production. Its Helicopter Division, which had been established in 1951 when Saro took over the Cierva Autogyro Co, developed the latter's two-seat Skeeter and built it in quantity. It also derived from it the more powerful P531, progenitor of the Westland Scout and Wasp. By building the revolutionary SR-N1 Hovercraft, the world's first practical cushion craft in 1959, Saro entered a completly new field of transport. With these craft its history as an independent company came to an end, for in 1959 it was absorbed into Westland Aircraft Ltd. Simultaneously, Saunders-Roe (Anglesey) at Beaumaris and another subsidiary, Saro Laminated Wood Products Ltd, became part of the de Havilland company.

Right: the Skeeter was a light two-seat observation, liaison and training helicopter. It was used by the RAF, the British Army and the army and navy of West Germany. Production ended in 1961.
Below: the P531 first flew on 20 July 1958 and was developed by Westland into the highly-successful Scout and Wasp.
Bottom: the SR53 was the first British aircraft to employ both turbojet and rocket propulsion. Built as an experimental interceptor under a government contract, two prototypes were tested

Builders of the Air Armadas

**A famous line of Savoia-Marchetti flying boats was
followed by the finest Italian bomber of World War II**

SIAI or Societa Idrovolanti Alta Italia started work at
Sesto Calende in northern Italy in mid-1915. The original
intention was to specialise in flying boats and only later
was the name changed to Societa Italiana Aeroplani
Idrovolanti to provide for landplane production.

After French FBA flying boats, technical director
Ing Conflenti built 172 of his own S 8 biplane design in
1917–18. He then produced in rapid succession the higher-
powered S 9, long-range S 12 and single and two-seat
versions of the S 13. Greatest success was the S 16, displayed at the 1919 Paris Aeronautical Salon. Built in
large numbers, both as a six-seat passenger aircraft and as
a Regia Aeronautica bomber-reconnaissance machine
(with 7·7mm bow gun and racks for 200kg (440lb) of
bombs), its Fiat 300hp A 12bis engine was replaced by a
400hp Lorraine in the S 16ter.

Schneider Trophy challengers

Savoia flying boats were brilliant Schneider Trophy
contestants. A clipped-wing, single-seat S 13 completed
the 1919 Bournemouth course in solitary splendour, only
to suffer disqualification. However, Luigi Bologna made
amends in 1920 at Venice, taking first prize with a modified
S 12. The streamlined S 21 and twin tandem-engined S 22,
specially designed for the 1921 Trophy were not ready
in time.

The S 23 trainer flying boat was Conflenti's swan song.
Having finished the design of the twin-engined S 24
(which was never built), he departed for the French
CAMS firm to design their Schneider contenders. His
successor, Alessandro Marchetti, maintained the seaplane
tradition. Up until this time SIAI designs had borne the
generic name 'Savoia', but this was now changed to
Savoia-Marchetti. For the 1922 Schneider race Marchetti

*Top right: the S 8 was the first of a series of highly-
successful flying boat designs built by SIAI from 1917.
Above right: the Marchese de Pinedo's S 16ter under
tow on the Swan River, Western Australia, during his
record 54,700km (34,000 mile) world flight in 1925.
Below: S 59bis flying boats of the 182ª Squadriglia*

produced both the S 50 twin-float variation of his own 1917 MVT scout and the beautiful S 51 sesquiplane flying boat. The S 50 crashed during a test flight, but Alessandro Passaleva piloted the S 51 into second place.

With a single aberration, the 300hp S 52 landplane fighter, Marchetti confined his designs to flying boats. The S 53 twin-engined bomber was followed by the unique and hugely successful S 55. The successful S 56 of 1924 was a two-seat, side-by-side school biplane amphibian with a tractor propeller and 50 were produced under licence in the United States. The S 57, of which 19 were built, was a two-seat, light fighter-reconnaissance boat, while the S 58, an experimental single-seat fighter, broke the world seaplane altitude record in 1924, when Adriano Bacula reached 5,829m (19,125ft) with a 250kg (550lb) payload. The 400hp Lorraine-engined S 59 and 500hp Asso-engined S 59bis, three-seat developments of the S 16, were produced in civil and military versions. The S 59bis reached 210km/h (130mph) and equipped Italian maritime reconnaissance *squadriglie* for a decade, carrying out a spectacular 1929 mass eastern Mediterranean cruise.

The single-bay 500hp Asso-engined S 62 bomber was developed into the 750hp Asso-engined S 62bis. Several 'show-the-flag' flights created a reputation for dependability and orders came from Italy, South America Romania, Spain and the Soviet Union. The last three countries all built the S 62bis under licence, the Russians producing 29 as the MBR-4 and Spain producing 40. The 1933 S 78 had a 955hp Asso RC 35 engine, automatic Handley Page slots along the length of the upper wing leading-edge and an improved hull. Like the S 62bis it was a three-to-four seater with midships and bow gunners' cockpits; 60 served with the Regia Aeronautica.

Air Armadas

The S 55 was the world's most successful inter-war flying boat. Its unique layout – twin hulls with a shoulder wing containing the pilot's cockpit in its centre section leading-edge, two fins and three rudders on the horizontal tailplane

carried on twin booms extending from the hulls—led to some official hesitation, but, one year after the 1925 maiden flight, series production commenced. Many modifications were introduced; the tandem twin engines supported by twin N struts were, at first, 400 hp Lorraines, then 550 hp Assos, then Fiats, either 600 hp A-22Rs (on the S 55A) or 700 hp A-24s, and finally with 750 hp Assos on the S 55X of 1933. Aerodynamic improvements were incorporated and hull enlarged and its shape modified. Construction was largely of wood, although Piaggio built seven S 55Ms with metal hulls.

The civil S 55C and S 55P, seating ten to twelve passengers, operated on a number of regular routes in the Adriatic and Mediterranean for a decade. Military versions of the S 55 had four defensive gun positions, one in the bow and stern of each hull, and had an offensive load of bombs or torpedoes, weighing up to 1,000 kg (2,200 lb). Maximum speed gradually improved from 210 km/h (130 mph) to 280 km/h (174 mph). Over 200 S 55s were built.

with three 600 hp A 22R engines, each with a four-bladed pusher propeller, and the one-off S 77 of 1937 with three radials and tractor propellers. The S 63 was an experimental single-hull development.

The S 64 monoplane was a triumphant record-breaker and a landplane. Fuel accounted for two-thirds of its loaded weight. The thick-section wing was attached to a small fuselage with booms extended from the upper wing surface and the undercarriage fairings to support the single-fin-and-rudder tailplane and its 590 hp Fiat A 22T engine was carried above the wing on a pair of N struts. On 1 June 1928 Capitano Ferrarin and Maggiore Del Prete established a world closed circuit endurance record of 58 hours 53 minutes and 15 seconds' continuous flight, covering 7,667 km (4,764 miles). Next the S 64 captured the straight-line distance record, making a landfall in Brazil after flying 7,189 km (4,467 miles). In May 1930, fitted with a variable-pitch propeller and redesignated S 64bis, Marchetti's extraordinary aircraft won the closed circuit record a second time.

Above left and below: S 55 flying boats undertook spectacular long-distance formation flights led by General Italo Balbo. Left: an early S 55 serving as a patrol flying boat with the Regia Aeronautica. Right: one of three S 74 airliners to serve with the Italian carrier Ala Littoria

The S 55 made several outstanding flights, including de Pinedo's odyssey, flying the *Santa Maria* to South America and the United States in 1927, when he used the Mississippi and various lakes to reach far inland. In 1928 Maddalena's S 55 made mercy flights to the survivors of Noble's ill-fated airship *Italia* stranded in the Arctic. It was, however, the great mass flights by S 55s, hailed in the world's Press as 'Air Armadas' which established Savoia-Marchetti's place in the annals of aviation. A distance of 10,400 km (6,460 miles) was covered at an average speed of 185 km/h (115 mph) by a formation of 14 S 55As ('A' for Atlantic) which left Italy in December 1930 and reached Rio de Janeiro in Brazil. Three years later 25 S 55X machines overflew the Alps, alighting first at Amsterdam, then flying by stages to Chicago for the 1933 World's Fair. These flights, remarkable achievements for their day, were led by Italo Balbo, Mussolini's son-in-law and made him a national hero, while bolstering the myth of Fascist aerial might. The S 55As of 1930 and the S 55Xs of 1933 had extra fuel tankage to increase endurance and bore impressive paint schemes, incorporating international registration letters based on the name of each aircraft's captain. The 1933 flight commemorated the tenth anniversary of the independent Regia Aeronautica—thus accounting for the 'X' suffix in the designation—and it covered 9,761 km (6,065 miles) in 48 hours' flying time.

Twin-hulled S 55 developments included the 1932 14-passenger S 66, 22 of which were built for Ala Littoria,

The 1929 S 65 twin-float, low-wing monoplane was to be Marchetti's final attempt to win the Schneider Trophy. Its slender pilot's nacelle had 1,000 hp Isotta Fraschini engines fore and aft, while a pair of booms carried the tailplane with its single fin and rudder. However, disaster struck when the famous Dal Molin crashed into Lake Garda and was drowned.

Two S 67 single-seat shipborne monoplane flying boats were briefly tested in 1930. The S 80 of 1933 was a sporting high-wing cabin flying boat amphibian with a single 150 hp tractor engine. One example of the S 80bis version with twin pusher 75 hp Pobjoy engines remained airworthy into the 1950s.

Trimotor transports

The S 71 transport was the first of the sumptuous Savoia three-engined landplane airliner family. A ten-passenger, high-wing monoplane, it established a world record in 1931, climbing to 6,540 m (21,460 ft) with a 2,000 kg (4,400 lb) payload; production aircraft operated on Ala Littoria domestic routes. Adriano Bacula flew the S 73 prototype for the first time on 4 July 1934. The first Marchetti three-engined, low-wing cantilever monoplane, 48 S 73s were produced, including seven by SABCA in Belgium, with a variety of power plants, equipping Belgian and Czech airlines as well as Ala Littoria and Avio Linee Italiana, setting new standards of passenger comfort. Of typical Marchetti construction—wooden wings wedded

Top: the SM 81 bomber-transport fought in Abyssinia, Spain and during World War II. Centre: produced for export, the S 79B was a twin-engined derivative of the S 79 trimotor. Above: this S 79 was captured by the British at Sidi Barrani

to metal fuselage–the S 73's main fixed undercarriage wheels were 'spatted' and, carrying 18 passengers, it cruised at 269 km/h (167 mph). In addition three 22-passenger high-wing, fixed undercarriage S 74s with four 700 hp Piaggio P X RC engines, flew on Ala Littoria prestige routes.

In November 1937 the prototype of the S 75 was first flown and a total of 94 was built. Featuring retractable undercarriages, they carried up to 42 passengers and possessed considerable range. Most early S 75s operated on routes to North and East Africa, but four went to the Regia Aeronautica. Production continued after Italy's declaration of war in June 1940, the military version carrying 24 fully-equipped troops and having a dorsal turret with 12·7 mm Scotti machine gun.

The prototype S 83 transport also flew in November 1937, production ending with the 23rd machine in 1940. Resembling the S 79, its very long range was intended for the South Atlantic passenger route, fuel tanks containing a maximum 6,105 litres (1,343 gallons). However, after 59 scheduled flights, World War II ended the prestigious

service of the type although Italian-owned machines operated the wartime LATI routes to Lisbon and Algiers.

The SM 82 Marsupiale military transport and bomber prototypes were built, Alessandro Passaleva test-flying the former on 30 October 1939, followed by the bomber on 5 February 1940. Defensive armament included a 12·7 mm gun in a Caproni-Lanciani dorsal turret and two single 7·7 mm weapons firing through lateral hatches. The bomber version had a retractable gondola beneath the control cabin housing both bomb-aiming post and rearward-firing 7·7 mm gun. The bomb-bay accommodated a 4,000 kg (8,800 lb) load. While isolated SM 82s made surprise long-distance night attacks on British-held cities and ports, the main function of the 720 built was transport. They accommodated 40 fully-equipped soldiers or a single disassembled fighter or up to six aero-engines; freight loading was through ample doors in the rear fuselage floor.

Initially powered by three 950 hp Alfa Romeo 128 radials, SM 82 was a mid-wing monoplane with a deep fuselage and retractable undercarriage. Maximum speed was 370 km/h (230 mph) and normal range 3,000 km (1,860 miles). After the Italian Armistice, the Germans eagerly seized all available new and existing examples of this outstanding load-carrier. After the war the SM 82 had a new lease of life powered by Pratt & Whitney engines and the last SM 82 flight was on 2 August 1960.

The high-wing S 72, Marchetti's first landplane bomber, had three 550 hp Bristol engines. The prototype established an altitude record with 5,000 kg (11,000 lb) payload on 15 June 1934 and the Nanking Chinese Government ordered 20 examples for use against the Japanese.

The S 81 Pipistrello (Bat) bomber, which was a parallel design to the S 73, first flew on 8 February 1935. It had a semi-retractable bomb-aimer's gondola under the nose, retractable twin-gun dorsal and ventral turrets and single 0·303 in Lewis guns firing through side hatches, plus a 2,000 kg (4,400 lb) bomb-load. With Alfa 125 radials maximum speed was 340 km/h (211 mph) at 4,000 m (13,100 ft). Four other engine types were also employed. Orders totalled 534 and as with the S 55, S 62 and later the S 79, production had to be sub-contracted. The first S 81s entered service in April 1935, establishing a reputation for reliability over Ethiopia and Spain, but by June 1940 were relegated to night bombing and transport duties.

The successful Sparrowhawk

The S 79 Sparviero (Sparrowhawk) ousted the S 55 as Savoia-Marchetti's most famous aircraft. The eight-seat prototype of the S 79P powered by two 610 hp Piaggio radials which was originally built for the London-Melbourne Race, flew in November 1934 and broke several international records. The first bomber prototype, powered by three 750 hp Alfa 125s, flew on 2 September 1935. With its prominent raised fairing behind the pilot's cockpit–with a fixed forward-firing 12·7 mm gun and a flexibly mounted weapon of the same calibre under a sliding hatch–it was aptly nicknamed 'Gobbo' or hunch-back. A rear ventral gondola housed the bomb-aimer and a 7·7 mm machine gun. Another 7·7 mm weapon could be fired through either port or starboard lateral hatches. The internal bomb-bay carried a 1,200 kg (2,645 lb) load. The S 79, a world-beater with its maximum 430 km/h (267 mph), reached first-line units in October 1936. In early 1937, 65 were dispatched to fight in Spain. That August the first three places in the Paris-Damascus-Istres Air Race were taken by S 79Cs (which closely resembled the S 79P), With an eye to publicity, the five S 79Cs were

Savoia-Marchetti SM 79 of the Regia Aeronautica

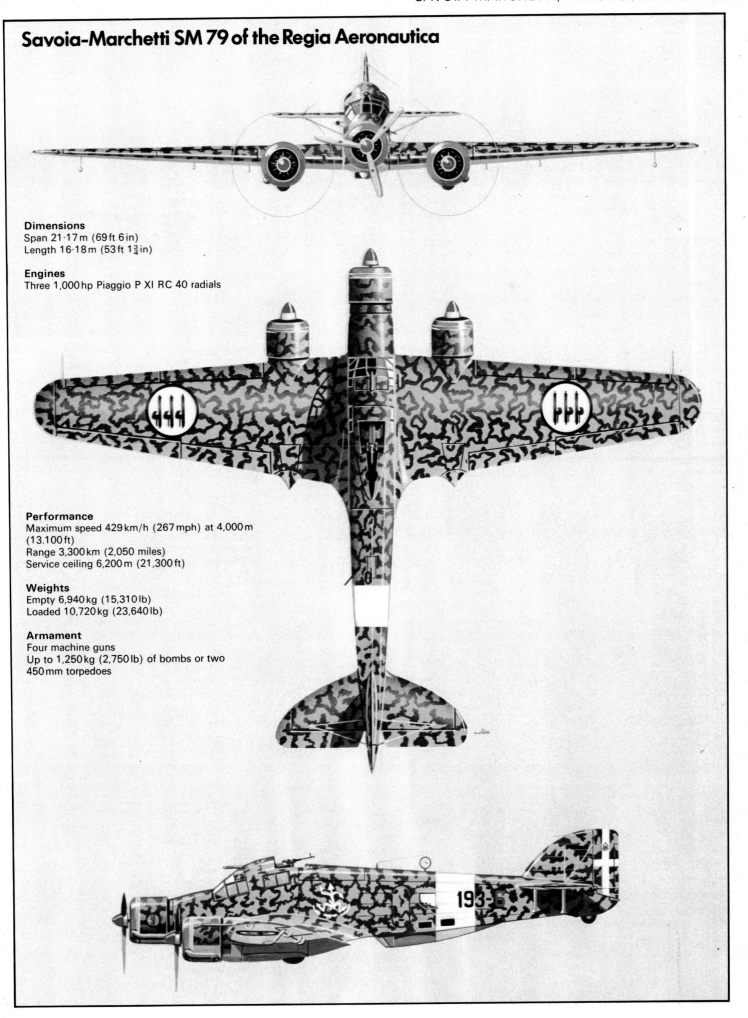

Dimensions
Span 21·17 m (69 ft 6 in)
Length 16·18 m (53 ft 1¾ in)

Engines
Three 1,000 hp Piaggio P XI RC 40 radials

Performance
Maximum speed 429 km/h (267 mph) at 4,000 m
(13.100 ft)
Range 3,300 km (2,050 miles)
Service ceiling 6,200 m (21,300 ft)

Weights
Empty 6,940 kg (15,310 lb)
Loaded 10,720 kg (23,640 lb)

Armament
Four machine guns
Up to 1,250 kg (2,750 lb) of bombs or two
450 mm torpedoes

allocated civil registration letters based on the abbreviations of their pilots' names (as with the transatlantic S 55s) and bore the 'Sorci Verdi' insignia – three green mice – which became famous throughout Italy. Redesignated S 79T, three 'Sorci Verdi' covered the route from Rome to Rio de Janeiro on 24/25 January 1938 in 24 hours 20 minutes flying time.

Over 1,200 S 79s served with the Italian air arm and Yugoslavia bought 45 in 1938. S 79 aircraft powered by 1,000hp Piaggio P XI RC 40 engines equipped specialist Italian torpedo units. The S 79 torpedo bomber was acknowledged as the finest land-based torpedo bomber of World War II. The type led attacks on Malta and operated widely over the Balkans, Mediterranean and North Africa. The final version with ventral gondola deleted served as a torpedo bomber with the Fascist RSI regime after the Armistice of September 1943.

For the export market, Alessandro Marchetti designed the experimental twin-engined S 81B and the S 79B, with glazed nose for bomb-aimer and forward gunner, a small gondola for the ventral gunner and two Gnome-Rhône K 14 Mistral radials. Four went to Iraq and 24 to Romania, which subsequently received 24 S 79JRs with no ventral gondola, a redesigned fin and rudder and Junkers Jumo 211D inline engines, 16 more being built in Romania by IAR at Brasov.

The original S 84 was an experimental 1934 twin-engined transport, but the SM 84 was a bomber with twin fins and rudders. Marchetti was determined to produce a true bomber, avoiding the problems inherent in the S 79, which was modified from a civil design. SM 84 lost the hump of the S 79 and had a dorsal turret with a 360 degree field of fire. The ventral gunner held an S 79B-type gondola and the bomb-aimer a retractable position below the flight deck. However, with 1,100hp Piaggio P XIs it achieved only 432km/h (268mph) at 4,000m (13,000ft), little better than the S 79. Between 1940 and 1943, 309 SM 84s were completed, but were unpopular with aircrew despite notable torpedo bombing successes, including damage to the battleship HMS *Nelson* in September 1941.

Postwar renaissance

Thirty-two disastrously underpowered production twin-engined SM 85 dive bombers operated ineffectively out of the tiny island of Pantelleria in June/July 1940, but were soon ignominiously withdrawn. The prototype S 86 development was tested operationally in late 1940, but a production order for 97 machines had already been cancelled.

The SM 89 engined with two 1,500hp Piaggio P XIIs, was a powerful attack bomber with fixed forward armament of two 37mm cannon and three 12·7mm machine guns supplemented by another 12·7mm gun in a dorsal turret, but development was abandoned after September 1943. The SM 91, a twin-boom two-seat fighter with central crew nacelle, achieved a maximum 575km/h (357mph) with twin 1,475hp DB 605A inline engines. Test flying began in March 1943 and continued through the Armistice, the sole prototype being removed to Germany a month later. The SM 92 had no central nacelle and the crew located in the port boom. Flying in November 1943, it crash-landed after being fired on by RSI fighters and was never repaired. The SM 93 low-wing two-seat dive bomber with one DB 605 engine flew on 31 January 1944, reaching an impressive 542km/h (337mph), but was abandoned in the critical war situation.

After the war, SIAI-Marchetti was permitted to build

the 18-seat SM 95 transport to meet chronic shortages. The first prototype had flown in May 1943 with four 860hp Alfa 128 radials and a second was built under German supervision. A total of 18 aircraft, powered by Bristol or Pratt & Whitney radials, was completed up to 1946. A few were exported, despite the design being hopelessly outmoded. The 1947 six-seat, single-engined SM 101 cabin tourer had no buyers and export orders for the twin-engined, light, eight-seat SM 102 transport/liaison aircraft were cancelled, the bulk of production going to the Italian Aviazione Militare; not surprisingly, SIAI was forced into liquidation. However, the company started work again in 1953.

In the past twenty years SIAI-Marchetti has produced large numbers of outstanding light aircraft. Twin-boom Nardi FN 333 Riviera amphibians were followed by more than 500 S 205 single-engined, four-seat, low-wing cabin machines for military and civil use and 44 of its S 208 variant. The S 210 twin-engined machine and the S 202 Bravo light trainer were followed by 100 SM 1019 high-wing, turboprop-powered liaison aircraft for the Italian army. The three-seat SF 260 low-wing cabin monoplane, developed from Stelio Frati's 1964 F 250, is remarkably still in production. Military and civil versions have been sold in Italy and abroad and SIAI is currently meeting foreign orders for the trainer SF 260C and the tactical support SF 260W Warrior.

Top: the SIAI-Marchetti SF 260 has proved popular with both civil and military customers.

Above: developed from the Cessna O-1 Bird Dog, the SM 1019 turboprop light liaison and forward air control aircraft is operated by the Italian army air arm

With RAF Bomber Command committed to a night offensive against Germany and enemy-occupied territory from the early days of World War II until Hitler's final defeat, it was inevitable that the Luftwaffe would produce a number of very high-scoring individuals in the non-stop night air battle over Europe. No fewer than 39 such pilots attained scores of over 40 night victories, two men exceeding 100–Helmut Lent with 102 and Heinz-Wolfgang Schnaufer with 121. What made Schnaufer's achievement so remarkable was that his entire score was amassed during no more than 164 sorties. At the end of the war he was a *major*–and still only 23 years of age.

An efficient team

Born at Calw near Stuttgart on 16 February 1922, Schnaufer joined the Luftwaffe in 1940 and after a year's basic training opted to join the night fighter arm, being posted to II Gruppe, Nachtjagdgeschwader 1 in April 1942, and teaming up with Unteroffizier Fritz Rumpelhardt as radio operator and Oberfeldwebel Wilhelm Gänsler as gunner. It was the extraordinary ability of these three young men to work as a team that soon set them apart from other night fighter crews. The period between 2 June 1942, when they scored their first victory, and mid-1943 witnessed the advance of the German night defence system to a point where it threatened defeat of Air Marshal Harris's bomber offensive against the Ruhr. Dependent upon the Kammhuber Line of Würzburg ground radars, the Lichtenstein-equipped night fighters were in the ascendancy over British bombers which were still operating without the benefit of sophisticated radar and 'Window' jamming. During that year, flying Messerschmitt Bf 110s from Saint-Trond airfield in Belgium, Schnaufer and his crew destroyed 21 RAF bombers. He also flew occasionally with Leutnant Doktor Baro and Oberfeldwebel Erich Handke as alternative radio operators. From July 1943 conditions for the German night fighter arm changed with the introduction of 'Window'. This was the code-name for metalised foil strips which effectively jammed German radars and deprived the fighters of ground control.

The Midnight Ghost

Heinz-Wolfgang Schnaufer destroyed 121 RAF bombers in 164 night-fighter sorties

In August 1943 Schnaufer, now an *oberleutnant*, was appointed Staffelkapitän of NJG 1's 12 Staffel in time to operate against RAF Bomber Command's raid on the German rocket establishment at Peenemünde on the night of 17/18 August. Five Bf 110s of NJG 1's IV Gruppe were directed towards the bombers, but instead ran into a number of the RAF's No 141 Squadron Beaufighters which were equipped to home onto the Germans' airborne radar. There followed a unique air battle between radar-equipped night fighters, in which the Germans emerged second best. The Messerschmitts of Feldwebel Vinke and Oberfeldwebel Georg Kraft were both shot down by No 141 Squadron's CO, Wing Commander 'Bob' Braham, another Bf 110 was also shot down, a fourth had to return to base with engine trouble while the fifth, flown by Schnaufer himself, was fired on by German flak but managed to regain Saint-Trond.

Mounting score by night

British bomber tactics were now quickly improving and soon the German night fighters were often forced to operate virtually blind–so effective was RAF jamming– added to which, with improved bombing aids, the British were frequently able to mount raids in weather that would normally prevent German fighters from taking off. However, on 16 December, Schnaufer took off in very bad weather against a raid on the German capital, shot down four of the raiders, and landed safely under a 30m (100ft) cloudbase. With 42 night victories to his credit, Schnaufer was awarded the Knight's Cross on the

Schnaufer (fourth from right) pictured during an inspection of Luftwaffe night fighter crews by Reichsmarschall Hermann Goering. Josef Kammhuber (second left), the General der Nachtjagd, looks on

last day of 1943.

Early in the new year Schnaufer was promoted *hauptmann* and appointed Kommandeur of NJG 1's IV Gruppe–no mean achievement for a 21-year-old. By the end of March 1944 he had shot down 50 aircraft in the course of just over 100 combat flights. On 25 May, during an RAF attack on Antwerp, he shot down five Lancasters in the space of 14 minutes; his award of the Oakleaves to the Knight's Cross, announced on 24 June, was recognition of this feat. Much to his embarrassment, however, Schnaufer failed to score on the night of 30/31 March during the disastrous RAF raid on Nuremburg when more than 100 Lancasters and Halifaxes were destroyed by Luftwaffe night fighters.

When the RAF switched its attacks to targets in the Low Countries immediately after the Normandy landings, the 'Midnight Ghost of Saint-Trond'–as Schnaufer had been dubbed in the Luftwaffe–stepped up his execution of British bombers, and at the end of July both Rumpel-hardt and Gänsler were awarded the Knight's Cross; this was the only instance in which all members of a three-man crew wore the coveted decoration. On 30 July Schnaufer himself received the Swords to the Knight's Cross when his night score reached 89.

Geschwader commander

In November 1944 he left Nachtjagdgeschwader 1 to take command of NJG 4, and by the end of the year he had emerged as Germany's top night fighter pilot with a score of 106. He had been awarded the Diamonds to the Knight's Cross on 16 October when he reached his century–then second only to Helmut Lent who died shortly after a flying accident on 5 October.

During the early hours on 21 February 1945, Major Schnaufer shot down two RAF heavy bombers during a raid on Dortmund, and early the next night went on to destroy no fewer than seven Lancasters within the space of 17 minutes during a raid on Duisburg.

Of his final score of 121 victories, Schnaufer had 'shared' one hundred with Rumpelhardt and two fewer with Gänsler. He survived the war only to lose his life in a motoring accident in France in July 1950. The tail unit of his aircraft, displaying his victory tally, was put on show at the Imperial War Museum in London after the war as a tribute to a very remarkable young fighter pilot.

Left: the victory tally on the port tail fin of Schnaufer's personal Messerschmitt Bf 110G attests to this pilot's remarkable skill in destroying RAF bombers. Below: the Bf 110G was produced in both day (illustrated) and night fighter versions from 1942 and the type formed the backbone of the Luftwaffe's night fighter arm until the end of the war

HIGH-SPEED SEAPLANES

The Schneider Trophy contestants were among the fastest aircraft of their era

Jacques Schneider had a passion for speed, a love of the sea and a fascination for flying. These interests led to his announcement at the Gordon Bennett Cup Race banquet in 1912 of the Coupe d'Aviation Maritime Jacques Schneider—a trophy to be awarded annually for hydro-aeroplanes, together with a cash prize of £1,000. The rules were straightforward: the contest had to take place over a distance of at least 150 nautical miles. Entries had to be seaworthy; each country could enter up to three hydro-aeroplanes sponsored by the sport aviation body of that nation, while any country winning three times in five years would hold the trophy permanently.

The first contest for the Schneider Trophy was held at Monaco on 16 April 1913. The 28-lap race was over a triangular course of 10 kilometres (6·2 miles) starting and finishing off the mouth of Monaco's yacht harbour. Days of storms eventually cleared for the postponed Grand Prix, but weather and eliminating trials had taken their toll of contestants. Just four aeroplanes were entered for the final contest: a Deperdussin flown by Maurice Prévost, a pair of Nieuports flown by Doctor Gabriel Espanet and the American Charles Weymann, and Roland Garros'

Jacques Schneider's coveted Trophy (right) was secured for Britain in 1931 by the Royal Air Force's High Speed Flight and its Supermarine S 6B racing floatplanes (below)

Morane-Saulnier. As in all subsequent contests, competitors started one at a time after drawing lots, so that they raced against the clock rather than each other. The contest was won by Prévost for France.

According to Schneider's rules, each year's winning nation was to organise the next contest. Thus Monaco was the venue again in 1914, when the contest attracted entries from America, Britain, France, Germany and Switzerland. Nieuport pilots Gabriel Espanet and Pierre Levasseur started first on the calm morning of 20 April, followed by Ernest Burri from Switzerland flying an FBA flying boat and Englishman Howard Pixton piloting Tommy Sopwith's Sopwith Tabloid floatplane. Pixton's lap time for the first circuit was four minutes 27 seconds—nearly 24 km/h (15 mph) faster than the Frenchmen, who were forced to pull out on their 16th and 17th laps respectively with seized engines. Pixton's 100 hp Gnome Monosoupape also began to falter and his times slowed; he lasted for the full 28 laps, however, and then flew two more to set a new floatplane record over a 300 km (186·4 miles) closed circuit course. Pixton thus took the Schneider Trophy at 139·66 km/h (86·78 mph) with Burri second some 56 km/h (35 mph) slower.

Postwar competition

The Royal Aero Club's opportunity to organise a Schneider Trophy contest in Britain was delayed until 1919. In the meanwhile aircraft and engines had developed radically from the machines which had competed at Monaco. The chosen venue was Bournemouth, on the south coast, with a 20 nautical mile triangular course of ten laps. On the morning of 10 September a thick blanket of sea mist covered the whole area. As the spectators began to throng the beaches from Bournemouth to Swanage it cleared slowly, but visibility was very poor and the start of the contest was successively postponed.

At 1700 hours, with the crowds beginning to head homeward, the race committee announced that a start would be made. The French protested that they could not be ready, and few of the pilots thought that the weather was suitable for flying. Harry Hawker, whose beautifully-streamlined Sopwith Schneider seemed certain to retain the trophy for Britain, refused to start, so Lieutenant-Colonel Vincent Nicholl went off first in his Fairey IIIA, only to retire after one lap because of bad visibility. Behind him went Basil Hobbs in a Supermarine Sea Lion, then Hawker, who changed his mind when he saw the

Above: the Supermarine S 6B in which Flight Lieutenant J. N. Boothman won the 1931 contest to claim the Trophy outright for Britain. Italy's entrants were forced to withdraw, leaving Boothman to fly the course uncontested.
Right: the 1923 contest was dominated by America's Curtiss CR-3 floatplanes which, flown by US Navy Lieutenants Rittenhouse and Irvine, claimed both first and second places.
Below: Rittenhouse's Curtiss crosses the finishing line at Cowes, Isle of Wight to register his country's first Schneider Trophy victory

other competitors leaving. Last to go was Guido Janello in an Italian Savoia S 13. Before long both Hawker and Hobbs were back on the water, forced down by thick mist in the Swanage area, and all three British contestants tried to persuade the organisers that the race should be abandoned that day.

Janello meanwhile continued to fly around the course returning consistent, if unusually fast lap times. He landed on the sea after completing 11 laps and was towed back to Bournemouth by launch to learn that observers on the Swanage marker boat had not seen him all afternoon. He had been turning around a spare marker boat left anchored in Studland Bay; he was thus disqualified and the entire race declared void. Despite protests that the event had been a fiasco because of poor organisation and bad management in difficult conditions, the Federation Aéronautique Internationale (FAI) agreed that Janello could not be awarded the Schneider Trophy, but by way of compensation, invited the Aero-Club d'Italia to organise the 1920 contest.

After the 1919 *débâcle* the Italians were determined to run their Schneider contest properly, with unambiguous rules to prevent the kind of misunderstandings which had robbed them of victory in England. A fine course was set out, beginning off Venice's Porto di Lido, the triangular run around the Adriatic clearly marked with captive balloons. Only one thing was missing: contestants. The Germans were unable to prepare an aircraft due to restrictions imposed by the Treaty of Versailles, and neither Britain, France or Switzerland put forward an entry. Of the four Italian entries, three were withdrawn, leaving Lieutenant Luigi Bologna to fly his Savoia S 12 around the course entirely alone on 21 September 1920, winning the fourth Schneider Trophy meeting unopposed with an average speed of 172·55 km/h (107·22 mph).

Italian 'walk-over'

Bologna's victory assured Italy of the 1921 contest, again held at Venice, but over a modified course of 16 laps of 13·3 nautical miles, with the start/finish line adjacent to the Excelsior Hotel. Again there was a disappointing response. The sole non-Italian entrant, Frenchman Sadi Lecointe, damaged his 300 hp Hispano-Suiza-engined Nieuport-Delage during navigability trials and withdrew. When the contest was held on 7 August 1921 there were just three Italian Macchi flying boats left – a pair of M 7s flown by Giovanni de Briganti and Piero Corgnolino and a Fiat-engined M 19 flown by Arturo Zanetti. The M 19 was fastest, but a failed crankshaft and subsequent engine fire forced Zanetti down after a few laps. Corgnolino looked set to win when his engine, too, gave up on his penultimate lap, leaving de Briganti to cruise home at

189·6km/h (117·8mph). Another Italian win and the Coupe Jacques Schneider would be theirs in perpetuity.

This fact became apparent to the British and French, who began preparing to offer a challenge at the 1922 contest, held at Naples. The British entry was provided by the Supermarine company, with the aid of Napier engines, Shell Oil and General Steam Navigation who agreed to transport whatever aircraft the company produced to and from Italy. The British entry was a modified Supermarine Sea Lion II flying boat, reworked by designer Reginald Mitchell with a 450hp Napier Lion engine. With a maximum speed around 200km/h (125mph), the Sea Lion hardly seemed a serious contender, but Mitchell removed every unnecessary fitting, reduced its wingspan by 1·2m (4ft) and streamlined the biplane's struts in the quest for speed. Two French CAMS 36 boats were withdrawn before the initial trials, leaving Mitchell's modified Sea Lion as the only threat to an outright win for Italy.

The Italians fielded three contestants, two flying Macchi M 17s, and the third flying a new and beautifully streamlined Savoia S 51 sesquiplane flying boat powered by a 300hp Hispano-Suiza engine. This aeroplane shipped water and capsized during the navigability trials; the machine should have been eliminated, but Supermarine's managing director Hubert Scott-Paine sportingly raised no objection to its being repaired, and all four aircraft were ready on the warm, sunny morning of 12 August 1922. Henri Biard, Supermarine's chief test pilot was flying the Sea Lion; Corgnolino and Zanetti were again flying the Macchis, while Alessandro Passaleva was aboard the Savoia. Biard flew off first, completing his first lap at over 241km/h (150mph), and neither of the Macchis could hope to challenge it. The S 51's spell in the sea caused its laminated wood propeller to begin separating, forcing Passaleva to fly at less than maximum available power. Nonetheless, as the four aeroplanes roared around the Bay of Naples, the Savoia's lap times began to equal and eventually to overtake those of the Sea Lion. The vibration worsened, however, and the Italian was forced to accept second place, 122·6 seconds behind Biard, who brought the Trophy to Britain again with an average speed of 234·48km/h (145·7mph).

British indecision

Entries for the seventh contest, to be fought out at Cowes, Isle of Wight in September, were scheduled to close on 1 March 1923. Three American, six French and three Italian aircraft had been registered on that date, but not a single British machine. The closing date was extended to 1 August, but still no entry was forthcoming. Questions were asked in the House of Commons; why was there no Government sponsorship in this matter of national prestige? Eventually a Government offer to purchase the winning aircraft–if it was British–for the less-than-generous sum of £3,000 was made. At the last moment Supermarine again put forward the Sea Lion, and after a further time extension Robert Blackburn entered his Pellet and Harry Hawker the rebuilt 1919 Schneider machine, which was renamed Rainbow, but was wrecked in tests before the event.

The Americans entered a pair of Curtiss CR-3s and a Wright NW-2. A landplane version of the Curtiss had won the 1922 Pulitzer Trophy Race at 331·2km/h (205·8 mph) and the aircraft were seen as a great threat, though British observers concluded that the large floats installed for water operation would substantially reduce their performance. The Italians, lacking a more powerful

engine to increase the performance of the Savoia S 51, which was to be their prime challenger at Cowes, withdrew altogether, throwing away the chance to keep Jacques Schneider's trophy once and for all.

The course was 37·2 nautical miles long and the contest consisted of five laps, heading out eastbound from Cowes to Selsey Bill and back westwards along the beaches at Southsea to the Isle of Wight. Two French entries were eliminated before the navigability trials and the American NW-2's engine exploded after the aircraft threw both a propeller blade and its pilot into the water; the Blackburn Pellet porpoised and sank during the tests.

The Grand Prix thus was contested between the Sea Lion, now with a 550hp engine, a CAMS 36bis, CAMS 38 and Latham L.1 from France, and the Curtiss CR-3s of US Navy Lieutenants Rutledge Irvine and David Rittenhouse. The Americans started first, followed by Biard, and Maurice Hurel in the CAMS 38, his compatriots both having withdrawn with damage during the manoeuvring at the start. The thousands of onlookers gathered on the south coast beaches on 28 September 1923 soon discovered that the times being recorded by the sleek, 465hp Curtiss D-12 engined American racers exceeded the speed calculation graphs so thoughtfully provided in their programmes, which went no higher than 275km/h (170mph). Rittenhouse averaged 285·5km/h (177·38mph) over the course, topping 320km/h (200mph) at times, with his colleague Irvine not far behind at 279·2km/h (173·46mph), while Biard in the outmoded Sea Lion gamely finished third at 252·9km/h (157·17mph).

European contenders

The convincing American victory at Cowes clearly showed that if the trophy was to return from across the Atlantic, European contenders had to act quickly to rethink their aircraft designs. Fortunately for these countries, the US National Aeronautic Association sportingly declared their planned 1924 contest at Baltimore void when Britain, France and Italy failed to have contenders ready in time. The Americans might easily have flown the course unchallenged and strengthened their chance of a third, outright win in 1925.

By that year serious efforts were being made in Britain. The Air Ministry commissioned the Gloster Aircraft Company and Supermarine to build high-speed racing seaplanes which were to be loaned back to their manufacturers for the Schneider Trophy event, again scheduled for Baltimore between 24-29 October 1925. Reginald Mitchell designed a completely new monoplane the Supermarine S 4, which was constructed secretly at the company's Woolston works near Southampton, Hants.

From Gloster came a biplane seaplane, the Gloster III, which also had the Lion engine but was much smaller than the Supermarine monoplane. Two Glosters–to be flown by Hubert Broad and Bert Hinkler–and the S 4, which was Biard's mount, were shipped to Baltimore, Maryland, where the Americans had a trio of Curtiss R3C-2s, which were smaller, cleaner developments of the winning 1923 Curtiss biplanes. The Italians were competing with a pair of Macchi M 33 flying boats.

The course was laid out in Chesapeake Bay, southeast of Baltimore, and both British competitors caused the Americans some concern during practice because of their great speed. Then, three days before the race, tragedy struck. Biard, rising from his sick bed where he had suffered a bout of influenza, lost control of the fast-moving S 4 at an altitude of about 240m (800ft) and crashed into the sea. Luckily he managed to escape from the wrecked,

Right: Venice was the venue for the contest in 1927 by virtue of Mario de Bernardi's victory in America the previous year. This time, however, Britain took the leading and second places.
Below right: Lieutenant Jimmy Doolittle led the Schneider field in 1925 in a streamlined Curtiss R3C-2 biplane. He was later to achieve greater renown as leader of the Tokyo Raid in World War II.
Bottom: Britain's entries in 1929 were three Supermarine monoplanes. The pictured S 6, piloted by Flying Officer H. R. Waghorn, was the only aircraft to complete the course successfully

submerged aircraft with broken ribs and stomach injuries, but the British challenge had been considerably weakened.

A further blow was struck when Bert Hinkler, carrying out the navigability trials in the hastily-prepared reserve Gloster III, was eliminated when heavy waves pounded the float struts, causing them to collapse and damage the floats themselves. First away in the actual speed contest was the brilliant young US Army pilot Lieutenant James H. Doolittle, whose Curtiss clocked 359·13 km/h (223·15 mph) for the first lap, and fully ten miles per hour faster on the second.

His team-mates Lieutenants George Cuddihy and Ofstie were considerably slower than Doolittle and both were forced to retire with engine troubles before the end of the seven-lap race. Hubert Broad in the Gloster was lapping at speeds of around 320 km/h (200 mph) and with the departure of the two Americans was placed comfortably second behind Jimmy Doolittle, who won with an average speed of 374·3 km/h (232·6 mph). Broad's Gloster averaged 320·5 km/h (199·2 mph) and the Italian de Briganti was placed third at 271 km/h (168·4 mph).

Two-country contest

A year later at Hampton Roads, Virginia, the British were not to be seen. Unable to prepare a competitive machine in time, the Royal Aero Club had urged the Americans to postpone the event until 1927, but the Americans were bent on an all-out victory and, having once accommodated the European challengers in this fashion, determined to go ahead. The 1926 Schneider Trophy was thus a straight race between the United States—which fielded a pair of Curtiss R3Cs and a Curtiss F6C-1 Hawk—and a trio of elegant Italian Macchi M 39 low-wing seaplanes.

The Italians regained the Trophy on Saturday 13

November, but the contest was not without incident. Major Mario de Bernardi, lapping at nearly 386 km/h (240 mph), was slowing with an overheated engine towards the end of the seven-lap race and George Cuddihy in the Curtiss R3C-4 was racing neck-and-neck when his engine stopped on the final lap. De Bernardi won at 396·7 km/h (246·5 mph), with American Frank Schilt second and Italian Adriano Bacula third.

Back at Venice in 1927, the Aero-Club d'Italia had

A poster published shortly after Britain's third victory at Venice in 1927. From then on, the Trophy was defended every second year; thus the three wins in five years required to claim the Trophy outright had to be obtained in successive contests

redesigned the speed course around a 27 nautical mile circuit, with aircraft crossing the start line in the air for the first time. No official American entry was made, but Britain, having had two years' breathing space, put up four aeroplanes – a Gloster IVB, a Short-Bristow Crusader and a pair of Reginald Mitchell's Supermarine S 5s. The Gloster was a biplane, not dissimilar to the American Curtiss racers, while the Crusader and Supermarines were monoplanes.

The race itself resulted in a British victory. While the Italian crowds became dismayed as, one after another, their scarlet Macchis dropped out with engine failures, Flight Lieutenants Webster and Worsley lapped the lagoon circuit not just to win the Schneider Trophy, but also setting new world speed records for both seaplanes and landplanes. Webster's average speed was an astonishing 453·28 km/h (281·65 mph); Worsley's was 439·3 km/h (273 mph). Only a sixth lap failure of the Gloster's engine prevented Britain taking the first three places.

In 1928 it was finally agreed that the Schneider contests should be defended every two years, as the advances in technology demanded could simply not be accomplished

in 12 months. Jacques Schneider, who started the quest for speed over water, died in May 1928.

High Speed Flight

After its victory at Venice, the High Speed Flight was disbanded and was not reformed until early in 1928 in an effort to win back the world speed record snatched by de Bernardi in November 1927. Flight Lieutenant Sam Kinkead made the record attempt in a Supermarine S 5 from Calshot in March 1928. He was killed instantly when the aircraft flew into the mirror-smooth surface of the Solent at high speed, probably because he misjudged his height over the glassy sea. Flight Lieutenant A. H. Orlebar took command of the High Speed Flight in 1929, with an entirely new team, consisting of Flight Lieutenants D'Arcy A. Greig and G. H. Stainforth and Flying Officers R. L. Atcherley and H. R. Waghorn.

The Italians, once again the only challengers, revealed plans for two revolutionary designs – the Savoia S 65, which had two 1,000 hp engines in the then-unique 'push-pull' configuration, and the Piaggio P 7, which was intended to ride on hydrofoils driven by a marine propeller linked to its 850 hp Isotta-Fraschini aero-engine. Not surprisingly, development problems prevented either of these interesting aeroplanes from taking part and, when the contestants lined up at Calshot on 7 September 1929, the Macchi M 52R and a pair of improved M 67s were the Italian team's mounts.

Despite an overnight engine block replacement on one of the Rolls-Royce power plants, all three Supermarines were ready on the day. The start and finish point for the race was at Ryde Pier on the Isle of Wight, with a diamond-shaped course laid out with turns off Seaview, Hayling Island, Southsea and West Cowes. Waghorn was first off in an S 6 followed by Dal Molin in the M 52R. Waghorn was starting his last lap when he ran out of fuel; he glided down to cross the finish line, not knowing that he had miscounted and had actually been on his eighth lap. Atcherley took off in the other S 6, but with spray-covered goggles cut inside a turn at Seaview and was eliminated, although he set up the fastest lap of the event at 534 km/h (332 mph), unaware of his mistake. Both M 67s, flown by Remo Cadringher and Giovanni Monti, retired on their second laps, leaving Waghorn the victor at 528·8 km/h (328·6 mph). He was subsequently awarded the Air Force Cross for this feat.

And so to 1931, and the prospect of a third and final British victory. Amazingly, neither the Government or the Air Council was willing to sponsor the defence of the title, at an estimated cost of more than £100,000. Bitter political lobbying and harsh press criticism failed to sway Prime Minister Ramsey MacDonald, who remained adamant that any British entry for the Schneider Trophy would have to look to private enterprise for finance. Just as the acrimony reached its peak, Lady Houston, patriotic and public-spirited widow of a wealthy shipping magnate, sent the Royal Aero Club a cheque for £100,000; thus Britain's defence of the trophy was assured.

In the event, this defence became a formality when the Italians, beset with problems with the tandem-engined Savoia S 65 and the favoured Macchi M 72, pulled out of the contest. Thus on 13 September 1931 in front of a crowd estimated at one million people, Flight Lieutenant John Boothman lapped the Solent circuit in his 2,350 hp Supermarine S 6B alone, capturing the Trophy for all time with a speed of 547·3 km/h (340·08 mph). That same day George Stainforth broke the world speed record in another S 6B, reaching 610·02 km/h (379·05 mph).

Black Thursday

The high losses suffered by the Schweinfurt raiders forced the USAAF to re-examine its strategic bombing doctrines

The concept of strategic bombing–the destruction of an enemy's war industry through aerial attack–originated during World War I but was not truly put to the test until the latter years of World War II. The two powers that made major efforts to develop strategic strike forces were Britain and the United States, but they did so along quite different lines. The Royal Air Force concentrated on weapons and equipment for use under cover of darkness, believing that daylight operations would render heavy bombers too vulnerable to enemy interceptors. On the other hand, the US Army Air Corps–later Army Air Force –planned to operate by day, as it was only then that accurate bombing could really be achieved. For its bombers to survive in daylight against enemy defences, the four-engined Boeing B-17 Fortresses and Consolidated B-24 Liberators were heavily armed with machine guns and flown in massed formations to confront interceptors with formidable firepower. The development of turbo-supercharged engines allowed the American bombers to operate at the then very high optimum altitude of 7,600 m (25,000 ft) and, by using a Norden precision bomb-sight, great accuracy could be obtained in target strikes even from such a great height.

Daylight penetration

The USAAF campaign of daylight strategic bombing was principally carried out by the Eighth Air Force in England. Early missions showed promise that the Fortresses and Liberators could carry out attacks on targets in Germany and occupied territories without prohibitive losses. The

Right: Eighth Air Force groundcrew collect machine gun cartridges from a Boeing B-17 after a raid on Germany. Below: a German fighter is shot down by B-17s on their first mission to Schweinfurt on 17 August 1943

real test did not come until the summer of 1943 when the Eighth Air Force had received sufficient B-17 groups to conduct far-ranging missions into Germany, chiefly against the enemy's aircraft industry. At this time the Luftwaffe, aware that early attempts to turn back the USAAF formations by fighter interception had not met with much success, made strenuous efforts to bolster its fighter forces for the defence of the Reich and to evolve better tactics.

Strategic experts in the Allied camp held that one of the most profitable target systems to attack would be the German bearing industry which, vital to the manufacture of all military vehicles and aircraft, was concentrated in a few locations, chiefly around Schweinfurt, a town in south central Germany. Successful destruction of the major bearing plants could cause a critical situation in German war production. A major obstacle to launching such an attack was the distance involved – a 1,450 km (900 mile) round trip from England, with the bombers in 'hostile skies for six hours where heavy losses could be expected. A plan was devised whereby two separate forces would be sent into Germany; the first would attack the Regensburg fighter factory near the Austrian border and then turn south across Italy and the Mediterranean to land in Allied North Africa. The second force, flying a similar penetration course and ten minutes behind the Regensburg

bombers, would hit Schweinfurt. In this way it was hoped to divide and confuse the enemy defence whose interceptors had limited flight duration. Good visibility over the target area was an essential requirement if good bombing was to be achieved and such weather was finally predicted for 17 August 1943 when the mission was flown.

Delayed departure

Matters did not go well from the outset for dawn found a thick ground fog over much of the eastern part of England, making take-off dangerous. Eventually the 4th Wing's B-17s – which were to fly to Regensburg – had to be dispatched to ensure their arrival over Africa in daylight. Their bases were near the east coast where the fog had thinned, but it persisted further inland delaying departure of the 1st Wing force for Schweinfurt. The timing of the two forces was planned so that enemy fighters attacking the first would not have time to refuel to meet the second and thus some of the anticipated opposition would be dissipated. With the delay this advantage was lost and the 1st Wing bombers were held until American fighters that had given the Regensburg force penetration cover to the German border had had time to return and refuel.

The Schweinfurt bombers eventually departed three-and-a-half hours behind those attacking Regensburg and consisted of 230 B-17s in four combat formations. The

Below: B-17s of a depleted formation bomb Schweinfurt on 17 August 1943. The results of the bombing were unsatisfactory and losses were heavy. The timing of the mission became dislocated, the escort was inadequate and the weight of the bomber force was further dissipated by prolonged fighter attacks. Right: bombs strike the bearing complex at Schweinfurt during a daylight raid on 13 April 1944 by USAAF bombers

first fighter attacks were encountered soon after crossing the Belgian coast and these continued intermittently to the target and back to the coast, some 200 enemy fighters being involved. Attacks were concentrated on the leading elements from which 21 of the 36 B-17s lost by the whole force were shot down. The disruption of the leading formation had the effect of causing some of the bombing to be off target although a considerable number of hits was obtained on factory buildings. Although claimed as a success by the American authorities, later examination of reconnaissance photographs showed the damage at Schweinfurt to be far from the crippling blow required.

Second attempt

A return mission to Schweinfurt was planned using the whole Eighth Air Force bomber establishment to ensure maximum destruction within the target area. Other commitments and poor weather delayed this raid until 14 October 1943 when 420 B-17s and B-24s were scheduled. The number would have been higher but for heavy attrition during recent missions. Weather over home bases again interfered and the small B-24 formation was unable to assemble on time and therefore flew a feint over the North Sea. Even the Fortresses were fewer than planned with a total of 291 departing England in two divisional forces.

The 1st Division took what was a more or less direct route and the trailing 3rd Division followed a zig-zag course to deceive the enemy into believing it was heading for a different target. This was successful, for the 3rd Division encountered little concentrated fighter activity until it had bombed the target and was on its way home. The 1st Division was not so fortunate, coming under continuous fighter attack as soon as the US escort had withdrawn. Confusion during the assembly in poor weather over England had resulted in some combat wings being scattered and it was on these that the enemy concentrated his forces. The 305th Bomb Group was almost annihilated, only three of its B-17s surviving. From the combat wing in which this Group was flying, half the strength dispatched had been lost by the time the target was reached. Despite the intensity of the opposition, good bombing

results were achieved with three of the five plants at Schweinfurt receiving heavy damage. There was no let-up in the Luftwaffe attacks on the return journey and vicious assaults were made on the leading elements of the 3rd Division. Late in the afternoon the first Fortresses began to reach England and soon it was known that the cost of the raid had been 60 B-17s missing in action, five more had crashed in England and 133 were damaged, some so badly that repairs were not economically worthwhile. A total of 600 men was missing and there were five dead and 43 wounded on returning bombers. Against this terrible loss was the claimed destruction of 288 enemy fighters and the laying waste of three bearing factories. The claims of enemy aircraft were obviously exaggerated through the confused nature of the air battle (actual losses were about 50 fighters), but the bombing could be verified by photographic reconnaissance. The attack cost the Germans a 50 per cent fall in bearing production and it was six months before production returned to the pre-raid level. However, despite this achievement, the USAAF day bombers had taken what was to be the highest percentage loss to a major task force during their campaign and, coming after a week of similarly costly raids, this convinced most dedicated supporters of the self-defence bomber mission that such tactics were no longer tenable.

Diminishing importance

Although the 14 October raid had considerable success, a follow-up attack could have had a more telling effect on the German war economy. The bearing complex was not attacked again until the following February and by this time the Germans had had time to disperse their bearing production to a number of smaller sites. While another 14 bombing raids were made on the Schweinfurt plants during the war, none caused so much disruption to the supply of ball-bearings as the first two strikes.

The third attack on Schweinfurt, carried out by 238 B-17s of the 1st Division, took place on 24 February 1944. Only 11 Fortresses were lost but the formation had the benefit of long-range fighter support. RAF Bomber Command visited the scene that night and 663 Avro Lancasters and Handley Page Halifaxes unloaded over 2,000 tons of bombs over the factory complex. Heavy attacks by Eighth Air Force bombers were carried out on 21 July and 9 October 1944, only by this date Schweinfurt was no longer of major importance to the German bearing industry – a fact not then fully appreciated by Allied intelligence. Further attacks were carried out, the last by medium bombers of the Ninth Air Force in April 1945.

The Schweinfurt raids resulted in a reappraisal of the whole concept of US Army Air Force strategic bombing. It was evident that success depended upon gaining air superiority over Germany. This belated conclusion hastened the introduction of the North American P-51 escort fighter which was capable of missions to Berlin. Secondly, the Allied air commanders were effectively convinced that targets should be repeatedly attacked in a more co-ordinated, massive and continuous campaign.

When an American armoured column captured Schweinfurt at the end of hostilities the Nazi flag flying in the town was sent to the Eighth Air Force in England to be donated to the unit that had suffered most grievously over this infamous target. The flag was given to the 305th Bomb Group which had lost 14 bombers on the second raid. While the bombing of the German bearing industry failed to realise the hopes of the strategic planners, the name Schweinfurt has become famous in popular history as the epic mission of the Eighth Air Force.

Mildenhall to Melbourne

The England-Australia air race of 1934 was won by Charles Scott and Tom Campbell Black

Long-distance navigation fascinated Charles Scott from an early age. Born in London, he spent much of his youth sailing and after a spell as a sugar planter in British Guiana, returned to England in 1923 and obtained a short-service commission in the Royal Air Force. He was a brilliant, but undisciplined pilot and six years and three courts martial later he left the Service and journeyed to Australia where he worked as a salesman in Melbourne before joining Queensland and Northern Territories Aerial Services as a mail-run pilot.

In 1931 Scott returned to England and on 1 April that year he set off from Lympne Aerodrome in Kent for Port Darwin, flying a de Havilland Moth. He reached Australia

Ten thousand pound prize

Soon after Australian millionaire Sir MacPherson Robertson announced his plan for an England-Australia air race to commemorate the city of Melbourne's centenary, Scott and Campbell Black met at the Royal Aero Club in London. Despite the differences in their personalities, the two fliers became firm friends and resolved to compete together for the ten thousand pound first prize being offered to the winners of the race, which was scheduled to start on Saturday, 20 October 1934.

There was, however, one problem: neither Scott nor Campbell Black had an aeroplane. Their first attempts to find a sponsor failed, but fortuitously, as they were leaving

nine days, three hours and forty minutes later, clipping twenty hours off the record held by Charles Kingsford-Smith. Seven weeks later Scott returned, breaking the record for Australia to England with a time of ten days, thirteen hours. In October 1932 he flew from London to Melbourne in eight days, twenty hours, 47 minutes, a record which was to stand until 1934 – the year of the great England-Australia Air Race.

Tom Campbell Black learned to fly in 1917 with the Royal Naval Air Service before joining the RAF and eventually moving to airline flying. He pioneered commercial flying in East Africa and formed Wilson Airways of Nairobi, Kenya.

the Royal Aero Club after a fruitless meeting over dinner with a prominent banker, they met Mr A. O. Edwards, managing director of the Grosvenor House Hotel. He agreed to put up the money for a suitable aeroplane, stipulating only that it should be named *Grosvenor House*.

Revolutionary racer

Shortly afterwards came an announcement from Captain Geoffrey de Havilland. His company would build a new racing machine with range sufficient to cover each of the five stages of the race non-stop, at a maximum speed of not less than 320 km/h (200 mph), and he would sell limited numbers of the aeroplanes for the low price of five thousand pounds apiece. Jim Mollison ordered one, followed quickly by Edwards and Bernard Rubin. The revolutionary racer built by de Havilland was the DH88 Comet, a beautiful, twin-engined two-seat machine with thin, tapered wings and retractable undercarriage, powered by a pair of 230 hp Gipsy Six R engines driving the then unusual variable-pitch propellers.

The first Comet flew only six weeks before the race was due to start, but when the competitors assembled at Mildenhall in Suffolk during the week prior to the race, three Comets were ready: the Mollisons' black-and-gold *Black Magic*, Rubin's unnamed green machine which, its owner having fallen ill, was to be flown by Lieutenant Owen Cathcart-Jones and Ken Waller, and Scott and Campbell Black's red-and-white *Grosvenor House*. The late delivery of these aircraft left little time for the crews to become acquainted with their handling and during the days leading up to the start the problems of landing an aeroplane whose propellers could not be returned to fine pitch caused the Comet crews some anxiety.

Race day started bitterly cold and cloudy, but despite this, sixty thousand spectators journeyed out to Mildenhall long before dawn to await the 0600 hours start. The first

rays of sunlight were just appearing as Sir Alfred Bower, acting Lord Mayor of London, dropped the flag and the Mollisons took off in *Black Magic*, followed by Roscoe Turner and Clyde Pangborn in a Boeing 247, Cathcart-Jones in the second Comet, Asjes and Geysebdorfer in their Panderjager and then Scott and Campbell Black in *Grosvenor House*. They were joint second favourites with Turner and the Mollisons, with the KLM Dutch Airlines crew's Douglas DC-2 leading the betting odds at ten to one.

A number of competitors were forced down by bad weather across France and mechanical problems and others duly checked in at the optional stopping points at Marseilles, Rome, Athens and Aleppo in Syria, but the three Comets headed straight for the first control point at Baghdad. At 1910 hours the Mollisons arrived, having flown 4,072 km (2,530 miles) at an average speed of 444·18 km/h (199·77 mph). One hour and thirty-five minutes later they took off again, just before Scott and Campbell Black arrived. The latter two had had a nightmarish journey, seeing nothing after leaving England until they reached the Danube. They flew through heavy rain and thunderstorms over Turkey and became lost over Syria. After landing at RAF Kirkuk in Iraq for fuel they

Left: Tom Campbell Black pictured in 1934. Below: the DH88 flown to victory by Charles Scott and Campbell Black in the 1934 England to Australia air race is preserved in England by the Shuttleworth Trust. Below left: Scott and Giles Guthrie (right) with the Vega Gull in which they won the 1936 Portsmouth to Johannesburg air race

completed the 210 km (130 miles) to Baghdad where they learned that only the Mollisons were ahead of them and set off in pursuit just 31 minutes after landing.

Grosvenor House was to head direct for Allahabad in India, while Jim and Amy Mollison stopped off at Karachi, which they reached in record time. However, undercarriage trouble and the prospect of a night landing at Allahabad delayed them and the lead was lost to Scott and Campbell Black's Comet. This touched down at 0918 hours in time for them to have a quick meal before taking off again 40 minutes later, four hours before Koene Parmentier arrived in the DC-2. Meanwhile the Mollisons had become lost *en route* from Karachi and in an effort to catch up Jim Mollison made an all-out dash. This burned out six cylinder heads and pistons in one of the Comet's Gipsy Six engines and at Allahabad they were forced to retire.

Grosvenor House sped onwards towards Singapore, heading out over the Bay of Bengal where both pilots had to handle the controls as the Comet battled between layers of storm clouds. Scott and Campbell Black landed at Singapore downwind, 40 hours after leaving England. Their Comet was 1,930 km (1,200 miles) ahead of Parmentier's Douglas, which was then at Rangoon, while Turner and Pangborn were still at Allahabad and Cathcart-Jones and Waller in the other Comet were at Karachi.

England-Australia record

An hour's rest and Scott and Campbell Black were airborne again, aiming for Darwin, 3,354 km (2,084 miles) out across the Timor Sea. As night fell, the clouds lowered and *Grosvenor House* was forced down to within 300 m (1,000 ft) of the water's surface. At that altitude the Gipsy engines–like those of the Mollisons' Comet–were being pushed too hard and the oil pressure dropped to zero. Although the danger was averted by an immediate climb, the port engine failed 320 km (200 miles) out from Port Darwin. However, they managed to reach the airfield, where thousands of jubilant Australians threatened to

destroy the Comet and engulf its weary crew. They had set up a new record for an England-Australia flight of an astonishing two days, four hours and 38 minutes.

The engine trouble was traced to a clogged oil filter which delayed *Grosvenor House* more than two hours before its crew could start for Charleville, but their nearest rival, Parmentier, was still eight hours behind. Further delays at Charleville while the Comet's engines received more attention ate into their lead, but at length Scott and Campbell Black were able to set course south for Melbourne, where they dived between the finishing pylons on Flemington Racecourse 71 hours after leaving the airfield at Mildenhall.

In December, Scott and Campbell Black returned to England to face a tremendous welcome and an exhausting round of public appearances and celebration dinners, which the flamboyant Scott took to with gusto. In March 1935 Campbell Black married the actress Florence Desmond, and shortly afterwards, while attempting a new record to Cape Town, crashed his Comet in the desert near Khartoum. He escaped alive and the following year he was to have competed in the Schlesinger Race from England to Johannesburg in a Percival Mew Gull. On 19 September 1936 he flew the aircraft to Liverpool *en route* to Portsmouth for the start of the race. On the tarmac at Speke Airport an RAF Hawker Hart taxied into the Mew Gull and one of its propeller blades penetrated Black's lungs; he died within half an hour.

Ironically, his erstwhile partner Charles Scott won the race in a Vega Gull, and continued the round of dinners and celebrations begun after the 1934 victory. He played the role of public hero to the full, found the obscurity of wartime service hard to accept and, having divorced his second wife and taken to alcohol, committed suicide on 15 April 1946. Of that famous race in 1934, only one victor has survived–*Grosvenor House*. This is now in the hands of the Shuttleworth Trust at Old Warden, Bedfordshire, and is being restored to fly again in time for the 50th anniversary of Scott and Campbell Black's epic flight.

Flown by Koene Parmentier, the Douglas DC-2 of KLM, the Royal Dutch Airline, was a leading contender in the England-Australia race. Pictured while being retrieved from soft ground after a forced landing, the DC-2 eventually finished second overall to Scott and Black

LEADING LADY

Former actress Sheila Scott captured the headlines with her solo flying exploits

Born in Worcester on 27 April 1927, Sheila Scott's early life gave no indication that her name was to become synonymous with women in modern-day aviation. A joy-ride on her sixth birthday from Sir Alan Cobham's barnstorming Circus had introduced her to flying, but seemingly struck no ambitious chord in the youngster who, on her own admission, was a rebellious child. At the outbreak of World War II Sheila was still at school; after completing her studies, she was able to assist the war effort with a spell of auxiliary nursing with the Royal Navy at Gosport. The following 14 years were spent in repertory as an actress, with varying degrees of success.

Introduction to flying

In 1959, however, came the event which was to change the course of Sheila Scott's life when, for a wager, she had her first flying lesson. Despite the curiosity and, occasionally, ridicule to which the few women pilots of the day were subjected, Sheila persevered with her new pursuit. Basing herself at Thruxton Airfield, Hampshire, she soon demonstrated a hitherto-unsuspected aptitude for flying and, having obtained her Private Pilot's Licence (PPL), she became the proud owner of a light aircraft. This was a Thruxton Jackaroo, a de Havilland Tiger Moth biplane to which a four-seat enclosed cabin had been fitted, resulting in a decidedly strange, hump-backed hybrid. Such was the aircraft which Sheila Scott acquired at the turn of the decade; finished in blue and silver and named *Myth* (supposedly a female Moth), this was the means by which Sheila intended to gain experience to accomplish her next objective–the acquisition of a Commercial Pilot's Licence (CPL).

Gaining an appetite for competitive flying after participating in the 1960 King's Cup air race, Sheila and *Myth* soon became familiar sights at rallies and aviation meetings around Britain. Dark financial clouds loomed,

however; these were dispelled by Cessna Aircraft, who granted the use of several of their latest lightplanes for publicity purposes following the award of the Jean Lennox Bird Trophy by the British Women Pilots' Association. This double boost to her fortunes was timely and renewed Miss Scott's determination to join the small but *élite* band of women commercial pilots. Despite her Cessna connections, her next aircraft was to be the Piper Comanche, a racy, single-engined monoplane several generations removed from the Jackaroo.

It was 1964 when Sheila Scott first determined to write her name in aviation's record books. After considering retracing the steps of two illustrious aviatrices, Amy

Left: pictured prior to her initial round-the-world flight in 1966, Sheila Scott had captured her first records two years previously with solo flights to five European capitals. Below: Myth Too, Miss Scott's Piper Comanche, carried two long-range fuel tanks in its six-place cabin, more than doubling the type's original capacity. Full airways radio and navigational aids were also installed

Sheila Scott and Myth Too shared in no fewer than 94 world records established during the latter half of the 1960s. Sold to a flying group to finance the purchase of a twin-engined Piper Aztec, Myth Too is scheduled to be preserved at the end of its flying career

Johnson and Jean Batten to the Antipodes–a plan abandoned through both lack of funds and a suitable air-craft–Sheila decided at length to attempt a feat within the range of the Comanche. This was a bid to capture the light aircraft speed records between London and five European capitals. Although established by one man, the previous records had taken two-and-a-half months to complete; Miss Scott's aim was to break them all consecutively within the space of 36 hours.

The morning of 19 May 1965 dawned bright and sunny as Sheila and *Myth Sun Pip*, her 400 hp Piper Comanche leased from its makers, lifted from the runway at Northolt in Middlesex *en route* for The Hague. Brussels and Paris followed, both outward and return journeys setting new inter-capital records for all three destinations. Despite adverse weather conditions, the trips to Belfast and Dublin were completed in like manner, permitting Sheila to arrive at Northolt amid the glare of television lights on 20 May with no less than 15 records under her belt, the whole being accomplished in some 36 hours.

Round-the-world flight
Heartened by her unqualified success in this first venture, Sheila decided later that year that her next project would be a flight around the world. *Myth Sun Pip* lacked the economy required for such a flight: despite her wish to use a British aircraft, Sheila decided that a lower-powered Comanche with additional tankage would be the ideal type. Thus a 260 hp Lycoming-engined aircraft was acquired and was named *Myth Too*.

After touching Alcock and Brown's statue as a last superstitious gesture, Sheila Scott boarded her Comanche on 18 May 1966 at London's Heathrow Airport. It was no ordinary light aircraft: full Airways and High Frequency long-range radio installations were fitted, together with

two radio compasses, an instrument landing display and other navigational aids. Two massive 295 litre (65 gallon) fuel tanks filled the six-place cabin giving, together with two smaller wingtip and standard wing tanks, a total capacity of 1,136 litres (250 gallons). A dinghy, emergency beacon and life jacket jostled for space with clothes to cater for every conceivable climate. The only non-essential items for which room could be found were the lucky charms with with Sheila had been entrusted by numerous well-wishers; the most notable of these was a toy rabbit named Buck Tooth, who was to be her only companion for the next month.

Following an irritating six-hour delay due to a radio failure, *Myth Too* finally became airborne for Rome, which was reached at midnight. A further radio and auto-pilot failure *en route* necessitated another, longer wait on arrival while replacements were ordered and fitted. Continuing via the Middle East to Delhi, which was reached on 25 May, the time lost had still to be regained. Stormy weather dogged her course from Calcutta to Bangkok, obliging *Myth Too* to force-land on a military airfield near Rangoon. Sheila's reception was friendly, however, as it had been throughout the flight so far: indeed, an armed guard had been necessary at some ports of call to ward off the attentions of souvenir hunters.

Diverting via Singapore and Bali to escape the worst of the weather, Sheila eventually arrived in Darwin, Australia. Crossing to Auckland, New Zealand, she was delighted to be given Jean Batten's Harmon Trophy to carry for luck. Coincidentally, Miss Scott was to receive the Trophy (awarded for an outstanding feat of aero-nautical achievement) at the conclusion of her own passage. This joined Amy Johnson's jewel box–a gift several days before take-off–as a memento of the flight.

The final leg of the Pacific crossing, involving a flight

of 3,862 km (2,400 miles) over water from Honolulu was fraught with anxiety when a fuel leak in the cabin developed. Swift action in switching to the damaged tank minimised the danger, but the lights of San Francisco were a welcome sight in the early morning. Feted across the United States, Sheila faced one final obstacle–the Atlantic crossing from Gander, Newfoundland to Europe. After carefully supervising the filling of the cabin tanks– the previous leakage had been traced to an overflow valve– Sheila staged to Lisbon via the Azores and thence to London, arriving on 20 June to a tumultuous welcome. A distance of over 49,890 km (31,000 miles) had been covered in approximately 189 flying hours.

Amid a blaze of publicity, Sheila's life became a round of receptions, speaking engagements and television appearances. *Myth Too* was partially dismantled–much to Sheila's displeasure–and displayed outside the offices of the *Daily Mirror*, to which her story had been sold in her absence by her manager. Despite the adulation, Sheila's financial position was still precarious, but help–in the shape of Ken Wood, a wealthy industrialist–was at hand. At his suggestion, it was decided to attempt to beat Amy Johnson's record from London to Cape Town, South Africa, established in 1936. A change of plan, when permission to overfly the African state of Chad was refused, caused the first attempt on 29 June to be abandoned, but a second–rerouted–flight from 6 July to 9 July was more successful. The return journey, accomplished on 30 July to 1 August was timed at 67 hours 42 minutes.

Transatlantic air race
The North and South Atlantic records were next to fall in October 1967, the former being notable in that the Shannon-Gander leg was accomplished in the face of prevailing headwinds. The following year was distinguished by the announcement in the New Year's Honours List of the award of the Order of the British Empire (OBE)–a treasured addition to Sheila's collection of trophies. The year 1969 saw the *Daily Mail*'s 'Top of the Tower' transatlantic air race, commemorating the 50th anniversary of Alcock and Brown's non-stop passage. The illustrious roll of competitors included Max Conrad, Prince Michael of Kent and racing driver Stirling Moss, while aircraft participating ranged from the Hawker Siddeley Harrier vertical take-off jet and the Mach 2 McDonnell Douglas Phantom to Sheila Scott's tiny Comanche.

With the assistance of a couple of Aston Martin sports cars and helicopter transport, Sheila's time from the top of London's GPO Tower to New York's Empire State was 26 hours 54 minutes and 20 seconds, ensuring her a class victory. The next challenge in December 1969 was the England-Australia air race, covering 19,310 km (12,000 miles) from Gatwick to Adelaide. The female record from London to Darwin stood at 5 days 21 hours; thus when Singapore was reached in under 3 days despite a multitude of equipment malfunctions, the target still seemed within reach. Bad weather, combined with a near-total radio blackout and a forced landing in the inhospitable Celebes Islands all but prevented this, however, and it was a typically stubborn display of flying skill which enabled Miss Scott to reach her goal, later continuing via the United States to London.

Myth Too, the faithful Comanche which had taken Sheila to 94 world records, was forsaken for her next project in 1971, in which she planned to make the first FAI-recognised flight in a light aircraft via the North Pole. Charles Blair had overflown the Pole in 1951 from Norway in a North American P-51, but FAI rules stipulated that

flights should be routed from equator to equator to qualify for ratification. A twin-engined Piper Aztec was selected for the mission and named *Mythre*; the type's normal range of 1,770 km (1,100 miles) was extended to 4,830 km (3,000 miles) by extra tankage. This had the unhappy side-effect of ensuring that failure of one Lycoming piston engine would mean almost certain disaster.

The problems posed by this historic venture were numerous and included the combating of frostbite and the necessity for complex polar navigation conversions to stay on a steady course. The aircraft's air inlets were sealed to keep out the freezing atmosphere, while special heaters were found which produced no harmful carbon monoxide fumes while maintaining cabin temperatures. The National Aeronautics and Space Administration (NASA) installed a heart monitor and a special push-button console to gauge Sheila's alertness and fatigue. It was a heavily-laden Aztec which departed Heathrow on 1 June for Nairobi, Kenya, from where the flight proper was to commence.

The Polar weather became increasingly unfavourable from April onwards, when warmer weather caused icing fog. Thus it was with some trepidation that Sheila took off after several delays on 23 June from Bodö on the edge of the Arctic Circle *en route* for Point Barrow, some 4,830 km (3,000 miles) distant. That the flight was accomplished is testimony to Miss Scott's resourcefulness and courage, for a mainwheel which refused to retract forced a diversion to weather station Nord–a tiny community inaccessible by land. Pressing on regardless she reached her destination after an additional 17 hours' flying, continuing down through the American continent to Canton Isle, just below the equator. From there, Sheila staged to Australia and thence to Britain, thus completing her third round the world flight.

The first FAI-recognised flight by a light aircraft over the North Pole was accomplished in June 1971. Mythre, a much-modified Piper Aztec, was chosen by Miss Scott for the venture, in which she was monitored by America's National Aeronautics and Space Administration (NASA)

Prestwick Pioneers

Formed as a flying school, Scottish Aviation graduated to produce some noteworthy aircraft

In August 1935, the Marquess of Clydesdale and David MacIntyre, members of No 602 (City of Glasgow) Squadron and the pilots of the 1933 Everest expedition, formed Scottish Aviation Ltd in association with the directors of the de Havilland Aircraft Company. A government scheme had been launched to train men in their first 50 hours as civilians before joining the RAF as pilots and completing their training. Thus selected firms were awarded contracts to open Flying Training Schools. The new company was established at Heathfield, near Prestwick, on 64 hectares (157 acres) of land, and an additional 77 hectares (191 acres) were bought to allow for expansion. Construction of a hangar, lecture rooms and a control tower was completed by the end of 1935, the airfield opening on 17 February 1936 as No 12 Elementary Flying Training School with 16 de Havilland Tiger Moths, eight instructors and 30 to 40 pupils.

Wartime expansion

Prestwick's excellent weather record enabled some courses to be completed several weeks ahead of schedule, and larger training contracts were awarded, including the beginning, in 1937, of RAF Volunteer Reserve pilot training, utilising the Hawker Hart for advanced training. The following year, No 1 Air Observers Navigation School (AONS) was opened with Avro Ansons, and Scottish Aviation began to manufacture aircraft parts and carry out modifications.

More hangars and buildings were erected and, at the end of August 1939, the AONS fleet was enlarged by the acquisition of three four-engined Fokker airliners, two F-XXII aircraft and the only F-XXXVI built; one F-XXII survived the war and was broken up in 1952. War inevitably brought expansion to Prestwick and to Scottish Aviation. Modification and repair work was much in evidence, initially on Blackburn Skuas and Rocs and Westland Lysanders, but later on Hawker Hurricanes and Supermarine Spitfires; 50 radio-controlled Queen Bee target aircraft were built under sub-contract to de Havilland. With the coming of Lend-Lease, Consolidated B-24 Liberators, Boeing B-17 Fortresses and Lockheed Hudsons began to appear in the modification bays and an ever-increasing stream of aircraft across the Atlantic kept the company busy on maintenance contracts. A workshop was built at Greenock to maintain Coastal Command flying boats.

David MacIntyre, Manager of Scottish Aviation was also Officer Commanding RAF Prestwick for a time during the war. He campaigned for the airport's postwar expansion as an international terminal for several years without success, until his efforts were rewarded in 1945 and Prestwick was designated Britain's second international airport. As the war ended, so the aircraft industry slumped. Warplanes were no longer needed, but homes were in desperately short supply, and the Scottish Aviation factory became involved in the manufacture of plumbing units for prefabricated houses and the assembly of caravans, coaches and double-decker buses.

Although it had never built an aircraft of its own design, Scottish Aviation was sufficiently interested to

The Scottish Aviation A4/45, the company's first design, was not ordered into production by the Air Ministry. It was, however, developed into the Pioneer, whose exceptional short take-off and landing characteristics led to adoption by the RAF as a casualty evacuation and communications type

produce a single-engined high-wing monoplane to meet Air Ministry Specification A4/45 for a light communications aircraft capable of operating from confined spaces. The three-seat aircraft was powered by a 240hp DH Gipsy Queen 34 inline engine and first flew in 1947, but did not attract a production order. Following the installation of the much more powerful 520hp Alvis Leonides 502/4 radial engine the prototype flew again in June 1950 as the Pioneer, now with accommodation for the pilot and a total of four passengers.

First STOL transport

With a take-off run of 68m (75yds) and landing in a mere 60m (66yds), the Pioneer became Britain's first STOL (short take-off and landing) transport, and was ordered for the Royal Air Force which received 40 aircraft designated Pioneer CC Mark 1. The first unit to be equipped with the type was No 267 Squadron in February 1954, based at Kuala Lumpur in Malaya, while other Pioneers operated in Singapore, Brunei, Aden, Cyprus, Germany and the United Kingdom. Unarrested deck landings on the Commando carrier HMS *Bulwark* were carried out by two Pioneers from No 209 Squadron based at Seletar, Singapore, in November 1961.

Pioneers were also supplied to the Royal Malayan Air Force and Royal Ceylon Air Force, while the Sultan of Muscat's Air Force received two ex-RAF aircraft and two civil examples went to the Iranian Customs Authority. Total production of the Pioneer amounted to 59, including the prototype which was eventually re-engined to standard Pioneer configuration and delivered to the RAF. By modern standards, production of the Pioneer was on a very small scale, but outstanding success in the roles for which it was intended paved the way for a successor, a twin-engined STOL aircraft named, not unexpectedly, the Twin Pioneer.

In the meantime, Scottish Aviation had lost its battle with the Ministry of Civil Aviation against compulsory purchase and in 1953 the company became a tenant on what had been its own property, while development of Prestwick continued with plans for a new terminal and runway improvements. Design work on the Twin Pioneer began in 1952, and the aircraft emerged as a high-wing monoplane with triple fins and rudders, powered by two 540hp Alvis Leonides 514 engines and with accommodation for 16 passengers.

The prototype flew on 25 June 1955 appearing at the SBAC Display at Farnborough in September; Scottish Aviation received an RAF order for 20 aircraft, to be designated Twin Pioneer CC Mark 1. The first military aircraft flew on 29 August 1957 and the order was eventually increased to 39, with the last seven being manufactured to CC Mark 2 standard. The last three RAF aircraft were military equivalents of the civil Series 3 Twin Pioneers with the more powerful 640hp Leonides 531 engines. All Twin Pioneers were retrospectively modified to this standard in 1961. RAF deliveries were made between early 1958 and March 1961, first aircraft replacing the single-engined Pioneers of No 78 Squadron at Aden.

The Twin Pioneer was known as the 'Twin Pin' in RAF service. Serving alongside Hunting Percival Pembrokes with No 152 Squadron, based in Bahrein, the type took part in the Kuwait operations of July 1961. In Kenya the four Twin Pioneers of No 21 Squadron operated closely with infantry on security duties and in October 1961 flew 146 relief missions during Operation Tana Flood. No 209 Squadron's Twin Pioneers flew supply missions in Borneo during the conflict of 1962–66.

Demonstration flights

A number of overseas demonstration flights were made by Twin Pioneers, one covering the Middle East, Far East and Australia, while another visited the United States, Caribbean and South America. During the 1957 Paris Air Show, a Twin Pioneer operated a passenger service between Le Bourget Airport and the heliport at Issy, where it flew from the grass area normally used by helicopters. Although this gave a 777m (850yds) strip, the Twin Pioneer required only 119m (130yds) to 'unstick' and 311m (340yds) to clear 15m (50ft). The aircraft made five flights a day in each direction and spent the rest of each day in the static exhibition at the show.

The company suffered a great loss in December 1957 when a Twin Pioneer crash at Tripoli, Libya, resulted in the death of Managing Director and co-founder David MacIntyre, together with the pilot, engineer and three passengers. Mr T. D. M. Robertson became the new Managing Director, production of the Twin Pioneer continuing until around 90 had been built.

The largest overseas customer for the type was the Royal Malayan Air Force, which initially received four Series 1 aircraft and in 1962 took delivery of ten Series 3s worth some three-quarters of a million pounds. A conversion training programme had been provided by Scottish Aviation for the RMAF aircrews, and on completion of the 12,870km (8,000 mile) delivery flight in June 1962

Top and above: the RAF operated 39 Twin Pioneers between 1958 and 1968. The type served with six squadrons, operating from Britain, Kenya and the Middle and Far East as a multi-purpose STOL aircraft. The Twin Pioneer also found limited success on the civil market

Scottish Aviation Twin Pioneer CC Mark 1 of No 230 Squadron RAF

Dimensions
Span 23.3 m (76 ft 6 in)
Length 13·8 m (45 ft 3 in)

Engines
Two 550 hp Alvis Leonides 514

Performance
Maximum speed 265 km/h (165 mph)
Range 640 km (398 miles)
Service ceiling 6,100 m (20,000 ft)

Payload
Sixteen passengers, eleven infantry or
nine paratroopers

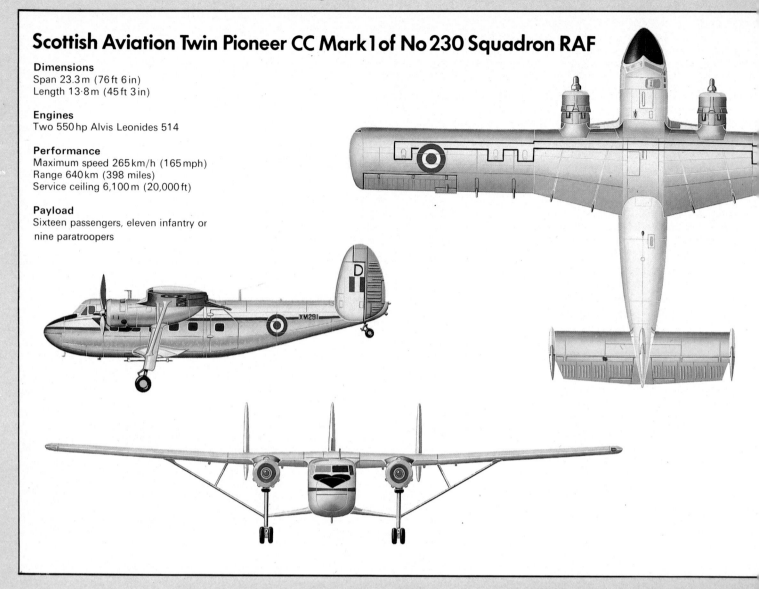

Opposite above: developed by Beagle from the civil Pup and taken over from that company on its liquidation, the Bulldog military trainer was ordered by the Royal Air Force and the air arms of several nations.
Right: originally designed and marketed by Handley Page, the Jetstream began its life as a civil feederliner and executive transport. The type has also served with the Royal Air Force and Navy

by the new aircraft the four Series 1 aircraft were returned to the manufacturers for conversion to Series 3 standard. The first production Series 3 Twin Pioneer was delivered to the Iraq Petroleum Company in October 1959, and this model soon became the standard type.

The Series 2 resulted from a Philippine Air Lines order for five aircraft, with the stipulation that they should be fitted with Pratt & Whitney R-1340 engines of 600 hp, and able to carry 19 passengers. The change of engine necessitated considerable modifications to the engine nacelles to accommodate the larger engine, the prototype Series 2 flying on 31 August 1958. An early customer for the Twin Pioneer was the Swiss Federal Air Office, which used one for aerial survey work. This aircraft has been presented to the Swiss Museum of Transport in Lucerne.

Maintenance and overhaul work
A twin turboprop 40-seat passenger airliner, the Turbo-Pioneer, and a single-engined aircraft, the Pegasus, were projected, but neither was built and for some years Scottish Aviation undertook no aircraft production. A period of diversification followed, with repair and maintenance work for the Royal Canadian Air Force on North American F-86, Lockheed T-33 and Avro Canada CF-100 aircraft, started in 1955, continuing at a high level. As the earlier types were phased out of service, the programme continued with work on the Lockheed CF-104 for the Royal Canadian Air Force (later restyled Canadian

Armed Forces).

Scottish Aviation had long been active in engine overhaul work; with Rolls-Royce commitments to turbine engines becoming rapidly larger, the Prestwick company was given a substantial contract in 1961 to take over work on the Merlin and Griffon piston engines. Work also continued on repair and overhaul of Pratt & Whitney R-1830 engines and in late 1961 the company merged its interests in this field with Air Engine Services of Lingfield, Surrey, with the founding of a new company, Scottish Air Engine Services Ltd.

Production under the new company doubled and, within a year, overhaul facilities for the larger R-2000 engine were available. There was also a considerable amount of activity on aircraft overhauls, in particular with the Douglas DC-3 since Scottish Aviation was a Douglas-approved overhaul and modification centre. The latter seal of approval was to prove valuable in 1962, when the company secured a seventy-five thousand pound contract from Sweden for the overhaul and conversion of 12 ex-Royal Navy Douglas Skyraiders for target towing duties. These replaced Fairey Fireflys with Swedish Air Service Limited, the contract including pilot and engineer conversion training.

In May 1962, Scottish Aviation introduced a comprehensive checking and servicing scheme and, within ten months, more than 30 operators had used the new system, with aircraft types ranging in size from a Piper Tri-Pacer

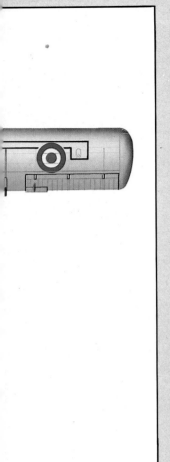

lightplane to Lockheed C-133 Cargomaster aircraft of the USAF. A significant event in 1965 was the award of a contract for the manufacture of sections of the C-130 Hercules for the American Lockheed company; each assembly comprised six large fuselage sections, two main undercarriage panels and two wing pylons. The company announced the delivery of the 100th such set in May 1968. Over 200 further sets were subsequently ordered.

The award of a half-a-million pound contract in December 1966 for the production of Handley Page Jetstream wings was hailed in a contemporary press release as 'a valuable Christmas present'; this programme was terminated, however, with the collapse of Handley Page in early 1970. The company became part of the Cammell Laird Group in 1966 and once again became an aircraft manufacturer in 1970. The voluntary liquidation of Beagle Aircraft Ltd in January 1970 came at a time when the Swedish air force had virtually completed its evaluation of the prototype Bulldog trainer and had decided to place an order.

Bulldog production

Scottish Aviation reached agreement with Beagle's liquidator to acquire design rights for the Bulldog and Beagle 206, with the understanding that they would provide full technical support services for operators and similar support for the Beagle Bassett, then in RAF service. Beagle had already flown a prototype of the Bulldog, developed from the Pup as a military trainer, in 1969. The second prototype was completed by Scottish Aviation and flown in February 1971, by which time the production line had been running for three months. The Lycoming IO-360-A1B6 engine developing 200 hp was chosen as the power plant for the aircraft.

The Swedish order included 58 Bulldogs and the provision of spares for ten years. The contract was at that time worth one-and-three-quarter million pounds, and deliveries began in July 1971. A subsequent order covered 20 Bulldogs for the Swedish army. The first 98 Bulldogs were Series 100 machines, subsequent aircraft being given Series numbers for different customers. Orders in 1978 numbered over 300, the aircraft being supplied to Malaya, Kenya, Ghana, Nigeria, Jordan, the Lebanon, Hong Kong and the RAF.

Following the collapse of Handley Page, Scottish Aviation acquired complete design, production and marketing rights for the Jetstream twin-turboprop transport in August 1972. The first of 26 Jetstreams for use by the RAF as multi-engined pilot trainers flew in April 1973. Deliveries of all these aircraft had been made by the spring of 1976, but a change in RAF requirements led to them being placed in storage. In October of that year it was announced that eight Jetstreams would be used by the RAF for the role originally envisaged, while 16 would be converted to T Mk 2 standard for observer training with the Royal Navy, replacing the Hunting Sea Prince aircraft currently in service. The Navy Jetstreams carry airborne weather and terrain-mapping radar in a nose radome, thus altering the aircraft's familiar profile.

Bulldog production continued in 1978, together with the manufacture for Lockheed of TriStar doors and Hercules fuselage sections, with some 600 sets of the latter delivered. In fact, every Hercules built since the 66 ordered for the RAF in 1966 has had Scottish-built fuselage sections. Maintenance for the Canadian Air Force continues, as does aero-engine work, and the Prestwick factory employs some 1,400 people as British Aerospace's Aircraft Group Scottish Division.

Storm over the Sealanes

Air attacks against shipping have frequently proved decisive in maritime warfare

RAF Bristol Blenheims flying low over Holland to strike the port of Rotterdam in July 1941. Strikes against enemy shipping at sea and in port became routine after the RAF began offensive operations over Europe in summer 1941. In that year a third of the total tonnage of bombs delivered on Europe by Bomber Command was expended against naval targets

Such is the nature of modern warfare that vast quantities of *matériel* are transported by sea and both world wars have been characterised by constant efforts by every belligerent nation to interrupt this flow of men and supplies both by naval action and from the air. Indeed it has been in the nature of modern war that Great Britain has faced her gravest dangers in the threat to her maritime lifelines by belligerent powers.

The air-launched torpedo

To destroy a ship at sea, be it a warship or merchant vessel, special tactics and weapons are called for and this is no more clearly emphasised than in the history of air attacks against shipping. The air-launched torpedo has remained the principal anti-shipping weapon and such are its shape and weight that special aircraft have usually been developed to deliver it. The first recorded success achieved by an aerial torpedo was the sinking of a 5,000 ton Turkish supply ship near the Dardanelles on 12 August 1915 by a torpedo dropped by Flt Cdr C. H. Edmonds in a Short 184 seaplane from HMS *Ben-my-Chree*. Unfortunately this claim was put in question when a British submarine commander claimed to have launched his torpedo simultaneously. However, five days later Edmonds torpedoed another Turkish supply ship and this time his claim was not disputed.

Very little success was achieved using bombs against ships during World War I and the 18 in naval torpedo remained the sole weapon in regular use by the land-based Royal Naval Air Service. Before the Armistice the

world's first flush-deck aircraft carrier, HMS *Argus*, was commissioned and embarked the first full squadron of torpedo-carrying aircraft–Sopwith Cuckoos–in October 1918; they were, however, too late to be used in action.

The widespread use of aircraft by naval air arms during World War I encouraged far-sighted officers in Britain and America to advocate development of specialised aircraft as vital anti-shipping weapon carriers, expounding a belief that in the presence of suitable bombing aircraft the days of the capital warship were drawing to an end. In the United States, Brigadier-General William Mitchell favoured the use of Army bombers in attack trials against warships, and succeeded in sinking several, including the 22,800 ton ex-German battleship *Ostfriesland* during a demonstration on 21 July 1921. Observers remained sceptical about the use of bombs dropped from medium altitude against moving targets, but were quick to notice that near-misses by heavy bombs frequently proved fatal.

Biplane bombers

In Britain the inter-war years witnessed a succession of biplane torpedo-carriers including the Blackburn Ripon and Shark and Hawker Horsley, culminating in the classic Fairey Swordfish, which was followed by the Albacore during World War II. It is perhaps interesting to note that anti-shipping attack training was the sole prerogative of the Fleet Air Arm and that shore-based RAF aircraft were almost totally excluded from this role. The result of this omission was that when, in the first days of World War II, Bomber Command aircrews of Nos 9, 107, 110 and

149 Squadrons were called upon to find and strike enemy shipping off the German coast, the raids were unsuccessful and seven bombers were lost. In further fruitless raids by Vickers Wellingtons of Nos 9, 37, 99 and 149 Squadrons in December 1939 losses proved so heavy that Bomber Command abandoned daylight attacks.

Indeed henceforth the whole offensive against enemy shipping at sea fell on the shoulders of Coastal Command and the Fleet Air Arm, with cross-Channel sweeps against enemy coastal traffic being undertaken by Fighter Command. Only once more did Bomber Command attempt to strike enemy warships at sea in daylight; after numerous attempts to hit the *Scharnhorst*, *Gneisenau* and *Prinz Eugen* while they lay in Brest, bomber crews were sent against the German warships as they escaped through the Straits of Dover on 11/12 February 1942. Not one bomb struck its target. The critics of Billy Mitchell's tests 21 years previously seemed to have been vindicated.

If the British had been caught short of suitable anti-shipping weapons at the beginning of World War II (Coastal Command aircraft only carried 250 lb bombs) the Fleet Air Arm still pinned all its faith on the Swordfish torpedo aircraft. The Blackburn Skua had failed to match expectations as a dive bomber and was employed more as a fighter before being hurriedly withdrawn from service. The Swordfish, however, succeeded against all probability with outstanding victories at Tobruk in July 1940, Taranto on 11/12 November 1940, at Cape Matapan on 28 March 1941 and against the battleship *Bismarck* in the Atlantic on 26 May 1941. In the memorable attack against the *Scharnhorst*, *Gneisenau* and *Prinz Eugen* of 12 February 1942 all six Swordfish led by Lt-Cdr Eugene Esmonde were shot down without inflicting any damage. For all its success the 'Stringbag' was an anachronism; it was flown with gallantry but inevitably succumbed in the face of determined enemy air defence. The Albacore fared little better, and the Fairey Barracuda monoplane entered service too late in the war to see anything but limited combat. Although first flown as early as December 1940, few saw service in the European Theatre.

Enemy strikes

Although the Axis sea routes between Italy, Sicily and North Africa were under constant attack by Allied forces, the Allies, being largely maritime powers, depended upon sea routes and provided infinitely more targets on the high seas than the European Axis nations. The Germans accordingly applied much greater effort against these targets from the outset of World War II. On the one hand the Luftwaffe established specific *küstenfliegergruppen* manned principally by naval aircrews whose operational role it was to concentrate against shipping and naval shore establishments; on the other hand some emphasis was also laid upon aerial mining of Allied waters by *minensuchsgruppen* and these operations certainly gained some success.

The dive bomber also achieved much greater effect in the Luftwaffe than in the RAF and Stukas sank a total of three battleships, a battlecruiser and 15 cruisers during the war, in addition to more than 50 other naval vessels and countless merchant ships. German and Italian torpedo bombers (predominantly Heinkel He 111s and Savoia-Marchetti SM 79s) also gained numerous sinkings, particularly among the Allies' famous Mediterranean and Russian convoys.

Perhaps the most interesting anti-shipping weapons of World War II were the range of air-launched guided missiles developed by Germany. The rocket-powered Henschel Hs 293 was used with limited success during the last three years, when Allied invasion fleets offered such lucrative targets. The destroyers *Boadicea*, *Dulverton*, *Inglefield*, *Intrepid* and *Vasilissa Olga* were all sunk by Hs 293s. Another successful weapon was the Fritz X armour-piercing missile. Carried by Dornier Do 217K-2s of III/KG 100, these missiles sank the Italian battleship *Roma*, damaged the *Italia*, severely damaged the battleship HMS *Warspite*, and sank the cruiser HMS *Spartan* and the destroyer HMS *Janus*.

In the Far East the Japanese followed their treacherous air attack on Pearl Harbour (where the American ships were stationary targets in port) with the sinking of the British battleships HMS *Prince of Wales* and *Repulse* of

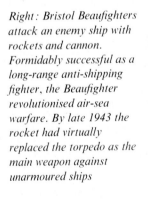

Right: Bristol Beaufighters attack an enemy ship with rockets and cannon. Formidably successful as a long-range anti-shipping fighter, the Beaufighter revolutionised air-sea warfare. By late 1943 the rocket had virtually replaced the torpedo as the main weapon against unarmoured ships

Above right: a painting by Richard Eurich depicting an attack on a British convoy by German Dornier Do 17 bombers.
Below: North American B-25J Mitchells of the 345th Bomb Group, US Army Air Force sank the Japanese destroyer Amatsukaze and two escorts (one illustrated) off Amoy on 6 April 1945 with 500 lb bombs

Force Z when torpedo bombers caught them 320 km (200 miles) north of Singapore without air cover. Japanese naval aircraft went on to sink the cruisers HMS *Cornwall* and *Dorsetshire* in the Indian Ocean on 5 April 1942. Off Ceylon HMS *Hermes* was the first aircraft carrier to be sunk by enemy carrier-borne aircraft.

Against this chapter of disasters in the Far East the Americans quickly responded with the successful employment of Douglas Dauntless and Douglas Devastator dive bombers (and later bomb-carrying fighters such as the Vought Corsair) and achieved a welcome success in the Battle of the Coral Sea on 7-9 May 1942 by sinking the Japanese carrier *Shoho*. In the decisive Battle of Midway on 4 June that year the Japanese suffered the loss of four fleet carriers, the *Agaki*, *Hiryu*, *Kaga* and *Soryu*–all victims of American carrier-based dive bombers.

Torbeau and Rockets

Yet it was the RAF that probably developed the most deadly shore-based anti-shipping strike tactics during the war. These stemmed partly from the successful use of low-flying, cannon-armed Hurricane fighters, which flew constant sweeps against enemy light coastal shipping in the English Channel during 1941 and 1942, and from the use of the purpose-designed Bristol Beaufort torpedo bomber of RAF Coastal Command. The latter performed a number of memorable attacks, including Flg Off Kenneth Campbell's torpedo hit on the *Gneisenau* in Brest harbour on 6 April 1941. As such attacks gained increasing successes against Axis shipping, the Germans deployed heavier and heavier air and surface defences to protect these targets, including flak ships and interceptor fighters, so that by mid-1942 such attacks had become fraught with extreme hazard and unescorted raids were invariably attended by heavy losses.

The Bristol Beaufighter was developed to carry a standard 18 in torpedo and later to mount three-inch rocket projectiles. Dubbed the Torbeau, the Beaufighter entered service with the first anti-shipping Strike Wing (consisting of Nos 143, 236 and 254 Squadrons) at North Coates in November 1942, gaining its first success on 18 April 1943. By the following year several such wings had been formed, each including rocket-armed 'Flakbeaus' and escorting Beaufighters on its strength.

Today the threat by potential enemy naval forces pose no small threat to the maritime nations. Consequently modern search and attack tactics and weapons are being constantly developed to a pitch undreamed of in the days of the Swordfish and the 250lb bomb. Among modern anti-shipping aircraft, the Soviet Backfire bomber and the US Navy's Lockheed P-3 Orion, armed with Harpoon missiles, are especially noteworthy.

SHIPS OF THE AIR

The firm founded in 1908 by the Short brothers has long specialised in marine aircraft

Shorts, or Short Brothers & Harland, as it has long been styled, has the distinction of being the oldest aeroplane manufacturing firm in the world, having been established in 1908. Its roots go back further still to April 1901 when the brothers Oswald and Eustace Short first set up business at Hove, Sussex, as manufacturers of aerial balloons. Within two years they had moved to a larger workshop in a mews in London, and in 1906 they transferred to still larger premises in the arches under the Battersea Bridge Station of the London, Brighton and South Coast Railway. In 1908 they were joined by the oldest Short brother, Horace.

Initial designs

Having already constructed balloons for the Indian Army and members of the Aero Club of the United Kingdom, the Short Brothers, whose firm was officially established in November 1908, gained their first order to build an aeroplane; this came from an Irishman, Sir Francis McClean. Design work was started by Horace in the autumn of 1908, in his mother's flat in Battersea. He had very little to guide him, and no price or specification had been agreed. Construction began early in 1909 and four weeks later sufficient progress had been made for the uncovered airframe to be exhibited at the first Aero and Motor Show at London's Olympia. Conjointly with McClean's aeroplane, Shorts designed and built a glider for the Hon C. S. Rolls. This first flew in August 1909, but McClean's aeroplane, a 12 m (40 ft) span pusher biplane superficially similar to the Wright Flyer but actually quite original in design, never did take to the air, since the engine – built for a motor car – proved far too heavy.

Meanwhile, in the same month that the three Short brothers had founded their partnership, Eustace had

visited Le Mans in France to see the Wright Brothers and had been taken up in the Flyer by Wilbur Wright. The Wrights had no manufacturing facilities or drawings for their Flyer, and to help satisfy the great demand for the machine they entrusted Shorts with the manufacture in England of six Flyers which had been ordered by members of the Aero Club. Horace Short spent several days at Pau in France in February 1909 making nearly 200 rough but fully-dimensioned sketches of the Flyer, and soon after his return to England he and his assistant, P. M. Jones, produced the first complete set of working drawings ever made of any Wright biplane. Today the time-worn leather-covered notebook containing Horace's rough sketches is held by the Royal Aeronautical Society in London.

Above: the S 27 Farman-type biplanes were the first Short aeroplanes to be built at Eastchurch, where the three Short brothers established a factory early in 1910.
Below: over 1,000 Short-designed seaplanes were supplied to the RNAS and RAF during World War I, many being built by a number of subcontractors. A Short 184 is pictured

Short Sunderland Mark II of No 10 Squadron Royal Australian Air Force

Dimensions
Span 34·36 m (112 ft 9½ in)
Length 26·78 m (85 ft 3½ in)

Engines
Four 1,050 hp Bristol Pegasus XVIII radials

Performance
Maximum speed 333 km/h (207 mph)
Range 4,330 km (2,690 miles)
Service ceiling 5,450 m (17,900 ft)

Armament
Eight machine guns
Up to 1,850 kg (4,960 lb) of bombs or depth charges

Short-Wright Biplanes

Although work on Flyer components was begun at Battersea, it was realised that the railway arches were too small to allow for final erection of aeroplanes, so a new factory was set up on a tract of level marshland at Leysdown on the Isle of Sheppey in Kent. The Flyer was also being built in France and Germany, but when the Wright Brothers visited England to inspect those under way at Shorts, they congratulated the firm on its workmanship. The six Short-Wright Biplanes all made their first flights in 1910 and 1911 and their owner-pilots competed successfully with them in early flying competitions.

In the spring of 1909 Shorts built a second biplane, designed by Horace, to the order of J. T. C. Moore-Brabazon who, on 30 October that year, flew it over the first circular mile ever covered by an all-British aeroplane,

winning the thousand pound prize offered by the *Daily Mail*. The engine of this pusher machine was a Green of 50-60 hp.

Shorts' activities developed at a considerable pace. As business grew it was obvious that Leysdown was too small for expansion. Furthermore, the marshy ground was not suitable for aircraft equipped with wheels, the first few types built there all having skid undercarriages and being launched from rails. A move was thus made, early in 1910, to Eastchurch in Kent, where a factory built of corrugated iron, rather than wood, was erected.

Expanding work-force

As Shorts' factories on Sheppey were some distance from any sizeable town, much of the labour was drawn from rural workers and carpenters, all the former having to be taught by Horace Short. The pay-roll had risen to 80 as early as August 1909, and by about 1911, not long after the move to Eastchurch, an emergency arose. The wage bill exceeded the firm's capital of six hundred pounds, which had been made up of a contribution of two hundred pounds from each of the three brothers in 1908. McClean came forward with a loan of five thousand pounds without interest, which helped finance the new factory.

Just prior to the move to Eastchurch, there emerged the first of a series of Short-designed and built box-kite biplanes generally similar to the French Farman and Sommers types. These quickly superseded the Wright type—which Horace Short considered to be 'a beast that needs some handling'—and were produced in some numbers, the final development model being ordered for training use as late as 1915. The series included some twin-engined variants, the first of which—the Triple-Twin as it was known because the forward engine drove two wing-mounted tractor airscrews through chain gears—first flew in September 1911. However, this was not the world's first twin-engined aeroplane as has been claimed.

Above: a Short Sunderland of No 201 Squadron takes off for an Atlantic patrol in March 1945. Based on Lough Erne in Northern Ireland, one of the Squadron's Sunderlands flew the last anti-submarine patrol of World War II.
Right: Paul Nash's painting 'Defence of Albion' portrays the unending battle with the elements which Coastal Command's Sunderland crews faced in maintaining their patrols

Sir Francis McClean bought several of Short's early box-kite biplanes and lent them to the Admiralty in 1911, for the purpose of instructing naval officers in aviation at Eastchurch, the flying-ground of what was by now the Royal Aero Club. Four officers were selected from more than 200 volunteers to undergo the first course: Lieutenants Samson, Longmore, Gregory and Gerrard. The course started in March and the instructor was another Royal Aero Club member, George Cockburn, one of the first Englishmen to fly. This marked the beginning of British naval aviation.

On completion of the first training course, the Admiralty set up a Naval Flying School at Eastchurch, bought two of the Short machines from McClean, and permitted Samson and Longmore to collaborate with Shorts in various experiments. Longmore, flying a Short biplane with air bags lashed to its chassis and tail, made a successful descent on the River Medway off the Isle of Grain on 1 December 1911. On 10 January 1912, Samson flew the same 'hydro-aeroplane' from Eastchurch to Sheerness, Isle of Grain, and later that day flew it off a platform erected on HMS *Africa*. Piloted by Gregory, the Short hydro took part in the Royal Naval Review at Weymouth in the following May, dropping a dummy 300lb bomb within sight of the Royal Yacht and diving on a submerged submarine – an unrehearsed and prophetic manoeuvre which caused much speculative talk in naval circles.

Triple-Tractor

Horace Short developed a two-seat tractor biplane in 1911. Powered by a 70hp Gnome rotary engine, it first flew in January 1912, piloted by its purchaser, McClean. He lent it to the Naval Flying School at Eastchurch before very long, and Longmore, with his mechanic as passenger, flew it for 277km (172 miles) in four hours on 11 March 1912, thereby winning the Royal Navy Mortimer Singer Prize of five hundred pounds. So impressed was the Admiralty that it immediately ordered two tractor biplanes suitable for use from either land or water by exchange of landing gear. First of these made its maiden flight as soon as April 1912 and eventually a 'Triple-Tractor' variant was also built, featuring two separate Gnome engines mounted in tandem in a tractor fuselage, the front one driving a direct-coupled airscrew and the rear one, facing backwards so as to rotate the opposite way, driving wing-mounted counter-rotating airscrews through chain gears. From these early tractor biplanes stemmed a long and famous line of Short single-engined, twin-float seaplanes, one early example of which achieved the distinction of becoming the first seaplane in Britain to drop a torpedo on 27 July 1914.

At Christmas, 1914, seven Short seaplanes, all with folding wings, were transported by seaplane carriers from Harwich to a point 19km (12 miles) north of Heligoland, from where it was planned that they should take off from the sea and bomb the Zeppelin base at Cuxhaven. In the event, they failed to locate the base but bombed other targets along the Kiel canal.

Eustace and Oswald Short had established a works in 1912 at Rochester on the right bank of the Medway, with facilities for seaplane launching. With a nucleus staff from Eastchurch, work was started to build the seaplanes in quantity for the Admiralty. Early in 1914 Oswald was sent to take charge of the Rochester factory and, when war came, Shorts were ordered to supply drawings of their torpedo and bomb-carrying reconnaissance seaplanes to nine subcontracting firms chosen by the Admiralty, and to give, where necessary, tuition to enable these sub-

contractors to build the aircraft in quantity. Vast production runs followed during the war years, notably of the famous Short Type 184, from which was developed the equally renowned Short landplane bomber of 1915–16. The latter, which was considered to be a long-range 'heavy' in its time, preceded the twin-engined Handley Page 0/100 'Bloody Paralyser' into RNAS service, and first went into action as a night bomber on 15/16 November 1916 when four aircraft, flying from Coudekerque in France and carrying eight 65lb bombs apiece, raided submarine pens at Zeebrugge on the Belgian coast. Fifteen others were attached to the newly-formed No 3 Wing RNAS at Luxeuil-les-Bains in France, whose task was to carry the war into the Saar Valley; from this unit grew the RAF's Independent Force of 1918, the lineal ancestor of Bomber Command.

Non-rigid airship

By the war's end, some 13 subcontractors, including the Phoenix Dynamo Manufacturing Co, Bradford (later English Electric), Saunders Ltd, Isle of Wight (later Saunders-Roe), and the Supermarine Aviation Co, Southampton, had between them built more than 1,000 Short seaplanes. Shorts themselves built a substantial quantity, also building 150 aircraft – DH9s and Felixstowe flying boats – not of their own design. The Eastchurch works had eventually been handed over to the Navy and Shorts' headquarters transferred to Rochester, from where a new activity had already developed.

In the early part of the war, certain naval officers had the idea of suspending an aircraft's fuselage beneath a streamlined gas-bag, so making a non-rigid airship or blimp. Partly because of Shorts' interest in blimps and partly because of their success in engineering, the company was induced to join the select company of airship builders during World War I. Shorts set up works at Cardington near Bedford and henceforth became known as Short Brothers (Rochester and Bedford) Ltd. At Cardington, Shorts completed three rigid airships – R31, R32 and R38 – all to designs supplied by the Admiralty, and had a fourth – the R37 – under construction when the Armistice came; it was never completed.

Horace Short died in April 1918, whereupon his brother Oswald succeeded him in the control of the company. The British aircraft industry went through a period of depression in the early postwar period; to help Shorts survive the slump, Oswald turned the Rochester works over to the production of barges, motorboats and motor bus bodies. Nevertheless, Oswald never lost faith in aviation, and soon gained additional fame for Shorts by pioneering stressed-skin duralumin construction in a form which has lasted unchanged to the present day.

The Silver Streak

The Silver Streak biplane, which was shown publicly at the 1920 Olympia Aero Show, had a metal monocoque fuselage and metal wing struts. Although the wings were not stressed-skin structures, being built on spars and ribs like wooden wings, it was nevertheless a complete metal structure. Revolutionary as it was, however, the all-metal stressed-skin technique was not immediately accepted by either military or civil customers; Shorts did receive, however, an order from the Air Ministry for a duralumin hull for a Felixstowe F.5 flying boat, followed by orders for five examples of an all-metal stressed-skin, two-seat fighter derivative of the Silver Streak; this aircraft was named the Springbok.

Shorts' first all-metal seaplane appeared in 1924 in

the shape of the Stellite. Later renamed Cockle to avoid confusion with Shorts' contemporary Satellite all-metal light monoplane, the type was a single-seat high-wing monoplane of just 11 m (36 ft) span and powered initially by two 700 cc Blackburne motor cycle engines. Just one example was built and a relation of it, which appeared two years later was the 85 hp Blackburn Cirrus-powered two-seat, light sporting monoplane known as the Mussel and flown in both seaplane and landplane form. Eustace Short, who took very little interest in air activities until after World War I when he renewed his interest and learned to fly, frequently flew the Mussel for his own pleasure. It was in a second, improved Mussel that he died in April 1932 from a sudden heart attack after making a perfect landing on the Medway at the end of a local flight.

All-metal construction for marine aircraft gained official approval in Britain in 1924, when the Air Ministry placed an order with Shorts for the Singapore twin-engined biplane flying boat. The first machine, known as the Singapore Mk I, was loaned by the Air Ministry to Sir Alan Cobham for his memorable 37,000 km (23,000 mile) flight round Africa in 1927–28. Having won favour in the RAF, the type was developed, via the experimental Mk II prototype, into the Singapore III four-engined version (560 hp Rolls-Royce Kestrels in twin-tandem layout) of which 37 were built between 1933 and 1937. The 233 km/h (145 mph) Singapore III was the immediate predecessor of the Sunderland and a few remained in RAF squadron service until as late as 1941.

The original Singapore provided the basic design of the Short Calcutta three-engined commercial flying boat which Imperial Airways operated over various routes – notably in the Mediterranean area – between 1929 and 1936. From the Calcutta came the Rangoon military flying boat of 1930. Both types, almost identical, were con-

sidered to be the best of their class in the world, and a licence to manufacture them in France was acquired by the Breguet Company, although in the event only Calcuttas were built. In due course the Calcutta was replaced by the four-engined Kent (or Scipio) class, another Short flying boat. Some time later, two landplanes based on the Kent design were also built, again for Imperial Airways, who named them *Scylla* and *Syrinx* and employed them on the Continental services. Seating 39 passengers and having a cruising speed of 169 km/h (105 mph), they were very comfortable and extremely popular with passengers.

Largest British aeroplane
In June 1932, some 17 months after the first Kent flew, Shorts claimed the honour of having built and flown the largest aeroplane ever to come from a British factory. This was the 34 ton six-engined Sarafand military flying boat of 36 m (120 ft) span – twice as big as any of its predecessors and only exceeded in size and weight by Germany's Dornier Do X twelve-engined flying boat. Designed to carry a crew of ten and built to the order of the Air Ministry, the 246 km/h (153 mph) Sarafand remained a one-off prototype. It was eventually scrapped at Felixstowe in 1936 after having proved remarkably trouble-free and viceless from its very first flight and furthermore, having had the best all-round performance of any large flying boat ever built.

In 1934 the British Government decided that, from 1937, all first-class mail from the UK for delivery along what were then termed the Empire routes would, so far as practicable, be carried by air without surcharge. This decision led to an enormous increase in the amount of mail to be carried by Imperial Airways and an urgent need for new fleets. It was decided to rely mainly on flying boats for the task, and Shorts were thus awarded a one-and-

A crew walks out to its Stirling. The first of the RAF's four-engined heavy bombers, the Stirling lacked the good altitude performance of the Handley Page Halifax and Avro Lancaster

Below: the Sperrin was to be an interim jet bomber prior to the introduction of the V-bomber, but was not produced. Two prototypes were built, the first flying on 10 August 1951. Lower: produced immediately after World War II, the Sandringham was a conversion of the Sunderland Mk V. It could carry 45 passengers in extreme comfort up to 3,700 km (2,300 miles)

three-quarter million pound contract for an initial fleet of 28 C class flying boats. Time did not permit construction of a prototype and modification of design, yet Shorts fully met the challenge: the order was placed in 1935 and on 4 July 1936 the first of the fleet, *Canopus*, was launched at Rochester. Three months later it was delivered to Imperial Airways; deliveries continued at an average interval of a fortnight, until the last of the 28 was handed over to the carrier early in 1938.

Very soon, the magnificent Empire Boats, as they became known, were ranging the world and opening a 'Golden Age' in the annals of British flying boats. Thirty-one examples of the first variant were built, including six for Qantas Empire Airways which operated the Singapore-Australia portion of the route linking Southampton and

Sydney. Powered by four 740/920 hp Bristol Pegasus radial engines and providing accommodation for 16 to 24 passengers and 1·5 tons of mail, these early Empire boats had a maximum take-off weight of 18,370 kg (40,500 lb), later increased to 23,800 kg (52,500 lb). Top speed was 320 km/h (200 mph). Modified variants operated an experimental transatlantic mail service, the flying boats sometimes being refuelled in the air by Handley Page Harrow tankers soon after take-off. This operation took place on both the westbound and eastbound journeys.

All told, 43 Empire boats were completed, including in addition to the machines supplied to Qantas, two for Tasman Empire Airways (TEAL) who used them from April 1940 onwards for maintaining the only passenger service of any kind between New Zealand and Australia during World War II. The Empire boats rendered extremely valuable service in both civil and military roles during the conflict, although many were lost in the process. When victory came, the survivors continued flying for some time, BOAC–the successor of Imperial Airways–operating its last Empire boat service in January 1947, and both TEAL and Qantas doing likewise before the end of that same year.

Three examples of a scaled-up development of the Empire boat were built and designated G class; they, too, became a most useful asset to BOAC and RAF Coastal Command alike during the war years. These Bristol Hercules-powered aircraft had a maximum all-up weight of 33,800 kg (74,500 lb) and a wing span of 40·95 m (134 ft 4 in)–6·2 m (20 ft 4 in) wider than that of the C class. After the war, the flagship of the G class, *Golden Hind*, operated

passenger services between Poole in Dorset and Cairo, Egypt, for about a year.

If Britain's need of civil flying boats was urgent in 1935, its need of military flying boats at that time was equally pressing. The interchangeability of function as between a civil and a military flying boat had twice been proven by Short designs, and as the Government had gambled one-and-three-quarter million pounds on a civil venture, there was sound reason for a military investment of a similar kind. Shorts were in fact given a contract for a military counterpart of their projected commercial flying boat late in 1934, about the time the first RAF expansion scheme began, and thus the immortal Sunderland was born. Although fairly similar in outline to the Empire boat, it was a much more sophisticated aeroplane, and the prototype first flew in October 1937. The type entered squadron service the following summer, and its achievements in World War II are now legendary.

Maritime watchdog

Despite the so-called Phoney War on land, the war at sea began at once with the sinking by a German U-boat of the liner *Athenia*. Anti-submarine operations were an immediate necessity and Sunderlands not only flew patrols on the first day, but also carried out the last of these sorties in the European theatre on 3 and 4 June 1945 in case any U-boats had failed to surrender at the official end of hostilities. A Sunderland claimed a share of the honours in the destruction of the first U-boat of the conflict. This was in January 1940, the vessel being scuttled by its captain after being harassed by the Sunderland and a British naval force in the vicinity.

By the war's end, Sunderlands of Coastal Command alone were officially credited with having destroyed 29 U-boats and to have had a hand in the destruction of six others. Though Sunderlands did not seek aerial combat, they could and did put up stiff resistance to hostile aircraft on occasion, as was seen in April 1940 when a machine of No 204 Squadron was attacked by six Junkers Ju 88s while escorting a convoy over the North Sea. The Sunderland shot down one of the enemy, forced another to land in Norway and drove the others off. After one or two costly encounters of this kind, the Luftwaffe dubbed the Sunderland the Fliegende Stachelschwein (Flying Porcupine). With a power-operated turret in the nose in most models, another amidships and a third in the tail, plus sundry hand-held and four fixed bow-mounted guns, the aircraft lived up to its nickname. A total of 749 Sunderlands was built.

In 1936 Shorts and the well-known Belfast-based ship-building firm of Harland & Wolff had jointly formed an associate company, Short & Harland Ltd, to produce aircraft in a new plant at Belfast. A new airfield was already under construction at Sydenham, adjacent to Harland & Wolff's shipyards, and the Air Ministry agreed to build and equip a new factory at Queen's Island, Belfast, to be managed by Short & Harland. Production began in 1938 with an initial contract for 50 Bristol Bombays, followed by an order for 150 Handley Page Herefords.

A total of 341 Sunderlands was built by Shorts at Rochester, 35 more by Shorts in a wartime dispersal factory at Lake Windermere, 133 by Short & Harland at Belfast; and 240 by Blackburns at a wartime dispersal plant at Dumbarton, Scotland. After World War II, RAF Sunderlands earned more laurels in the Berlin Airlift (when they operated into Lake Havel), the Korean War and the Malayan emergency. Not until May 1958 were the last of these famous flying boats withdrawn from RAF service. The Sunderland had been with the RAF for longer

The SC1 was a vertical take-off and landing research aircraft powered by five Rolls-Royce RB 108 engines, one for forward flight and four for vertical lift. It first achieved the transition from jet-borne hovering to forward flight on 6 April 1960.
Left: groundcrew pull away the chocks from the SC1 before flight.
Below left: with the forward propulsion unit idling and the lift engines at full thrust the SC1 lifts off.
Bottom: once airborne, the propulsion engine's thrust is applied and the SC1 accelerates forwards

than any other aircraft type. Other users at various times were the air forces of Australia and Canada, both of which had squadrons within the wartime RAF, France's Aéronavale, the South African Air Force and the Royal New Zealand Air Force, the last-named continuing to fly Sunderlands until as late as 1967.

First of the 'heavies'

The second major contribution made by Shorts to Britain's World War II air power was the design and development of the Stirling bomber, the first of the four-engined monoplane 'heavies'. The original design was tested by an exact half-size flying replica powered by four Pobjoy engines. This flew in 1938 and was followed a year later by the prototype Stirling, with Bristol Hercules engines. Re-equipment of Bomber Command squadrons with Stirlings began in August 1940 and the type first went into action in February 1941. The Stirlings soon proved themselves highly manoeuvrable and capable of absorbing much battle damage. However, largely due to their poor ceiling – a result of an Air Ministry stipulation that the wingspan should not exceed 30m (100ft) to allow them to be accommodated in the standard Service hangars – they were gradually withdrawn as increasing numbers of Avro Lancasters and Handley Page Halifaxes entered service, the later versions being relegated to glider-tug and transport duties.

In all, 2,375 Stirlings were produced by Shorts, Short & Harland and Austin Motors, the latter of which operated a shadow factory at Birmingham. In the glider-tug and paratrooping roles, Stirlings participated in every important airborne landing from D-day onwards. In 1945–46 they provided a military freight and supplies service between the United Kingdom and Ceylon, flying via Africa, Egypt, Karachi and Bombay, while in the passenger-carrying role they made a useful contribution to the airlift for demobilised personnel.

During the war Shorts also improved the Sunderland's performance to produce the Seaford; in civil form, this became the Solent, the flying boat which took over from the Empire boats after the war. In co-operation with Saunders-Roe, Shorts built the 77-ton military Shetland, at the time Britain's largest flying boat. Hopes were entertained that, suitably modified, it would find a place on the air routes, but these were unfounded. Spanning over 46m (150ft) and powered by four Bristol Centaurus engines, it had a 'double-deck' fuselage which could have been furnished to accommodate 70 passengers. The first of the pair which flew in December 1944 was later accidentally destroyed by fire; the second flew in September 1947.

Oswald Short resigned as Chairman of Shorts in 1943 due to ill-health, although he remained Honorary Life President until his death in 1970. His company had been nationalised in 1942 by Sir Stafford Cripps, Minister of Aircraft Production. The Rochester factory finally closed in July 1948, by which time the headquarters had moved to Belfast. Since the war, Short types have included the Sturgeon – the second aircraft of that name to have been built by the company – for naval target-towing work, a range of Sandringham civil flying boats based on the Sunderland, the Sealand 5 to 8-seat amphibian and the SB3 anti-submarine aircraft. In addition they have built the huge four-jet Sperrin bomber, the Sherpa research aircraft, the SB5 low-speed swept-wing research aircraft, the Seamew anti-submarine aircraft, the SC1 experimental VTOL plane and the mighty, 48 m (158 ft) span, four

The distinctive shape of the Skyvan short take-off and landing transport has long been a familiar sight in many of aviation's most inhospitable outposts. Originally powered by the French Turboméca Astazou turboprop as exemplified by the second prototype (left), production Skyvans utilise the more reliable Garrett-AiResearch TPE331

Rolls-Royce Tyne turboprop-powered Belfast long-range strategic freighter, ten of which served the RAF from 1966 to 1976.

From the outset, the company enjoyed a reputation for fine workmanship, and it is partly this which resulted in it having done a great deal of subcontract work for other manufacturers over the years. Mention has already been made of the DH9s and Felixstowe flying boats produced in World War I, while comparatively recent types built by Shorts under subcontract include the English Electric/BAC Canberra jet bomber and the Bristol Britannia turboprop civil and military transport.

Short-Mayo composite

The total list of aeroplanes which have emerged from Shorts' factories is a long one. Not all went into production; some were purely experimental, like the three-engined Valetta, which was embarked upon to test the relative merits of the large landplane and floatplane transport. Further examples, were the Shirl landplane torpedo aircraft of 1918, the Cromarty twin-engined military flying boat of 1921 (the first Short-designed flying boat), the Crusader racing seaplane, intended for the

Schneider Trophy contest of 1927, the Scion and Scion Senior civil transports of 1932 and 1935 and the Short-Mayo composite *Maia-Mercury*. *Maia* was a modified Empire boat which carried on its back a relatively small four-engined floatplane, *Mercury*, of 1938. In October 1938 *Mercury* set a world long-distance record for seaplanes: after separating from *Maia* near Dundee in Scotland, it flew 9,718 km (6,045 miles) non-stop to the Orange River in South Africa in 42 hours 5 minutes.

Today, Shorts operate one of the best equipped design and production complexes in Europe and have a broad-based work programme concentrated in the three main areas of aircraft, aero-structures and missiles. Aircraft activity covers the whole area of design, development and manufacture of the company's own aircraft projects, and this division is responsible for the highly-successful Skyvan short take-off and landing transport. This was being built in 1978 in two main versions: the Skyvan 3 freight/passenger transport and Skyvan 3M military tactical support vehicle. The wide-bodied SD3-30 Commuterliner, developed from the Skyvan, was also in production. As of September 1978 sales of Skyvan variants and the Commuterliner had exceeded 120 and 19 respectively. In recent years Shorts have greatly extended their international commitments by undertaking the manufacture of major aircraft components for other producers in Europe and America, specialising particularly in the business of engine-podding. Major firms with which Shorts are collaborating include Boeing and Lockheed in the United States, and Fokker-VFW and Rolls-Royce in Europe. In the missile field Shorts are acknowledged experts in close-range guided weaponry, their Seacat/Tigercat being the world's most widely used missile system, while their Blowpipe shoulder-launched supersonic missile is the most advanced weapon of its kind in service at the time of writing.

First flown in August 1974, the Short SD3-30 was intended for third-level commuter airliner operation. Retaining the plank-like wing and twin fins of the Skyvan, the aircraft accommodates 30 passengers in a wide-bodied fuselage and is claimed to be remarkably quiet in operation